Mind, Society, and Human Action

T0300479

Economics originated as a branch of the humane studies that was concerned with trying to understand how some societies flourish while others stagnate, and also how once-flourishing societies could come to stagnate. Over the major part of the twentieth century, however, economists mostly turned away from these humane and societal concerns by importing mechanistic ideas from nineteenth-century physics. This book seeks to show how that original humane and social focus can be renewed.

The many particular topics the book examines can be traced to two central ideas. Firstly, that economic theory, like physics, requires two distinct theoretical frameworks. One treats qualities that are invariant across time and place: this is the domain of equilibrium theory. The other treats the internal generation of change in societies through entrepreneurial action that continually transforms the ecology of enterprises that constitutes a society. Secondly, economic theory is treated as a genuine social science and not a science of rationality writ large. The book also explores ways in which life in society is understood differently once economics is treated as a social science.

The book is aimed at professional audiences who work with economic theory and who find that much of the hyper-formality that comprises economic theory these days fails to make reasonable contact with reality. It will be of interest to sociologists, political scientists, and researchers in law, public policy, Austrian economics, evolutionary economics, institutional economics and political economy.

Richard E. Wagner is Holbert L. Harris Professor of Economics at George Mason University, Fairfax, USA.

Routledge foundations of the Market Economy
Edited by Mario J. Rizzo
New York University
and
Lawrence H. White
University of Missouri at St. Louis

A central theme in this series is the importance of understanding and assessing the market economy from a perspective broader than the static economics of perfect competition and Pareto optimality. Such a perspective sees markets as causal processes generated by the preferences, expectations and beliefs of economic agents. The creative acts of entrepreneurship that uncover new information about preferences, prices and technology are central to these processes with respect to their ability to promote the discovery and use of knowledge in society.

The market economy consists of a set of institutions that facilitate voluntary cooperation and exchange among individuals. These institutions include the legal and ethical framework as well as more narrowly "economic" patterns of social interaction. Thus the law, legal institutions and cultural and ethical norms, as well as ordinary business practices and monetary phenomena, fall within the analytical domain of the economist.

Previous books in this series include:

1. The Meaning of Market Process
Essays in the development of modern Austrian Economics
Israel M. Kirzner

2. Prices and Knowledge
A market-process perspective
Esteban F. Thomas

3. Keynes' General Theory of Interest
A reconsideration
Fiona C. Maclachlan

4. Laissez-Faire Banking
Kevin Dowd

Mind, Society, and Human Action

Time and knowledge in a theory of social economy

Richard E. Wagner

Routledge
Taylor & Francis Group

LONDON AND NEW YORK

First published 2010
by Routledge
2 Park Square, Milton Park, Abingdon, Oxon OX14 4RN

Simultaneously published in the USA and Canada
by Routledge
711 Third Avenue, New York, NY 10017

*Routledge is an imprint of the Taylor & Francis Group,
an informa business*

© 2010 Richard E. Wagner

Typeset in Times by
RefineCatch Limited, Bungay, Suffolk

First issued in paperback in 2013

British Library Cataloguing in Publication Data
A catalogue record for this book is available from the British Library

Library of Congress Cataloging-in-Publication Data
Wagner, Richard E.
  Mind, society, and human action: time and knowledge in a theory of
  social-economy / Richard E. Wagner.
      p. cm.
  Includes bibliographical references and index.
  1. Economics—Sociological aspects.   2. Economics—Political
  aspects.   I. Title.
  HM548.W34 2010
  306.3—dc22   2009032979

ISBN13: 978-0-415-75001-1 (pbk)
ISBN13: 978-0-415-77996-8 (hbk)
ISBN13: 978-0-203-85840-0 (ebk)

Contents

Figures

Tables

Preface

In his *History of Economic Analysis*, Joseph Schumpeter (1954) explains that any adventure in economic analysis starts with a pre-analytical cognitive vision about the object of interest. The subsequent analytical challenge is to probe that vision and to articulate its contours, which requires the creation of a suitable intellectual architecture. In *Human Action*, Ludwig von Mises (1966) explains that people act to remove uneasiness. An author who combines Schumpeter and Mises will realize that analytical writing starts with uneasiness about existing theoretical formulations and poses the challenge of reducing that uneasiness within the contours of a sensible intellectual architecture. This is what I try to do in this book.

Due to a teaching gap created by Karen Vaughn's retirement in 2004, for four years I taught the first semester of a year-long graduate sequence titled "Austrian Theory of the Market Process." This book emerged out of that teaching challenge. I was not surprised at being asked to teach this course because I have always had an interest in Austrian-style economic theory. At the same time, however, I have never identified myself as an Austrian-style theorist. Nor have Austrian-style theorists identified me as one of them. For instance, Vaughn (1994: 118) describes me as "sympathetic to some aspects of Austrian economics," but not genuinely an Austrian. There is a good deal of neoclassical-style theory that I embrace, just as there is a good deal of Austrian-style theory that I avoid. So I decided to use my stint teaching this course to sort out my sense of what I regard as the appropriate relationship between Austrian and neoclassical styles of economic theory. This book emerged from that effort.

The predominant research program in contemporary economics has long been neo-Walrasian in character, as Roy Weintraub (1993) notes in his *General Equilibrium Analysis*. My aim in this book, as in the teaching effort that nurtured it, is to articulate some elements of an alternative research program which could be described as neo-Mengerian to maintain linguistic parallelism with Weintraub, though I think of it more as a program on emergent dynamics to stress affinities with other bodies of contemporary literature. Furthermore, I do not regard neo-Mengerian as equivalent to Austrian. Many Austrian formulations after Carl Menger melded in significant respects into Walrasian-style formulations, as Sandye Gloria-Palermo (1999) explains in her treatment of *The Evolution of Austrian Economics*. Eugen von Böhm-Bawerk (1899) did this in arriving at what is generally regarded as the canonical statement of Austrian-style capital theory. Ludwig von Mises (1912) and Friedrich Hayek (1932 and 1935) did this in their development of what became known as the Austrian theory of the business cycle: that theory starts from a position of general equilibrium, imposes an exogenous shock through an increase in the supply of money, and generates a sequence of boom-and-bust through an exercise in comparative statics. Israel Kirzner's (1973) treatment of entrepreneurship is largely an effort to make the postulate of general equilibrium seem empirically more reasonable than it might otherwise seem.

Menger was not a theorist of closed systems of equilibrium relationships who construed economic analysis as a set of exercises in maximization and comparative statics. He was a theorist of open systems characterized by ongoing processes of development where people have limited and individually specific knowledge. Where the neo-Walrasian vision construes society as a field of equilibrated relationships, a neo-Mengerian vision construes society as an evolving organism, though an organism that is neither a sentient creature nor is reducible to some average or representative individual. These contrasting visions were apparent to Menger, as is revealed in the correspondence between Menger and Walras collected in Jaffé (1965) and explored in Jaffé (1976). In one letter where Menger responded to Walras's argument that they were kindred spirits analytically speaking, Menger answered: "There is indeed a resemblance between us. There is an analogy of concepts on certain points but not on the deeper questions" (Jaffé 1965: 176).

A neo-Mengerian vision of the continual generation of knowledge and the turbulence that results does not blend with a neo-Walrasian vision of a steady state. An analysis centered on turbulent processes of development and change cannot be merged with one centered on steady states, for what it is that propels the turbulence—an inconsistency among the plans of different people—can have no place in any framework centered on steady states, which presumes consistency among those plans. The incommensurability of these analytical frameworks was recognized by John Maynard Keynes (1936) in the closing paragraph of the Preface to his *General Theory of Employment, Interest, and Money*, where he lamented: "The composition of this book has been for the author a long struggle of escape, and so must the reading of it be for most readers if the author's assault upon them is to be successful—a struggle of escape from habitual modes of thought and expression. The ideas which are here expressed so laboriously are extremely simple and should be obvious. The difficulty lies, not in the new ideas, *but in escaping from the old ones*, which ramify . . . into every corner of our minds [my emphasis]."

I organized my teaching effort during those four semesters around Washington Irving's (1819) tale of Rip van Winkle's 20-year nap. During the year preceding their taking my course, the students had taken the standard core courses on micro and macro theory. I asked the students to try as best they could to imagine that they started their studies by reading Carl Menger (1871, 1883), then fell asleep for over a century. The object of this experiment was to embrace Menger's vision of social economy without influence from the subsequent century and a quarter of economic theory. While this is, of course, an impossible task actually to accomplish, it does provide an alternative point of theoretical departure to that provided by contemporary theorizing. In my syllabus I stated the hypothetical situation this way: "Suppose you reached a state that Keynes thought he had reached—of having flushed Walrasian-style theorizing out of his mind. Having accomplished that, you develop your analytical inspiration from Carl Menger, realizing that Menger wrote long ago and we are writing now. The analytical challenge is to bridge the gap between Menger and us, so as to contribute to economic theory today. If Menger supplies one end of the bridge's anchorage, you might think of letting Oscar Morgenstern's (1972) commentary on contemporary economic theory supply the other end (for Morgenstern was a genuine Austrian who is not regarded as an Austrian these days, and yet his orientation toward economics fits clearly within a neo-Mengerian motif). As for the character of the roadway that will connect these two points of anchorage, that is what we will work on this semester."

This book embraces Keynes' lament, and pursues economic theory from within an orientation that I think is similar to Menger's. Within this emergent-dynamic research program, and in contrast to a comparative-static research program, human action is to a significant extent creative and open, and thus is not conveyed adequately by closed models of constrained maximization. Furthermore, the primary object of economic theory is societal interaction and the social configurations that emerge from that interaction, and with economic phenomena appearing as emergent reflections of continuing development and not as states of equilibrium. Almost nothing corresponds to the exogenous shocks that are so widely used in economic theory, for those so-called shocks reflect the emergent and turbulent character of human societies. In large measure they are the products of conflicting plans and the working out of those conflicts, only the parade of conflicts never ends because there is no equilibrium to offer respite from life itself.

While these alternative orientations are antithetical, they are not contradictory. Rather they are incommensurable, and with needless confusion and antagonism resulting when they are treated as being commensurable. After the fashion of yin-and-yang, these contrary orientations are complementary, with each capable of being employed to yield valid insight in its appropriate domain. They cannot, however, be unified into one encompassing orientation. Where the emergent-dynamic orientation seeks to illuminate the operation of actual social-economic processes in historical time, the comparative-static orientation seeks to uncover the logical structure of social configurations that are independent of any process of development through time.

Reality presents us with both structure and change. A theory that seeks to explain structure as an equilibrated pattern is not simultaneously suitable for explaining the ongoing process by which tomorrow differs from yesterday. The neo-Walrasian program seeks to uncover a logic behind the structure of contemporaneous observations that is valid outside of time. The neo-Mengerian program seeks to uncover a logic of process, whereby the world we experience changes through processes that nonetheless conform to invariant principles of human action. Where the neo-Walrasian program characterizes an equilibrated world devoid of profit opportunities, a neo-Mengerian program characterizes the pursuit and capture of profit opportunities as pivotal to the generation of a tomorrow that differs from what we experienced yesterday. These alternative observations are not contradictory, but rather reflect salient facets of non-commensurable analytical frameworks.

My analytical focus is on processes of motion that generate turbulence, with equilibrium being only one mental tool among many and most certainly not a representation of reality. Those processes, moreover, are characterized as partially connected chains of causation and not as simultaneously equilibrated relationships, which shifts the emphasis from a circular flow to a structure of production. Little use is made of comparative statics, which is a tool for planning in which multiple histories are entertained in the mind; instead, choice is irreversible, with entrepreneurship supplying the energy that propels history forward. These neo-Mengerian themes and intuitions are joined to various types of contemporary conceptual material that seem useful for advancing our understanding of the political economy of generally but not universally orderly turbulence. This material is represented by such scholarly areas as economic sociology, institutional economics, political economy, evolutionary economics, and agent-based computational modeling, all of which are used to illustrate and convey some of the substantive ideas concerning the emergent features of interaction in a world of widespread and deep heterogeneity among people. The value of this conjunction of old and new is, of course, for readers to judge.

I should note that this book treats its object of analytical interest as one denoted as social economy and not one denoted as economy. I do this in explicit recognition of my affinity with the nineteenth-century tradition of *Sozialökonomik*. This tradition treats both individual minds and society as ontologically real, and with causation running in both directions. This analytical orientation contrasts with the predominant orientation of contemporary economic theory wherein society is reduced to mind, either directly or indirectly. This reduction is accomplished directly through the employment of representative agent modeling where social observations are explained by modeling the choices made by some presumptively representative individual. This reduction is accomplished indirectly through a style of theoretical exposition that looks to societal averages and not to entire populations and their structures as the pertinent objects of explanation.

Put differently, I treat economics and sociology as complementary domains of inquiry even as I recognize that there will always exist regions of contestation along some of the boundaries. Regardless of the location and extent of those regions, I do not seek to reduce one to the other through some act of imperialistic subjugation. In this respect, my focus on emergent processes of mind–society interaction fits comfortably within the Germanic tradition of historically oriented scholarship that is often treated as the bête noire of Austrian thought. It should be recalled, however, that Menger regarded his 1871 *Grundsätze* as falling within while advancing the general contours of the Germanic scholarship of the time, even dedicating the book to Wilhelm Roscher. While the book's reception by some of the major German figures was not as warm as Menger had hoped, he nonetheless saw his work as fitting within that general stream of scholarship; his subsequent 1883 *Untersuchungen* did nothing to reverse this impression. In my judgment the complementarities between the orientations strongly outweigh the differences, as Menger recognized and despite a lot of revisionist writing to the contrary that treats the so-called *Methodenstreit* as some kind of clash among incommensurable worldviews when it was really a form of intra-family quarrel, though these types of quarrels can often be particularly intense in spite of or perhaps because of the closeness of the participants.

The book proceeds in eight chapters, each of which starts by reciting some neo-Walrasian orientation toward that material that the students would have encountered the preceding year, and with the remainder of the chapter exploring facets of a neo-Mengerian orientation toward that material.

Chapter 1 examines some matters of scope and method, both as these pertain to the contrast between the two research programs and as they relate to the relation between mind and society. **Chapter 2** explores the bi-directional relationship between mind and society, using property-governed relationships among people, along with their ongoing contestation, as the grammar for pursuing an emergent-dynamic research program. These two chapters set the stage methodologically for the rest of the book.

Chapters 3 and 4 treat human action as significantly open and creative, as against treating human choice as closed and pre-determined. These chapters treat a stylized Robinson Crusoe, though one who exists and operates within society, as against being a reduced version of society. Hence economics is located as a social science and not as a science of household management. **Chapter 3** explores economizing human action in light of the twin presumptions that (1) such action is open and not closed and (2) that such action is influenced significantly by social context, and with the emphasis placed on action as distinct from choice. **Chapter 4** examines the creation and organization of team-production processes and relationships, and does so in a context where present choices are based on projections about future conditions that are open-ended and where monetary calculation provides the language and grammar of economizing action.

Where Chapters 3 and 4 treat human action, Chapters 5 to 8 treat human interaction. Interaction among people is the domain of emergent phenomena and spontaneously generated ordering. **Chapter 5** treats prices and forms of market configuration as objects that emerge and change through interaction among participants, and not as data that inform individual efforts at optimization. Market configurations, like macro-level phenomena generally, are not objects of choice but are emergent products of interaction. **Chapter 6** treats competition as an open-ended process that operates continually to transform society, while at the same time recognizing that the particular contours of such competition can also influence the character of human relationships within a society. **Chapter 7** explores the bridge between micro and macro levels of theorizing by elaborating on the notion of an emergent ecology of enterprises, and of explaining that it is just as sensible to speak of macro foundations for micro theory as it is to speak of micro foundations for macro theory. **Chapter 8** explores political economy in terms of a mapping that replaces the common disjunction between economy and polity with one where an entangled web of connections between market-based and polity-based enterprises leads to a different orientation toward state activity.

During the academic year 2008–2009, I presented significant parts of the book at conferences sponsored by the Foundation for Economic Education, the Wirth Institute, and the Fund for the Study of Spontaneous Orders. I am grateful to the sponsors and the participants for valuable commentary and discussion. In alphabetical order I should like to mention, in particular, Stephan Boehm, Peter Boettke, Bruce Caldwell, David Colander, Daniel D'Amico, Richard Ebeling, Steve Horwitz, Sanford Ikeda, Roger Koppl, Peter Leeson, Peter Lewin, Roderick Long, Adam Martin, Jason Potts, Barkley Rosser, Jack Sommer, and Glen Whitman for particularly helpful comments. I am also grateful to Petrik Runst, who as my graduate assistant the past two years not only provided fine research assistance but also provided a valuable student's-eye examination of an earlier draft of the manuscript that led me to make a significant number of revisions and emendations.

1   Social economy

Some preliminaries on scope and method

All scientific inquiry involves a relationship between an inquiring subject and an object of inquiry. Contemporary economic inquiry largely construes its object as a mechanism that operates in predictable fashion, as noted in Mirowski (1989, 2002). In contrast, this book designates its object as a social economy and, moreover, treats that object as a living organism that is not adequately apprehended by the image of mechanism. This reference to social economy, the contours of which are explored more fully in Chapter 2, harkens back to the nineteenth century when *Sozialökonomik* designated a field of inquiry that spanned what we now understand as economics and sociology. A program of social economy differs from mechanism-based economic theory in two significant respects. First, the object of analytical interest is society and not individuals or households. Consequently, the central analytical framework entails interaction among individuals, as distinct from optimizing choice by individuals (Buchanan 1964). There is no reduction of society to some representative agent. Nor is social-level explanation confined to the articulation of relationships among societal averages, for significant explanatory work is done by the structured pattern of relationships that exist within a society.

Second, the relationship between minds and society is bi-directional. In one direction, interaction among minds generates such social configurations as property rights, contractual relationships, and organizational forms: this is the standard direction of movement for economic theory. In the other direction, however, those emergent configurations influence the substantive content of mind and hence the objects of human action. Mechanism-based economic theory portrays autonomous individuals who *act on* society or markets in two respects: they supply inputs to the market and they withdraw products from the market. Within this setting economic theory explores the pattern of market production in relation to consumer wants. In contrast, the theory of social economy explored here features individuals who *act in* society and not just on it. In consequence, societal configurations influence the content of individual action just as interaction among individuals is the source of those configurations.

This chapter examines a potpourri of methodological matters that set apart a program of social-economic theory from the mechanism-based program of economic theory.[1] It starts by considering the nature of the object of theoretical inquiry. This object is not directly apprehensible, but is itself constructed through theoretical effort. Mind and society are both real objects; they are distinct but non-separable realms of being. To speak of bi-directional interaction is to speak of a process that operates through time and not some equilibrium state that is imagined outside of time. Theories of social economy thus make greater use of ideas based on emergence than on ideas based on equilibrium.[2] This should not, however, be construed as a call for disequilibrium theory, which is a sensible construction only in the presence of an equilibrium theory; rather, it is a call for non-equilibrium theory, as illustrated by Katzner (1998). In other words, the object of theoretical examination is likened to a motion picture, perhaps taken of a performance by an improvisational jazz quintet, and not to a snapshot of that quintet. The analytical focus is on processes and not on states. This alternative focal point, I should note, is not a disjunctive choice; rather, it involves a relationship of foreground to background: processes involving change are moved into the analytical foreground while states of equilibrium are relegated to the background. Among other things, theories based on emergence entail the passing of time, and this in turn entails the creation of new ideas and plans which operate continually to modify social configurations.

Subject, object, and economic theory

There are two types of entities that can serve as objects of theoretical examination, and those objects can be denoted by the contrasting terms, simple and complex (Hayek 1967). Simple objects are those that can be apprehended directly by the observer. A chair, a diamond, and a worm are all objects that can be apprehended directly, even though observers can differ in their purposes of inquiry and the questions they ask about their objects of inquiry. One person might study the genetics of different kinds of worms; another might study the comparative attractiveness of those worms to brook trout. In either case, the object of examination is apprehended directly and not through some preceding act of theoretical construction or interpretation.

All subjects who examine those objects will agree that they are examining the same thing. They may hold different opinions about some properties of those objects, typically because of some lack of knowledge, but they will agree about the identity of the object of their disagreement. If the chair is made from wood, they might disagree about what kind of wood was used to make the chair because it is outside their competence to render such a judgment. If worms differ in apparent attractiveness to brook trout, some observers might suspect that this is due to differences in enzymes secreted by different types of worms while others might suspect that it arises because of different patterns of motion made underwater by the worms. Still, the apprehension of the chair or worm is independent of any choice made by the theorizing subject, even though such subjects might differ in the knowledge they bring to bear on their theorizing activities.

By contrast, complex objects are those that cannot be apprehended directly but can be apprehended only through some preceding theoretical framework. With respect to complex objects, the scientific enterprise involves a compound form of theorizing, what Hayek (1952) describes as the compositive method wherein one theoretical framework is used to construct the object that is then subjected to theoretical examination.[3] There are many objects of theoretical examination that can be apprehended only through the prior creation of some conceptual framework that brings those objects into view. The natural sciences contain many such objects: gravity, for instance, is such an object, in contrast to a planet which is directly apprehensible. The social sciences likewise are filled with objects whose exploration requires a preceding theoretical framework for their identification. Prices are objects that are directly apprehensible, but markets are not. There can be specific market settings that are directly apprehensible, as illustrated by a local farmers' market at some town square on a Saturday morning. But as the term is generally used by economists and other social scientists, market is an abstract noun whose existence can be inferred but not observed.

Many such objects appear to be directly apprehensible even though they aren't. Typically this is because the requisite interpretative act is so deeply embedded in culture and tradition that we are unaware of the intermediation of an interpretative framework to make sense of our observations. A ballet illustrates such an object. What is directly apprehensible is just the sight of some people moving about in the same vicinity. The pattern of movement is different from that presented by the crowd in front of a theater during intermission, but in both cases what is directly apprehensible is only a number of people moving about in proximity to one another. The ballet as an object of examination appears to be directly apprehensible even though it is not because its form is something of which we were previously aware. It is the same with prices and markets. We observe prices directly, and from this observation combined with scientific and cultural tradition we infer the existence of markets from the presence of prices.

When we come to objects like economy, polity, or society, we are dealing in large measure with objects that cannot be apprehended directly but which can be apprehended only with the prior assistance of some organized pattern of thought. To be sure, there are objects inside such objects that are directly apprehensible. A factory, a city hall, and a dance club are directly apprehensible objects that exist inside the objects we denote by such terms as economy, polity, and society. It is, of course, the same for the relationship between such directly apprehensible objects as planets and those like gravity which are not directly apprehensible. This situation is unavoidable, but it presents the problem summarized by Friedrich Nietzsche's oft-acknowledged references to looking through different windows: the appearance and qualities of objects that are not directly apprehensible may vary depending on the conceptual window through which they are viewed.

There are numerous ways of apprehending the objects and relationships of relevance to economic inquiry. One theoretical framework may define its objects as resources and the relationships as allocations of those resources among uses. An alternative framework might define its objects as people, their thoughts, and their relationships as these interact to generate organized patterns of activity. The former framework leads to an economic theory centered on things and their allocations; the latter framework leads to a social-economic theory centered on people and their thoughts and plans (Rosenberg 1960, Shackle 1972). The theory of social economy explored here places thoughts and relationships in the analytical foreground and sets resource allocations in the analytical background. The study of economy, polity, or society involves relationships between theorizing subjects and the objects they examine, only the object and its properties must be constructed through prior conceptual inquiry because they are not directly apprehensible. A market economy is an abstract noun that is invoked to incorporate various patterns of activity that economists think they observe when human interactions are ordered within the private law framework of property, contract, and liability (Eucken 1952).

Within contemporary universities, economics, politics, and sociology are distinct fields of study, each with separate academic departments and associated professional associations and journals. Together they comprise the core of the social sciences.[4] In general usage, the domains of the core social sciences would seem to be pretty clear: Economy deals with industry and commerce, with making a livelihood; Polity deals with governing, with keeping peace and order; Society is the residuum that holds whatever is not contained within economy and polity, mostly the domain of families and civic associations. According to this trichotomy, society can be decomposed into three distinct spheres of human activity: economics treats commerce, politics treats governance, and sociology treats everything else.

This approach to definition, while in common play, would seem nonetheless to be conceptually incoherent in light of the considerable commingling of human activity that occurs throughout those domains. Many people earn their livelihood in politics, so politics is economics. Corporate officials spend a good amount of their time dealing with political officials, so economics is politics. Corporate and political officials belong to clubs and churches, and also raise families, so economics and politics are both sociology. Society simply denotes everyone and their activities. Some of those activities involve people in seeking employment and establishing businesses. Other activities will find people running for elected office, campaigning for candidates, and writing newspaper editorials on issues that are topics of political controversy. Yet other activities will find people worshiping in churches and going to dances sponsored by country clubs. There would seem to be no coherent reason for the organization of churches to be the domain of sociology, the organization of legislatures to be the domain of politics, and the organization of corporations to be the domain of economics when the same principles of human action and social interaction are in operation across all of those domains.

Economizing action, spontaneous order, and economic theory

Economic theory originates in recognition that societies exhibit orderly patterns of human activity even though people are largely free to choose their patterns of activity, as against having their activities directed by some external authority. Economic theory seeks to explain how economizing action by individuals generates self-organized patterns of activity in society. With respect to those principles of human action, economic theory begins with the recognition that people act so as to attain what they believe to be more highly desired states of being. People can differ in the ends they seek, in the means they possess, and in their ideas or beliefs regarding how to traverse from means to ends. All the same, economizing action provides the point of departure for economic theory. But such action is only a point of departure for a field of study whose object of interest is society. The abstract noun economy points to that facet of society that contains interactions among economizing individuals, including various groupings that those individuals form.

The history of economic thought reveals several particular definitions of the domain of economic science, as Israel Kirzner (1960) surveys, though these particular definitions can be collapsed into two primary categories. One category distinguishes among types of human action, and limits economics to those actions that are aimed at the creation and use of wealth. This materialistic definition of subject matter leads to an emphasis on economics as an administrative science of resource allocation, which is readily susceptible to materialist images of choosing among objects according to their contribution to production or utility. This materialist definition, which is the prevalent definition in use according to various dictionaries, is one that links economics closely with industry and commerce. The world of industry and commerce is an arena of human action, with economics being the science that examines that arena. According to this definition, economics treats that subset of human activity where people are concerned with the creation and disposition of wealth. The remaining human activities represent something other than economic action, and to the extent those activities are nonetheless social, they involve such other social sciences as sociology and political science. It was in this respect that Colander, Holt, and Rosser (2004) explained that most economic theory rests on three presumptions: rationality, selfishness, and equilibrium, as elaborated in Koppl (2006).

This treatment of economics as the theory of commercial practice is incoherent in at least two respects. It is incoherent within the confines of the materialist definition of economics because politics and sociology are also relevant for the creation and disposition of wealth. With respect to political science, for instance, one famous definition was contained in the title of Harold Lasswell's (1935) *Politics: Who Gets What, When, How*. It is common to write a production function as describing a relationship between inputs and output. Some of those inputs are hired through ordinary market transactions, which might make them the domain of economics. Other necessary inputs, including regulatory permissions, are obtained through political transactions, which would seem to place production into the domain of political science. Furthermore, the skills and attitudes that people possess, and which affect the character of their productive activities, are acquired in families, schools, and other institutional settings within civil society, which would seem to render production a topic for sociology.

The materialist treatment of economics as the science of business practice treats economic action as synonymous with hedonism, as illustrated by a sharp distinction between self-interested action and altruistic action. The alternative, non-materialist definition recognizes that economizing action is present in all intentional human activity. Among other things, from the perspective of the acting subject there is no categorical distinction between self-interested and altruistic action. For one thing, action is always performed by an acting self; moreover, the content of that action depends on what it is that interests those acting selves: it is a self's interest that propels a self to act. There is no option to being self-interested, a point that is explained thoroughly and charmingly by Philip Wicksteed (1910). To say this, however, is not to invoke hedonism, for to do this would be to recur to the materialist construction of economics. It is only to invoke the purely formal principle that all human action is aimed at making the human organism feel better, as illustrated by Demasio's (1994) treatment of Descartes' error as well as by Nussbaum's (2001) treatment of the intelligence of emotions, where both reason and sentiment are coherent emanations from the human organism. As a substantive matter, what makes human organisms feel better varies widely among people and involves genetics and other people, the latter in the form of social processes and configurations.

Albert Schweitzer and Adolf Hitler were both selves who pursued their interests. The substance of their interests differed greatly, which led the former to become a figure of admiration and the latter a figure of revulsion. In his thirties, Schweitzer left behind a promising career as a theologian to study medicine and then practice it in Africa. At a similar age, Hitler decided to stay home and practice politics. While they pursued different ends, they each surely sought to be successful in their pursuits. The search for analytical coherence surely starts from recognition that each of us seeks to be effective in whatever we attempt. This proposition is by no means testable, for the negation of this proposition is simple nonsense. People act teleologically in using the means they can command to attain the ends they seek. People can differ in the means they can obtain, as well as in their ability to recognize means for what they are in relation to the ends they seek. People can differ in their talents for living just as they can differ in their talents for singing or playing golf (Alchian 2006: xiii–xv explains that golf is the quintessential sporting activity of a capitalist society). The ends people can seek are limited only by their imaginations, and it is common for people in a society to seek conflicting ends, even though much economic theorizing has been based upon some presumed harmony among ends, as illustrated by efforts to set forth sufficient conditions for the existence of a competitive equilibrium.

The alternative to the materialist definition of economics is the scarcity definition articulated by Lionel Robbins (1932) and Ludwig von Mises (1933). As set forth there, economics does not study the particular facet of human action concerned with the creation and disposition of wealth, but rather studies all intentional human activity, wherein people act continually to secure more highly desired states of existence in the face of a universal inability to satisfy all of their wants. Economic theory begins with economizing human action, and proceeds to explore how this economizing point of departure plays out within a society. While much economizing action results in the creation or use of wealth, it is the action and not the material results of such action that comprises the object of analytical interest; moreover, that action is not independent of either the actions or beliefs of other people but rather is influenced and channeled by those actions and beliefs.

There are people whom we apprehend directly and societies which we apprehend through some theoretical framework. Without some sensible theoretical framework, it makes no sense to designate one set of activities as economic, another set as political, and a third set as sociological. All of those activities are conducted by the same people; moreover, it is through interaction among those people that all of these activities acquire their characteristic features and organizational patterns. There is a unity to human action and social order that renders incoherent any effort to separate life into economic, political, and sociological spheres of interest and activity. What is directly apprehensible is recognition that there are people doing all kinds of things, and doing them in generally but not totally coordinated fashion. The analytical challenge becomes one of articulating coherence to those activities and patterns. This articulation can only occur within some particular theoretical framework, and in this respect options exist, as illustrated by the contrast between a snapshot and a film of an improvisational jazz quintet.

The customary approach to economic modeling is to treat individuals as autonomous and society as a landscape on which people act, but without being changed in any way by that landscape. This approach was set forth nicely by George Stigler and Gary Becker (1977) in asserting that economic modeling should take preferences as universal givens. In similar respect, there is a large Hobbes-like literature that seeks to explain societal formations as generated through interaction among adults, as represented lucidly by Peyton Young's (1998) treatment. Hence, a society is explained as a form of contract among the participating adults, perhaps as illustrated by the Mayflower

Compact. In similar fashion, market economies generate an array of goods and services that promotes the pre-existing desires of the members of the society.

A major problem with the Hobbes-like formulations is that adults can never arrive at adulthood on their own. Humans are reared in social groupings of some form where, among other things, habits of heart and mind are established. While we can always use our imagination to construct some primeval setting to denote some point of origin for a foray into social theory, there is no option grounded in experience to theorizing *in medias res*, as Randall Collins (1998) explains in his treatise on intellectual change. In this vein, and similar to Emil Durkheim (1893), Georg Simmel (1900), Vilfredo Pareto (1935), and Norbert Elias (1982, 1991), I work with a bi-directional relationship between mind and society. The interaction among acting people generates higher-order phenomena of various societal configurations. From one direction, the interaction among minds generates and transforms societal formations; this is the conventional order of economic theory. From the other direction, however, those formations both channel and shape the ends people choose to pursue, as well as the means they employ in doing so.

Society is not an individual spoken of in a loud voice. A society is comprised of individuals, and yet a society is an object in its own right. To say this is not to assert some organic notion of a sentient creature that reflects some kind of will, general or otherwise. Only individuals can act, but interaction among acting individuals generates societal formations that are not products of deliberate choice. Those formations, moreover, serve to regulate individual conduct, though there is considerable historical variation in the types of regulation that have occurred. In any case, the relation between mind and society is bi-directional, and with interaction among people serving to generate societal configurations that shape and channel the contours of human action.

Technology offers one arena for illustrating this bi-directional relationship, and other illustrations will be given later. Ideas originate in minds, but the technologies that emerge also shape the content of minds, as explained by Kass (1993). Consider such simple technologies as cell phones or email. These are products of human creation that allow people to accomplish things they could not have accomplished before, or at least not accomplished so easily. But this isn't all they accomplish. They also influence the expectations other people come to hold, and which, through societal interaction, can influence an individual's evaluation of options for action. At an earlier time a person could control the timing with which he or she dealt with the outside world: mail took time traveling in each direction; the recipient of a phone message might be away. No such excuses are possible any longer, and the new technology transforms expectations about the etiquette of electronic communication. While no act of legislation requires near-instantaneous responses, it is nonetheless clear that people tend to appraise and judge other people's conduct according to the quickness with which they respond to electronic communications.[5] From one analytical direction, interaction among minds generates social configurations; but from the other direction those configurations can also influence the content of minds as evidenced by the patterns of human action that result. In this respect, there is a long-standing claim that commerce might act to polish manners, a theme examined by Albert Hirschman (1977, 1982, 1992) and which fits within the framework explored by Norbert Elias (1982).

Alternative research programs for economic theory

Recognition that economic theory pertains to all human action and social organization, and not just to a hedonistically-driven subset of human action, does not compel a particular form or content for economic theory. Further choices are necessary to supply form and content to any program of research. Any such program will rest on a set of hard core propositions that are used to propel analysis but are not themselves subject to analysis. Such hard core propositions comprise the scientific equivalent of a *Weltanschauung* or world view, which has been sketched generally by Lakatos (1970, 1978) and explored for economics in particular in the essays collected in Latsis (1976).

With respect to the material of economic inquiry, we can recognize two distinct qualities of social life. At one level there is a sense of continual change; at the other level there is a sense of invariance. These distinct senses are expressed by the aphorism, "the more things change, the more they stay the same." On the level of invariance, we can recognize with Ecclesiastes that there is nothing new under the sun. At the level of change, we can recognize with Heraclites that it is impossible even to step twice into the same river. Recognition of these distinct levels of perception regarding social life suggests a bivalent logic for economic inquiry (Wagner forthcoming). One type of logic addresses the qualities of social life that are universal across time and place: this would be a theory of invariant pattern or structure. The other type of logic addresses the internal generation of change: this would be a theory of temporally-situated processes (Rescher 2000).

Both types of theory are reasonable objects of inquiry, but they are different objects of inquiry. With respect to a theory focused on invariant structure, the analytical hard core of such a research program is widely associated with León Walras's (1874) initial articulation of general equilibrium, though, as Roy Weintraub (1993) shows, general equilibrium analysis has developed in quite different directions from Walras's initial formulation. This type of research program is widely recognized by the designation neo-Walrasian, and will be explored in the next section. It suffices to note here that this hard core construes its object as exhibiting formal patterns that are invariant across time and place. To be sure, the orientation of the neo-Walrasian program was present in much of the preceding theologically-oriented scholarship that sought to articulate the order of creation (Viner 1972), and with that eternal order standing outside of time.

The alternative research program focused on the internal generation of societal change carries no such recognized designation among economists. In recognition of the teaching program by which this book came to be written that I set forth in the Preface, this alternative research program could be designated as neo-Mengerian, though this alternative orientation was also present in the theories of spontaneous order we associate with the Scottish Enlightenment (Daiches, Jones, and Jones 1986, Buchan 2004). It was also present in the German Historical orientation that is often ascribed as being the opposite of the Austrian orientation (Shionoya 2005, Reinert 2003, 2007), and with eyewitness testimony about the similarities from a student who studied in both Berlin and Vienna during 1892 and 1893 set forth in Seager (1893). Furthermore, the economic theory of Alfred Marshall similarly places a concern with emergent dynamics and not comparative statics in the analytical foreground (Groenewegen 2007, Sutton 2000, Keynes 1951: 125–217). Peter Lewin (1999: 113) distinguishes between the Ricardian and Mengerian traditions to convey the same sense of distinctiveness.

While the contrast between neo-Walrasian and neo-Mengerian will carry familiar meaning, it also invites misunderstanding due to its association with the common dichotomy between neoclassical and Austrian economics which is often given play (compare, for instance Rosen 1997 and Yeager 1997a). Menger and Walras had distinctively different orientations toward economic theory, and their names are typically associated with the appellations Austrian and neoclassical. But the philosophers of the Scottish enlightenment could hardly be called Austrians. Furthermore, a good deal of Austrian-inspired scholarship after Menger largely embraced a good deal of the Walrasian orientation that was antithetical to Menger's effort, as Gloria-Palermo (1999) explains.

Both types of research program start with recognition that there is some orderliness to the object of inquiry, for otherwise there would be nothing to theorize about. They differ, however, in the analytical questions they pose about that object. They erect different windows for viewing social-economic phenomena to capture the different phenomena of interest. Where the neo-Walrasian window presents snapshots of equilibrated images taken of life in prefabricated worlds, the neo-Mengerian window presents films depicting processes where people participate in creating the world they come to experience. The continual creation of knowledge and injection of novelty into society is what occupied the foreground of Carl Menger's vision of the economic process. This emergent-dynamic research program could alternatively be called an evolutionary program, as illustrated by Boulding (1978), Nelson and Winter (1982), Loasby (1991), and Witt (1992a, 1992b), as well as some of the essays in Backhaus (2003). This alternative program, moreover, is more concerned with plausible than with demonstrative reasoning, as explored in Clower (1995).

The neo-Walrasian research program

The neo-Walrasian research program construes an economy as an equilibrated system of field-governed relationships, and with a similar framework for sociology set forth by Talcott Parsons (1951, 1967). This framework illustrates nicely the interrelated character of human actions across markets. It construes an economy as a connected set of markets that can be separated into product markets where goods and services are exchanged and factor markets where inputs are obtained and incomes earned. A disturbance in the market for one product will also affect the market for other products, as well as the market for inputs used in the production of products. The neo-Walrasian framework shows crisply how changes at one point in the nexus of economic relationships will induce changes elsewhere in that nexus, as illustrated crisply by Starr (1997) and Shoven and Whalley (1992).

A distinction can be made between treating a theory as a tool of thought and treating it as reasonably descriptive of reality, recognizing that all theories can never be fully descriptive because they are necessarily abstractions from reality, and with Asik Radomysler (1946) presenting a lucid distinction between abstraction that illuminates and abstraction that obscures the object of inquiry. As a tool of thought, the neo-Walrasian metaphysics of general equilibrium is surely indispensable for economic theory because it conveys the general interdependence among economic relationships in a society. As a description of reality, the situation is not so clear. It is possible to set forth necessary conditions for the existence of a general competitive equilibrium. What comes out of these formulations is mostly a sense that reality does not match those conditions.

Whatever the relation between reality and Pareto efficiency, the neo-Walrasian program nonetheless has proven successful in inspiring and organizing much contemporary economic scholarship, as Weintraub (1993) explains. It is possible for a person to fail to be captivated by efforts to prove the existence of a competitive equilibrium and yet be sufficiently impressed by the vision of general interdependence to employ that vision as a tool for organizing economic research. One can embrace the hard core of the neo-Walrasian program without displaying much interest regarding the conditions under which a competitive equilibrium might exist because that program is thought nonetheless to provide a fruitful framework for pursuing economic research.

Any research program can be portrayed with imagery that resembles the solar system: it contains a hard core of metaphysical or ontological presumptions that is analogous to the sun and is surrounded by various theoretical constructions that emanate from that hard core and are supported by it. The hard core is meta-theoretical and hence not subject directly to empirical examination. It is, however, subject to internal checks on the consistency of logic through processes of proof and refutation, as described by Lakatos (1976). In contrast, the theoretical constructions that emanate from the hard core are subject to processes of conjecture and refutation, as portrayed by Popper (1962). Those theories, moreover, reside within a protective belt that not only protects them from easy assault but serves to give them meaningful content. For instance, one theoretical construction supported by a neo-Walrasian hard core would maintain that competitive equilibrium requires equal prices for the same service, say home delivery of groceries. Yet experience might show that those prices are higher in high-crime neighborhoods than in low-crime neighborhoods. The protective belt would insulate this theoretical construction from refutation by incorporating some such notion as equalizing differences into the supply of labor, which in turn would increase the supply price required to obtain the labor required to deliver groceries in high-crime areas.

During his thorough examination of what has emerged as the neo-Walrasian research program, Weintraub (1993: 108–14) describes the hard core of that program in terms of six presumptions that themselves are not open to empirical examination, but which provide the grammatical or metaphysical framework for constructing theories. Table 1.1 presents a listing of the neo-Walrasian hard core adapted from Weintraub's presentation so as to be easily comparable with a listing of the neo-Mengerian hard core that will be presented momentarily. Different listings could doubtlessly be articulated because there is no formal convention that ratifies or adjudicates any such list. However such a listing might be constructed, any theoretical inquiry will necessarily be based on some prior presumptions that when shared by a significant set of scholars constitute the hard core of belief common to those scholars. Any scholarly research program will have some such hard core that provides the point of departure for particular scholarly efforts.

Scientific research programs also operate with both positive and negative heuristics. The positive heuristics provide guidance for the construction of theories; those heuristics promote the construction of theories that are consistent with the metaphysical hard core of the research program. In his presentation of the neo-Walrasian program, Weintraub (1993) presents two positive heuristics: (1) theories should contain agents who optimize; and (2) theories should make predictions about changes in equilibrium states in response to specified exogenous changes in parameters. A similar articulation of a positive heuristic was articulated by Reder (1982), who argued that

Table 1.1 Hard core of neo-Walrasian research program

1	Relevant reality contains only economic agents
2	Autonomous agents have preferences over outcomes
3	Agents maximize utility subject to constraints
4	Markets are interrelated and modeled as fields
5	Agents know everything necessary to optimize
6	Observations pertain to equilibrium states

economic models should be based on two presumptions: (1) agents maximize and (2) markets clear.

The methodology of scientific research programs also includes negative heuristics about what to avoid in the construction of theories. The real work, though, is done through the positive heuristics, for it is in light of the positive heuristics that the scholarly work of constructing economic theories is accomplished. In contrast, the negative heuristics just tell someone what not to do and what to dispute about someone else's work. Negative heuristics counsel researchers on how to avoid entering what the hard core would reveal as intellectual swamps. Weintraub (1993) lists three such negative heuristics for the neo-Walrasian program: (1) do not allow irrational behavior, (2) do not work without an equilibrium model, and (3) do not be concerned with the realism of the hard core propositions because you need them to do your work.

A neo-Mengerian research program

In sharp contrast to Walras, Carl Menger's analytical vision suggested a generative or emergent orientation toward economic phenomena, wherein complex macro formations emerge out of interaction among simpler micro units.[6] Among other things, an economy is construed as a set of network-based and not field-based relationships. Menger was an incipient theorist of emergent complexity who was caught inside a disciplinary maelstrom that was dominated by the formal simplicity of closed-form modeling. For Menger, the move from the individual or micro level to the societal or macro level was an elevation in analytical level, with macro phenomena emerging out of interaction among micro units. In contrast, for neo-Walrasian theorizing the move from micro to macro is not a movement in the direction of increasing complexity; to the contrary, macro is simply micro spoken in a booming voice. There is no difference between explaining the actions of Robinson Crusoe alone on his island and explaining the aggregation of the actions of the billions of people who inhabit the globe today. Micro and macro are equally simple phenomena to be represented by simple functional relationships among variables of interest. An individual's demand for a product might be represented by a function that includes the price of the product and the person's income. An aggregate demand for everything is conceptualized similarly, only the price is not some particular price but some statistically-constructed index of prices.

A helpful sketch of such interrelationships, however, need not be equally useful at showing how such interrelationships come into existence and undergo change through time. The neo-Walrasian formulation requires all transactions in a society to occur at the same instant. Otherwise, it is impossible to demonstrate the possible existence of equilibrium because trades that are made at non-equilibrium prices wreak havoc with the neatly ordered relationships postulated by the neo-Walrasian formulation. Within this formulation, prices exist in advance of transactions, for otherwise consumers could not use their given incomes to maximize their utilities. There is no recognition that prices arise out of the efforts of people to conclude transactions: people take prices as given in making transactions; they do not generate prices through transactions. The neo-Walrasian formulation seeks to characterize an orderly economy in terms of consistency among various postulated relationships regarding such things as consumer demands and producer technologies. What consumers will demand depends on their incomes; those incomes depend on the prices paid for productive inputs; the value of productive inputs to producers depends on the desires of consumers to buy those products. What results is a circular system of reasoning that reflects its logical consistency but which cannot be used to generate those relationships.

The neo-Mengerian research program is the antithesis of the neo-Walrasian program.[7] Menger wrote long before such techniques as agent-based computational modeling had arisen, but it's clear that Menger's theoretical intuitions would have supported emergent and generative styles of theorizing, much as Vriend (2002) claims for Friedrich Hayek. This reduction of societal phenomena to objects of individual choice is antithetical to the Mengerian vision. When many Crusoes interact, patterns emerge that would never have occurred through isolated individual action. Property, contract, legislatures, legal proceedings, and money are all phenomena of interaction and not of choice. Institutional arrangements are a macro- and not a micro-level phenomenon, recognition of which led Collins (1988) to postulate a meso level between micro and macro and with this trichotomy carried into economics by Potts and Morrison (2007). These phenomena represent a new level of existence that arises through interaction at a lower level. Accordingly, variation through time in some aggregate measure of activity is not to be explained in the same way as one would explain variation in a single person's pattern of activity.

There is a parallel in this respect with object-oriented programming, as explained by Mitchel Resnick (1994). Imagine traffic flowing down a highway, with the drivers following the simple rule of driving as fast as possible until they reach some stipulated distance behind the preceding car, then keeping that distance. If one car suddenly slows down, a traffic jam forms as drivers reduce their speed. Time-lapse photography would show the traffic jam to be moving backwards. Yet each car continues to move forward. It makes no sense to speak of the traffic jam as a gigantic car moving backwards. The jam consists of individual cars each moving forward, but interaction among those cars creates a higher-level phenomenon that has different properties than that possessed by any of the individual cars. There is no gigantic car, and no individual car is moving backwards.

In the spirit of Weintraub (1993), Table 1.2 sets forth my version of a neo-Mengerian hard core. Since the neo-Mengerian framework is concerned with theorizing about the emergent properties of action over some duration of time while the neo-Walrasian framework seeks to give an account of

Table 1.2 Hard core of neo-Mengerian research program

1	Relevant reality contains both economic agents and social structure
2	Agent preferences have social as well as genetic sources
3	Agents choose ends in addition to economizing on means
4	Markets are interrelated and modeled as networks
5	Agent knowledge is incomplete and distributed among agents
6	Observations are reflections of plans in process

instantaneous observations, there is no good reason to expect their hard cores to have the same structure. Nonetheless, I have constructed this listing of a neo-Mengerian hard core in this manner to facilitate comparison between the programs. This type of enforced comparability might not be the best way to articulate a neo-Mengerian research program because it applies a neo-Walrasian grammar to the neo-Mengerian program; nonetheless I can see pedagogic value in proceeding this way because of the familiarity of the neo-Walrasian grammar.

The hard cores differ in all six elements, though they nearly come together with the fourth element. Both programs treat markets as interrelated; however, the neo-Walrasian program works with field-based models while the neo-Mengerian program works with network-based models, and with the distinction between the two types of models explained in Potts (2000). For the other five elements, the differences between the programs are more significant. Where element #1 postulates that economic reality contains only economic agents for the neo-Walrasian program, it also postulates the reality of social structure for the neo-Mengerian program. Society is conceptualized in terms of networks of relationships within the neo-Mengerian program, and the properties of any such network depend on how that network is constituted.

Where element #2 in the neo-Walrasian program postulates that agents operate with given preferences, its counterpart in the neo-Mengerian program postulates that some preferences arise through particular patterns of social relationships, while also recognizing that some preferences arise from genetic sources. Element #3 in the neo-Walrasian program postulates that agents act mechanically to maximize pre-existing utility functions. The neo-Mengerian program holds that agents choose ends as well as employ means; furthermore, the choice of ends both entails a societal component and is not reducible to just another instance of the choice of means.

Element #5 of the neo-Walrasian hard core holds that agents have all the knowledge necessary to solve their optimization problems, whereas for the neo-Mengerian program knowledge is incomplete within any single agent and is distributed among agents. This element prevents any reduction of society to a representative agent, for the way that knowledge is used depends on the structure of social organization. Element #6 of the neo-Walrasian program claims that observations are of coordinated equilibria, so that meaning can be derived from a snapshot. In contrast, the comparable element #6 of the neo-Mengerian program claims that observations at some instant are but slices of some unfolding process, so that meaning is not derived directly from observation because meaning requires the interpretation of actions and plans.

Much of the remainder of this book will entail comparisons of positive and negative heuristics across a variety of topics. With respect to Weintraub's two positive heuristics for the neo-Walrasian program, the neo-Mengerian program would seem similar on the first positive heuristic and divergent on the second. Where the neo-Walrasian program theorizes in terms of agents optimizing over known options, the neo-Mengerian program theorizes about agents acting to implement plans that can be only incompletely articulated because the effect of any plan will depend on the future circumstances that will be influenced by future knowledge.

It is the second positive heuristic where the more significant difference appears between the two programs. The neo-Walrasian program holds that theoretical statements should refer to changes in equilibrium states. This follows from the sixth hard core proposition that all observations are of equilibrium states. Distinct observations refer to distinct equilibrium states, and this presumption suggests use of the positive heuristic to make predictions about the effect of changes in exogenous variables on equilibrium states. In contrast, the neo-Mengerian program does not postulate that observations are of equilibrium states, but rather are blips on a historical screen whose pattern is something to be discerned, as explored in O'Driscoll and Rizzo (1985). Theories start from planning agents, as illustrated by the first positive heuristic, but the entire set of agents is never fully coordinated. To the contrary, plans are continually being revised or abandoned. Among other things, institutional arrangements arise to facilitate the revision and abandonment of plans, and the neo-Mengerian counterpart to the second positive heuristic would counsel the construction of theories that, while consistent with agent planning, render intelligible the ongoing generation of the institutional framework that governs human action and interaction.

Ontology, epistemology, and economic theory

Both the neo-Walrasian and the neo-Mengerian programs provide views of generally orderly patterns of activity. A purely instrumentalist notion of science would advise the scientist to use the window that is easier to work with, unless the other window provides insight that cannot otherwise be obtained. This seems to be a reasonable basis for choice, save that the two windows present different objects for examination and so the respective views are not directly comparable but rather are non-commensurable. Furthermore, this instrumental notion elevates epistemology over ontology: what matters is some notion of goodness of fit and not some notion of the ability of a theory to reflect more essential features of the object of interest.

This presumption regarding the primacy of epistemology is not as apparent as the numerous references to Ockham's razor might seem to suggest. Any effort at social theory starts from recognition that societies are orderly. People are able to navigate within society in generally orderly and coherent fashion, and without being directed by some outside person or agency. Their activities are self-directed and self-organized, and this self-organization has often been described by the image of an invisible hand. This image, however, is potentially troubling and corrupting in its ability to lead thought astray, as illustrated by the assertion of the primacy of the epistemological over the ontological, the modern-classic illustration of which is Friedman (1953), and with the primacy of ontological presumptions set forth in Lawson (1997, 2003) and Lewis (2004).

The simplest possible notion of orderliness is equilibrium. The neo-Walrasian program provides a view of a society as an equilibrated structure of relationships that is characterized by a set of prices that is consistent with market-clearing in light of consumer demands. You cannot get any more orderly than this. Much work in economic theory involves claims of market failure, which brings in claims that the observed degree of orderliness is not as complete as it could be. This claim of market failure, however, cannot be rendered intelligible without an ontological effort that would account for plausibility regarding the actual degree of orderliness within a society. The neo-Walrasian program makes no effort to develop such an account of plausibility. In contrast, the neo-Mengerian program is concerned directly with probing the realm of the plausible with regard to the experienced degree of orderliness within a society.

Equilibrium is a sensible even if perhaps peculiar notion to apply to an individual, for it merely signifies coherence in the person's planned pattern of conduct regarding the employment of means in the pursuit of ends. A plan of activity can be coherent because it stands outside of history. When plans are put in motion inside history, they often require revision. The revision, and the accompanying flexibility in action that revision requires, is so second-nature that often we do not even recognize that we are revising plans while we act. Such a simple act as going to a grocery store to buy a specific list of items often requires plan revision when it is necessary to make a substitution because one or more of the desired items is missing. People have no trouble doing this and do not think of themselves as adapting to market disequilibrium, and yet that is what they are doing.

It is an entirely different matter to apply notions of equilibrium to societies. A society is not an acting creature from which we would expect coherence, but rather is an arena within which acting creatures interact. It's true that societal processes unfold in generally orderly fashion, though not always and never completely. People seek to be successful in action, and have over the years developed various customs and conventions that facilitate such success. While there is a good deal of permanence in social life, particularly over relatively short periods of time, there is also a good amount of turbulence, much of which manifests itself through capital gains and losses and through revisions of plans. While repetition and reproduction are discernable features of social life, so too are creation, novelty, and turbulence. The neo-Mengerian program is particularly apt for social theorizing in a setting of continual and turbulent development.

Any analytical framework that distinguishes between universal principles and particular instances of those principles that can take on multiple guises is one that will involve both process and structure. Structure speaks to the universally recognizable features of the actions, both inventive and repetitive, that occur within society. Ecclesiastes speaks to universal structure; Heraclites speaks to the emergent dynamics of historical process. Both process and structure (or equilibrium) provide useful analytical orientation, but there is a question of which occupies the foreground. In a neo-Mengerian program, the foreground is occupied by process. The wrong turn in economics that Boettke (1997) describes is perhaps less of a wrong turn than a reversal of foreground and background.

Both a parade and a crowd of spectators leaving a stadium after an event illustrate orderly, coordinated social configurations. Ontologically, they are different types of configuration with different sources of orderliness. The orderliness of the parade is not reasonably explainable in the same fashion as the orderliness of the crowd. Both configurations involve connections among people, but the same theoretical framework does not explain both types of orderliness. The parade is an organization; the crowd of spectators is an order that is constituted through interaction among the spectators, each of whom is an organization within the order (Hayek 1973).

A parade is a coordinated movement of people, and with the coordination achieved by a parade marshal. Things can sometimes go wrong in a parade, and these would represent exogenous shocks to the marshal's plan. For instance, a horse might drop some dung that was neither cleared nor observed by a following trumpet player. On planting her left foot in the dung while turning right, the trumpeter slips and falls, sending some of the other band members collapsing into a heap. The parade is delayed momentarily and then continues, the exogenous shock absorbed into an error term that accounts for the above-average duration of the parade. Such exogenous shocks aside, a theorist who was asked to explain the variation in the quality or degree of coordination among parades would surely take resort to such considerations as the musical and marching abilities of the members, the instructional talents of the conductor, and the amount of effort given to rehearsal.

The departing crowd of spectators is likewise a coordinated social configuration, only it is not coordinated by some parade marshal. With the parade, every participant's location at each moment during the parade will be pre-determined by the parade marshal, save only for disruptions caused by exogenous events. With the spectators leaving the stadium, no such pre-determination is present even though the participants arrive at their desired destinations pretty much as they anticipated. It would be a metaphorical stretch to account for this outcome as if it were orchestrated by a parade marshal. It has none of those features of orchestration, and to invoke "as if" is to parade ignorance as knowledge. Coordination is instead achieved through some conjunction of intentional action by participants as mediated by such things as conventions regarding courtesy, the ability to understand and adapt to other people's actions, and police barricades. It is possible to observe exits that take place speedily and with everyone getting to their destinations about as quickly as one would imagine possible. It is also possible to observe exits where the movement out of the stadium is disrupted by the emergence of fights that perhaps even escalate into minor riots. Someone trying to give an account of the observed degree of orderliness would receive no help from taking recourse to such concepts as the skill of the parade marshal, the marching abilities of the spectators, or the amount of rehearsal time they devoted to practicing exits. Such concepts as these are irrelevant to explaining the orderly pattern of motion that is represented by the spectators leaving a stadium, even if they can be usefully applied to parades. Epistemological issues are important, but they must be addressed in ways that are suitable for the nature of the object being examined.

It is perhaps worth noting that if the exit of spectators were viewed while hovering in a hot-air balloon, it would resemble a parade. In both cases, everyone would be moving in the same direction, either down the boulevard or away from the stadium. The primary difference would be that the parade appeared to be better coordinated because no one would break ranks until some common destination was reached. With the crowd of spectators, however, people would be observed to break ranks now and then and leave the flow. And in doing so, they would sometimes disrupt the flow of those who were continuing down the boulevard. If the parade were treated as a model of perfect coordination, the crowd of spectators would be but imperfectly coordinated, illustrating a form of market failure when judged against this inapt standard.

As an ontological matter, societies are orders and not organizations. As orders, they contain many organizations within their domain. Organizations generally reflect the coherence of a plan, as illustrated by a parade and as will be explored more fully in Chapter 4. The orderliness of an order of organizations is not a reflection of a plan but is a product of continual interaction among multiple plans. To describe that orderliness as equilibrium is subtly to transform that order into an organization, as illustrated by images of an invisible hand. The equilibrium of market clearing has no turbulence. Reality has turbulence, for turbulence is a feature of an order. The degree of turbulence can vary but it cannot be eliminated. When economic theory is used to address temporality within history, as against addressing eternity outside history, the appropriate conceptual framework is of an emergent, dynamic order that is being generated through interaction among resident organizations, organized both as individuals and as teams of individuals.

Closed maximization, open action, and societal regularity

Social science starts with the perception of societal regularities, and from that starting point seeks to explain the character of those regularities. Both the neo-Walrasian and neo-Mengerian programs start from social-level regularity, but differ in how they relate that regularity to individual action at the micro level. The neo-Walrasian program assimilates societal regularity to regularity in individual action; the neo-Mengerian program assimilates it to the structured network of individual interactions that constitute a society. The neo-Walrasian program reduces society to an individual by theorizing either in terms of a representative agent or in terms of societal averages, as illustrated by speaking of a relationship between average scores on some reading exam and average amount spent on teaching reading. Within this program, the characteristics that are thought responsible for the social phenomenon under examination are presumed to be carried within the representative agent or average member of society. If pencils are observed to be produced within a society, a representative agent must be able to make pencils.

The neo-Mengerian program does not countenance this reduction. It is thus possible for pencils to be produced within a society even though no individual knows how to do everything necessary to make a pencil, as explained by Leonard Read (1958). The making of pencils, or of anything else, is not a matter of an individual's possession of knowledge but is a matter of the assembly of pieces of knowledge that is distributed throughout a society. No single person is capable of even describing all of the actions extending throughout the world across many years that must come together in coordinated fashion to produce pencils today. There is macro-level regularity, for pencils are made, but that regularity is located at the macro or societal level and not at the level of individual action: that regularity is a property of a rightly arranged nexus of relationships and not a property of individual action or rationality, as conveyed by Vernon Smith's (2008) treatment of ecological rationality in contrast to individual rationality.

The neo-Walrasian program employs an analytical window through which observations are ordered by the presumptions that individuals maximize given utility functions and that interaction among such individuals conforms to some equilibrium. Within the neo-Mengerian program, an alternative analytical window is used to order observations about societal phenomena. This window provides a different perspective on individual action as well as offering an alternative to equilibrium presumptions. Over some range of observations, the differences might appear small but they also point in opposing conceptual directions, much as the two parabolas X^2 and $-X^2$ have a common origin but point in opposing directions. The difference in analytical formulations is fundamentally a matter of whether one works with closed or open analytical concepts. The neo-Walrasian orientation looks through an analytical window that offers a framework of closed concepts; the neo-Mengerian orientation offers an analytical window that offers open concepts. For instance, the societal pattern created by a parade can be portrayed by closed concepts but the pattern created by the exit of spectators requires recourse to open concepts.

Economic models of individual action typically postulate closed and not open concepts. Closure brings tractability at the individual level, but at the price of rendering many social-level phenomena genuinely unintelligible through the accompanying presumption that all socially relevant information is contained within the individual unit. Within an equilibrium system, the creative injection of novelty can be accounted only as an exogenous shock or, equivalently, as some stochastic event. Within this closed framework, people do not truly make choices. They face a list of enumerated options in the presence of a well-defined utility function, and the outcome is inexorable, similar to involuntary reflexes. It is interesting in this regard to reflect upon the uneasiness many economists express for models that have multiple equilibria. The standard impulse in the presence of such multiplicity is to search for closure by tweaking the model in some fashion.

An alternative that comes into play when working with open concepts is to recognize that multiple equilibria speak not to structure but to process. We stand here today, and tomorrow will emerge though interaction among the various choices people make. In the presence of closed concepts, people will make the same choice each time and tomorrow will be the same tomorrow each time. This is what equilibrium signifies, and a model with multiple equilibria is an irritant for such a conceptual presupposition. With open concepts, however, people face genuine choices, in which case they could make different choices if it would have been possible to relive the scene multiple times. With everyone in the same position, multiple histories could have emerged. There are thus several tomorrows that could emerge out of today, depending on the particular choices people make and the resultant interactions that are set in motion. The social world can be rendered intelligible without being genuinely predictable, as set forth clearly and charmingly by George Shackle (1961).

A desire to render social life intelligible in terms of people pursuing plans stands in some contrast to claims that theory should seek to predict societal outcomes.[8] Prediction is a reasonable standard for any closed system to which equilibrium pertains. If someone makes a particular choice in the presence of a particular set of prices, the closed model of utility maximization requires that person always to make the same choice, for the requirement of transitivity brings closure to the model of choice. Alternatively, once we recognize that people can act creatively and experimentally, there is no necessity that they always make the same choice. They may very well want to explore and experiment. That exploration and experimentation can still be rendered intelligible even if it isn't genuinely predictable. For instance, a woman who walks home from work might have several possible routes available. These routes vary in their distance, as well as in the type of terrain traversed. An observer might well expect her to take the shortest and quickest route. And most likely she often will. But sometimes she might take a longer route to conduct some business. Or she might take some other route just to have a change of scenery. Her conduct would always be intelligible even if the prediction that she would take the shortest route to economize on travel time might sometimes be wrong. For an open system characterized by turbulence injected through novelty, the appropriate objective of theoretical activity is to seek to render social life intelligible in terms of people pursing plans within a societal setting.

In some respects, the distinction between prediction and intelligibility is a matter of the specificity of predictions, as conveyed by Hayek's (1967) treatment of pattern prediction. Where full-bodied prediction might seem to suggest prophecy, pattern prediction is something that the mind can understand when it appears even if it could not have prophesied its appearance. For instance, rent control creates a situation where the number of housing units demanded exceeds the supply of rental units. Without rent control, this excess demand would lead to increases in rents as potential tenants competed against one another for housing. Rent control makes impossible such increases in rent; however, rent control doesn't eliminate the competition among tenants. That competition will now move into different channels (Cheung 1975). We can recognize those channels when we see them even if we cannot prophesy their appearance. One oft-discussed channel is the creation of a tie-in between the ability to rent and the sale of furniture at an above-market price. Should such contractual forms be prohibited through legislation, we can expect the competition among tenants to play out along yet different paths. The identity of those paths is limited only by the imagination of the participants. It is possible to offer a generic or pattern prediction that rent control will lead to real prices that exceed the controlled prices without being able to prophesy just how that increased real price will be paid. Someone looking at the situation *ex post*, however, will understand why one owner might no longer offer free parking or storage, why a second owner might no longer heat a swimming pool, or why a third owner might reduce or even cancel a pest control service.

Theoretical vantage points: outside-in or inside-out?

Theorizing about people is different from theorizing about termites or trees because with respect to people, we live inside the objects we theorize about. For termites or trees there is no option but to theorize from the outside looking in, and the only test of reasonable theorizing must be some measure of the coherence between theoretical predictions and observed outcomes. We have no idea of what it feels like to be a termite, nor can we empathize with the various mental states that induce a termite to act. We can only theorize about termites as an outside observer. In contrast, the humane sciences can also call upon theorizing from the inside looking out because we have knowledge about our mental states and their connections to human action.

Indeed, much social theorizing can only be done from the inside looking out. The claim that people seek to be effective in applying means to the pursuit of ends is not a conclusion that is reached through outside observation and inference, but rather is a feature of our self-awareness.

The point of theorizing from the inside looking out is to render human action intelligible in terms of people forming and pursuing plans, as explained by Ludwig Lachmann (1977). Just as each spectator who leaves the stadium has a plan that organizes and guides action, so is the societal catallaxy constituted through an ecology of entrepreneurial plans. Theorizing from the inside looking out is an instrument that must be used with care, for a danger that comes with it is that it can turn into a battle among contending prejudices and intuitions. Yet there are many statements about human action that can be rendered intelligible in terms of a pure logic of choice because such a logic maps directly into a logic of successful conduct; moreover, we know from the inside that people do not seek to fail at what they try, even if their understanding of the relationship between means and ends might be incomplete, as illustrated by Carl Menger's (1981: 53–4) category of imaginary goods.

Claims of knowledge acquired from the inside must be capable of being rendered intelligible to other people. While such claims of personal knowledge (Polanyi 1958) might offer valid inputs into social theorizing, those claims must also be inter-subjectively communicable to avoid the assertion of dueling prejudices. Karl Popper's (1959) principle of falsifiability is one heuristic for doing this by rending statements inter-subjectively communicable. This heuristic remains valid even in the face of Duhem-Quine reasons (Quine 1951) regarding the impossibility of genuinely falsifying a hypothesis because what is tested will be a compound of hypotheses and not a single hypothesis. For this reason theories will necessarily be under-determined. While this situation suggests an unavoidable degree of ambiguity in appraising the relative merits of competing theories, it also brings into the foreground recognition that theories are adjudicated in a social setting that is not nearly as mechanical as a simple formulation of falsification might suggest. Reasoning, we should remember, involves a significant social component, as Annette Baier (1997) explains. That reasoning is to a significant extent a social skill means that it occurs within an environment of inter-subjectivity (Zanotti 2007).

Economic models are vehicles for conveying stories. For models that employ closed concepts, those stories are conveyed in the passive voice. People do not do anything in those stories, for they are responsive and not active: they are whipped into line by a meeting between a utility function and a given set of market prices. Markets clear and people are compelled naturally to optimize as their utility functions dictate. What is portrayed is a society without life or action, which is suitable for a theoretical framework that treats relationships from an end-of-history orientation. For instance, people take market prices as given and have done the best they can under those circumstances. This is economic theory pursued in the passive voice.

The open-concept alternative requires stories to be conveyed in the active voice. People actually do things, and with societal phenomena of various types emerging out of those actions and interactions. People choose one course of action while rejecting others. In doing so, prices change from what they otherwise would have been and people participate in generating the world they come to experience. From the *ex post* or outside position looking in, any choice can be portrayed through a closed formulation of utility maximization. But that construction isn't recognizable to participants, because from an *ex ante* or inside position looking outward people face and make choices, and the interaction among such choices generates the social world we experience. To state the point differently, the inside-out orientation seeks to penetrate social reality whereas the outside-in orientation seeks to stand outside or above that reality.

Why theorize? Understanding vs. control

There are two distinct objectives that can inspire an effort to theorize about some object. One is to acquire a better understanding about the object. The other is to act intelligently on that object. With respect to the study of societies, the former objective would be represented by social theorizing and the latter would be represented by systems design. Social theorizing and systems design are distinct activities that can be pursued by the same person, only not simultaneously. These two activities operate on different levels, and with social theorizing occupying a more foundational level than systems design.

Social theorizing seeks to give accounts of the objects of analytical interest so as to increase our understanding of the properties of that object. Someone could seek to do this purely out of curiosity. Many people, however, seek to make instrumental use of whatever knowledge they acquire. This instrumental use takes the form of systems design, or what is now called public policy. At the same time, however, public policy is an economic activity that can also be subjected to social theorizing at a different level of analysis. It is important to recognize that social theorizing and systems design do not refer to the same analytical level. What this hierarchy of analytical levels means is that any effort at systems design will have to be filtered through some framework of social theorizing before its consequences can be discerned, as was illustrated above with respect to rent control.

It is often asserted that institutions are like rules of the game, so changing the rules changes the characteristic features of the game. There is much merit in this assertion, but it also has some problematical features when it comes to politically-constructed rules in particular. Consider the American experiment with Prohibition starting in 1919, as explored in Thornton (1991) and Miron and Zwiebel (1991). If institutions are rules of the game accepted by the participants, Prohibition would have pretty much eliminated the production and consumption of alcoholic beverages throughout the United States. Consumption did fall modestly, by some estimates around 30 percent. That is not even close to prohibition. Numerous other changes also took place: low-alcohol beverages like beer and wine gave way to distilled spirits, and for readily understandable reasons regarding ease of concealment; politicians, police officials, and judges came often to receive two forms of compensation as bribes became supplements to salaries. Openness and trust receded in commercial and social relationships as surveillance, suspicion, and fear of entrapment came into play: after all, an offer to buy a drink might not be genuine but rather might be an effort to entrap. This picture, moreover, is repeated with the various contemporary forms of prohibition such as those against recreational drugs as well as the type of semi-prohibition involved in extraordinarily high rates of taxation on cigarettes and other tobacco products.

In contrast, policy measures regarding the flow of traffic generate pretty much the intended results. When it comes to traffic regulation, systems design through policy seems to act pretty much directly on society without calling for intermediation through social theorizing. For the various forms of pro-hibition, however, the effect of policy articulation can be gauged only by filtering it through social theorizing. The difference between the two settings harkens back to the claim that institutions are like rules of the game. In some respect or in some instances they are, when policy articulations are largely codifications that facilitate what people want to do anyway. People do not want to crash into other cars while driving through intersections, and they do not want to spend a lot of time sitting in idling cars. Policy articulation through traffic signals and rules of the road are pretty much agreeable to everyone and are recognized as assisting people in promoting their various personally-chosen activities.

Policy articulation works differently when policy seeks to promote the interests of some people at the expense of the interests of other people. Here, policy is an instrument of control and not of facilitation. Those who in various ways would be attacked and otherwise vexed through policy will seek other channels to accomplish what policy is seeking to prevent. In such cases, policy does not act directly on society as an object, but rather acts on particu-lar persons, nodes, and connections within a society and with the overall effect on society bring a product of emergent interaction. Prohibition did not abolish alcohol. Rather, it empowered police officers to make arrests, with the effects of that empowerment being an emergent phenomenon of societal interaction. With respect to something like traffic control, the mere articula-tion of rules of the road is pretty much sufficient to gain adherence; the presence of police is minor relative to the magnitude of the activity. People pass through intersections with four-way stops without visible police presence, other than a codification of ordinary rules of courtesy applied to driving.

We theorize both to understand and to control. Understanding, however, trumps control, in that the mere articulation of some policy measure will not exert the controlled change envisioned by that articulation. Whether it will, or how close it will come to doing so will depend on the understanding of the social processes that are called into play by that effort at control. One can seek understanding for instrumental purposes, but one facet of that understanding will be recognition that the law-like character of societal processes places constraints on the operation of systems design. To be sure, such constraints can prove vexing to societal reformers, as Randall Collins (1988: 54) explains: "The major problem that most prescriptive, action-oriented political philosophies face is precisely the fact that the macro world is a system that we are caught in, but it is not a goal-seeking system. Alienation may be a condition of teleological individual human beings making up a social system which is by no means as self-reflexive as themselves."

Societies are subject to economic laws, which both the neo-Walrasian and the neo-Mengerian programs seek to illuminate, only from differing orientations regarding time and knowledge. Where the former program involves scholars in seeking to make statements that are valid outside of time and place, the latter program involves scholars in seeking to make statements that illuminate continual societal transformation across time and place. One aspect of economic law explains that systems design is constrained by societal reality even as it might seek to shape that reality. A design that facilitates what people generally would like to accomplish will play out differently from one that seeks to control some people to promote ends desired by other people: this recognition, too, is rendered intelligible through a study of the law-like features of economic interaction.

2 Society, property, and human action

The conventional order of economic theory starts with Robinson Crusoe, who makes choices which are typically characterized by models of constrained optimization. Other people (Friday) are introduced only after Crusoe's optimizing activities have been explored. Economics is thus construed as a science of household management, and with the state being just one particular type of household. Constrained optimization provides the foundational template for economic theory in the neo-Walrasian motif, as illustrated nicely by Gary Becker (1976).

A neo-Mengerian program for economic theory requires an alternative point of departure due to its desire to render economics a science of society and not a science of household management. The prototypical problem setting is one of structured living together in geographic proximity; it is one of interaction among people in which societal processes involve both cooperation and conflict. Economics is thus a social science and not a science of individual rationality writ large or spoken loudly. Societies are orders and not organizations. Even the Soviet Union was an order and not an organization, only one with rules governing individual action and relationships that were not conducive to domestic tranquility or prosperity, as explained by Roberts (1971) and amplified by Boettke (1993). With society as an order of organizations, keeping in mind that people too are organizations, pivotal significance attaches to the rules by which organizations relate to one another (Vanberg 1994). A society is not reducible to an individual who is optimizing against nature because interaction among the individual members of society generates social configurations that are not products of individual choice and yet influence individual action (Merton 1936).

The relationship between mind and society is one of supervention, with social configurations supervening on individual minds as illustrated by the brief remark on cell phones and email in Chapter 1. For better or for worse, individuals exist and act within some social nexus, and that nexus can restrict as well as magnify individual accomplishment, and with the natural law traditions being particularly apt in this regard, as illustrated by Buckle (1991), Budziszewski (2003), and Miller (1995). Perhaps the most significant object of supervention for social-economic theory is property and rights of property, along with arrangements for resolving disputes over property. Property rights delimit the scope for allowable individual action within a society. Property rights are irrelevant to Robinson Crusoe living alone. They acquire significance only when multiple Crusoes encounter one another, for in this case it is notions of property that govern personal relationships. Property, after all, denotes propriety or proper-ness in action, and so it pertains to a social relationship and not an individual action. Most generally, property rights delimit the range of actions that a person can expect to take without encountering resistance from other members of society. That range, it should be noted, is determined not by the person taking the action but by third parties within the society. As a substantive matter, moreover, the content of rights of property is subject continually to challenge and change. The central problems of economic theory are thus problems of how people can live together and the circumstances under which they may do so, as noted lucidly by Asik Radomysler (1946).

Crusoe *as* society vs. Crusoe *in* society

Carl Menger (1883) distinguished two categories of economic theory: one category he described as "exact," the other category he described as "empirical-realistic." The former category dealt with simple phenomena, the latter with complex phenomena. This distinction between types of phenomena maps well into the distinction between praxeology and catallaxy. Praxeology refers to the idea that individuals act to remove uneasiness by forming plans to secure what they anticipate will be more desired states of being. Praxeology is exact in that it is not subject empirically to disconfirmation, and is sometimes described as a pure logic of choice. The proposition that people seek to act effectively and not ineffectively is an analytical proposition, based on recognition that the opposite assertion is nonsensical. This proposition does not assert that people necessarily act in ways they will not later regret, for knowledge is always incomplete and people know many things that are not true. It is only to assert that actors can ascribe to their intentional activities a causal connection between the means they use and the ends they seek.

Where praxeology denotes individual action or practice, catallaxy is the realm of social interaction. Typically it denotes exchange, but more generally it denotes all phenomena of interaction among acting agents, as illustrated by George Homans's (1958) treatment of social phenomena as arising generally through forms of exchange, and also by Bruno Latour's (2005) treatment of social phenomena as emerging through interaction among non-social entities. Catallaxy resides in the realm of history. It is contingent and empirical and not exact. A neo-Mengerian research program thus leaves plenty of room for empirical examination, though the forms of such examination would differ from the forms that would be employed pursuant to a neo-Walrasian research program.

Praxeology and catallaxy denote interrelated realms of activity. Most illustrations of praxeological action take place within catallactical settings. For instance, an entrepreneurial plan, which is a praxeological category, is articulated through monetary calculation, which emerges out of catallaxy. Preference and value are praxeological categories, but their representation through money and prices is possible only inside a catallaxy. Most illustrations of praxeological action involve other people, which is to involve catallaxy. Robinson Crusoe alone on his island would confront a variety of situations that could be portrayed praxeologically: whether to work on his tan or to look for food; what kind of food to look for, and where; whether to try to build such capital goods as a boat or a spear; along with many similar situations. Most of the interesting problems for social-economic theorizing, however, arise only within the catallactical setting of multiple Crusoes.

The distinction between praxeology and catallaxy is surely superior to the conventional distinction between micro and macro. The distinction between micro and macro is in significant respects analytically incoherent. Macro is generally described as being an aggregation over an entire economy, as distinct from micro, which pertains to parts of that aggregate. Yet most of the objects of conventional micro theory are also aggregates. An industry and a market, for instance, are aggregate concepts in that they pertain to actions undertaken by numerous individuals and organizations. If aggregate output is divided into ten industries, it makes no sense to describe the sum of the ten as denoting a macro unit while the ten smaller aggregates are each denoted as micro units, just as it makes no sense to divide a nation into regions and designate the former as a macro entity and the latter as a micro entity. All are macro entities in that each pertains to interactions among people, though with different principles governing membership within the different entities.

In this respect, Erik Lindahl (1939) characterized micro phenomena as products of choice and macro phenomena as products of interaction among choosers. Micro theorizing is thus the domain of praxeology while macro theorizing is the domain of catallaxy. One consequence of this distinction is that most economic phenomena are macro or catallactical and not micro or praxeological, and this reflects the position of economics as a social science. Crusoe as an isolated individual can formulate plans and make choices. But Crusoe will not face prices, will not calculate in money, will not trade, will not make contracts, and will not have disputes with other people. A solitary Crusoe will experience a much narrower range of situations and activities than will a Crusoe who lives within society. To be sure, the full story of Robinson Crusoe is far richer than tales of the autarkic individual of economic folklore, as Jack Wiseman (1989) explains, for the full story involved both open-ended action and the intrusion of social configurations.

Within catallaxy, other people in various ways feed into any particular Crusoe's plans, whereas for a solitary Crusoe only the elements of nature can be incorporated into his plans and activities (Swedberg 1994, Lijenberg 2004, Storr 2008). The incorporation of other people within catallaxy, moreover, runs in many directions. Some of those directions are denoted by notions of peaceful exchange and mutual gains from trade, but this is far from the only form of incorporation. In closing his play *No Exit*, Jean-Paul Sartre declared that "hell is other people." Crusoe alone might have a rough and uncertain life because he couldn't call upon other people within a division of labor. But neither would Crusoe be taxed, regulated, sued, or robbed. These other events also come with life within society.

When a famous bank robber, Willie Sutton, was asked by a reporter why he picked banks and not other targets, he is described as responding that he did so because that was where the most money was. While the accuracy of that report has been questioned, it is no accident that homes owned by wealthy people typically have more elaborate security systems than those owned by people of more modest means. It is likewise no accident that contact with lawyers, security firms, and insurance companies increases along with wealth. The presence of wealth invites plundering, which in turns calls forth greater effort to guard against being plundered, across nations as well as within nations (Thompson 1974). That plundering, moreover, can take different forms. Much of it takes the form of asset conversion, as illustrated by such activities as robbery and theft. For conversion to occur there must be settled rights of property that have been violated.

Plundering can also take place without what would be regarded as conversion, because it would take the form of a contest over the locus of some right of property. Legal actions often entail contests over the locus of specific rights of property, and the volume of those contests seems to rise with wealth. Once upon a time most people worked something like 14-hour days to support themselves. This is no longer the case. Yet the days have not shortened, so people have more time available for other activities than they did formerly. In asking what people do with such released time, the conventional answers run in terms of such private pursuits as reading books, visiting museums, golfing, and traveling. These are the leisure pursuits of retired people, and these activities would perhaps occur naturally to theorists who take household management as the object of economic analysis.

By contrast, new forms of activity suggest themselves if society is taken as the object of analysis. Social activity necessarily involves other people, and such activity can take many particular forms. It is common to think of social activity through some such pleasant communal image as dancing. But fighting is also a social activity, as is any activity that involves a plurality of people. Meddling with other people is a social activity, not as directly violent as outright fighting, but it takes the same form all the same. When technological progress makes it possible for people to reduce their work effort, people must necessarily increase the effort they devote to other activities. It is reasonable to expect people to devote more time to sport. Golfing and hiking are some such activities, but so are filing legal suits and participating in causes and campaigns of various types. It is surely quite reasonable to think that some people like to interfere with other people for the sport of it. Such activities can be pleasurable, interesting, and challenging. With 14-hour work days there wasn't much time for this kind of activity. It's different now, so to some extent litigation and so-called public interest activity become modern forms of sporting activity, gentler than the gladiatorial games of old to be sure, but still sport all the same.

When economics is treated as a science of household management, the market denotes an object that a household uses to pursue ends by supplying inputs to the market and removing outputs from the market. The market is an instrumental object that multiplies the ability of individuals to attain their desired ends. Some market settings will be superior and offer more commodious living than other settings, but the key point in any case is the presumption that markets are technical instruments that transform an individual's inputs into a bundle of consumer goods and services.

When economics is treated instead as a social science, social relations acquire particular analytical significance. Among these social relations, those represented by property rights are of paramount significance. Social relationships bring a number of considerations in their train, some positive and some perhaps negative. On the positive side, people can learn from one another, with some of that gain manifesting itself in more commodious living through a finer division of labor and knowledge. On the negative side, people have expectations and preferences about one another and some people can seek to impose their preferences on others. A restaurateur may want to operate a place that is open throughout to smoking, as a reflection of his use of his private property. But other people might like to see that use of private property restricted if not eliminated from society. How this clash of desires plays out is a contingent piece of history that can follow any of several paths. One path might entail legislative restrictions on the ability of restaurants to allow smoking. Another path might involve judicial action as lawyers try to create causes of action that might secure desired rulings in particular cases, often changing the characteristics of property rights in the process, as explored by Arthur Hogue (1966) and Harold Berman (1983). However that clash plays out, it illustrates the presence of third party determination regarding the domain over which private property operates.

Private property and the market ordering of social relationships

The pure theory of a market economy explores the logic of human interaction when those interactions are governed by the principles of private property and freedom of contract, as explained nicely by Noyes (1936), Dietze (1963), Alchian (1965), and several of the essays collected in Blumenfeld (1974). These principles mean that all market activity is voluntary within the framework of those principles. Anyone who wants to establish a commercial enterprise is free to try. The ability to try does not, of course, guarantee success, for success requires cooperation from other property owners. The promoter of the enterprise will find it necessary to convince investors or lenders to support the enterprise. That accomplished, it will be necessary to convince other participants to provide labor, supplies, places of work, and all of the other inputs that the enterprise will require. And it will be necessary to convince yet other people to buy the enterprise's products and services.

The core of economic theory explains how complex patterns of economic organization emerge through interactions among people whose individual actions are governed by adherence to the disjunction between mine and thine that we characterize as private property. The theory of an unhampered market economy (Mises 1966) is an ideal type of construction within which people can form organizations under whatever constitutive arrangements they choose. They can create profit-seeking firms, but they can also establish non-profit firms and clubs. They can also set whatever requirements for participation in those firms and clubs that they choose. Within the parameters of these institutional arrangements, all activities are mutually agreeable to the participants. This is not to say that those arrangements were agreed upon by everyone, for most of us are born into some ongoing set of arrangements. It is only to say that all subsequent action is agreeable to the participants, taking those arrangements as a point of departure. Private property limits one's freedom of action while common property does not, but for the most part we sense that private property contributes to good order, but not always and not for everyone, as explained with especial clarity by Armen Alchian (2006: 3–67) and Yoram Barzel (1989).

Human societies are orderly just as are societies of ants and termites, and of social insects generally (Wilson 1971, 1975, Tullock 1994). But the source of orderliness differs due to differences in the natures of humans and social insects. The nature of social insects allows them to participate in the life of their colonies without questioning or challenging their roles in their colonies. It is different with humans, and in this respect we are nothing like the social insects. Social order is still based on an acceptance of roles and rules, but acceptance is only in part attributable to genetics. It also depends on volition regarding property-based relationships. For humans, social order is based on acceptance of some disjunction between mine and thine. Conflict arises when the boundary of that disjunction is contested (Bowles and Gintis 1993, Hirshleifer 2001, Dixit 2004, North, Wallis, and Weingast 2009). Our very natures require property as the framework for governance, along with procedures for resolving boundary disputes that are also part of our natures. Property provides a simple framework for human governance that allows complex patterns and arrangements to emerge through the contracts and associations that can be put together through property-governed relationships (Epstein 1995).

Much of the content of property rights can be conveyed by the image of a bundle of sticks, which conveys the notion that property rights can be divided in myriad ways. The ability to make such divisions can accommodate enormous complexity in social arrangements. If ownership of land is conceptualized as a bundle of sticks, it is possible for the entire bundle to be held by one owner. In this case the owner would have the exclusive right to determine how that land was used. But it is also possible for that owner to alienate some of the sticks in that bundle. For instance, the owner might allow people to camp on part of that land for a nightly fee. Alternatively, the owner might provide an easement that allows an adjacent owner to build a path over the property. That owner could also allow someone to graze cattle over a portion of the property, while also allowing the owner of the cattle a right to enter the property to tend the cattle. Similarly, the owner of the land could also alienate the right to pump water from an artesian well on the property. The presence of exclusive ownership in conjunction with the ability to partition ownership into shares and with the ability to dispose by sale all or parts of that right of ownership allows for the generation of considerable complexity in social configurations, as Richard Epstein (1995) explains.

It is also possible for social processes to restrict alienability through legislation, judicial ruling, or convention, as illustrated by Georg Simmel's (1900) treatment of continual change in the domain of alienability. For instance, you might be prohibited from draining a marsh on your property and putting rental housing on the site. Externally-imposed limits on what you can do to your property will often be in place. You might be able to drill a well on it without encountering objection from anyone else, and yet you might encounter objection if an adjacent landowner dislikes your effort to build a house close to the property line. For instance, that adjacent landowner might claim that the height of your house might diminish the volume of sunlight reaching the solar panels on his house, as illustrated by *Prah v. Maretti* (321 N.W. 2d 404 (1982)).

The distinction between private and common property has been a long-standing dichotomy in economics, going back at least to Frank Knight's (1924) model of the overuse of good relative to bad roads, and with Scott Gordon (1954) providing the modern-classic statement in the context of fishing grounds. The comparative-static analytics of private and common property is straightforward and is illustrated by Figure 2.1. In keeping with Angello and Donnelley's (1975) examination of oyster harvesting under different property rights, let W denote the market wage that is relevant for labor that would be supplied to oyster harvesting. Under private ownership of oyster grounds, E_p of effort would be devoted to harvesting oysters, which would produce a market price of P and with $PWab$ denoting rent to the ownership of oyster beds. By contrast, if oyster beds were owned in common, additional labor would be attracted into harvesting oysters until employment reached E_c, in which case oyster beds would yield zero rent. Private property economizes on what otherwise would be an excessive exploitation of superior resources, when superiority is judged from the perspective of yield per unit of effort.

Under the assumption that the functions depicted in Figure 2.1 are monotonic, the marginal return to labor employed in harvesting oysters at E_c is

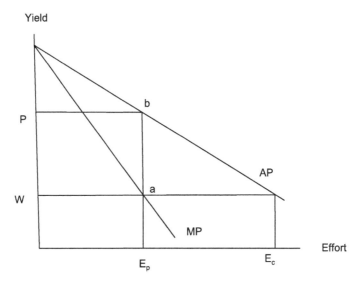

Figure 2.1 Comparative statics of common and private property.

negative. This situation illustrates what Garrett Hardin (1968) described as the tragedy of the commons. The comparative statics of these ownership forms illustrates this tragedy nicely; however, two things should be said about the appellation "tragedy" when it is conveyed by such models as that illustrated by Figure 2.1. First, it is costly to define, record, and monitor property rights, so the tragedy must reach a certain degree of intensity before some form of conversion to private ownership becomes economically sensible to the participants, as will be explored more fully below.

Second, the comparative-static analysis excludes from consideration most of the interesting social-level phenomena that would accompany escape from the tragedy. The tragedy of the commons will manifest itself in quarrels, as people try to practice forms of exclusion. In the absence of quarrels there is no tragedy: it is quarrels that point to the tragedy and not the other way around. Traditional lines in the sand will be contested, with new patterns of lines in the sand emerging, as Elinor Ostrom (1990) notes with particular aptness and clarity in her numerous studies of actual governance arrangements in common property settings. For instance, a common pasture may no longer be subject to open grazing while still being held in common; rather than open and unlimited grazing, limits might be placed on who can graze cattle and on how many cattle they can graze. The portrait presented by Figure 2.1 is timeless: it does not treat the process by which E_c changes into E_p, or vice versa. Figure 2.1 treats comparative statics and not emergent dynamics. To treat emergent dynamics it is necessary to replace the outside-in theoretical posture with an inside-out posture, as illustrated by Thébaud and Locatelli's (2001) model of the emergence of property rights over driftwood.

While in some instances some type of social control may be placed on use of the commons while maintaining the inalienability of common property, in other cases some conversion to private property is possible. Any such conversion, however, will entail the resolution of several micro-level issues that are ignored by the customary comparative statics. The macro entity denoted as private property will be constituted through some form of micro structure that emerges through resolution of the conflict. In her detailed analysis of such situations, Elinor Ostrom (2005) advances seven types of rules that must be combined to create what we recognize as private property. For instance, some rules will govern who has standing to participate in particular situations while other rules will govern the types of actions that different participants can pursue in the presence of conflict. If each of these seven rules were to have five options, there will be $5^7 = 78,125$ micro-level paths by which common property might be transformed into what we would denote as private property.

There are, moreover, numerous forums through which conflicts might be resolved and property rights established or amended. These forums also provide material for analytical examination. One common distinction is between legislation and adjudication, though there is also mediation and arbitration. Each of these forums, moreover, is a macro-level entity that is capable of being constituted in various structural forms. Private property can thus be constituted under numerous particular institutional arrangements. The propriety of individual action is determined largely through conflict resolution by third parties. While much of that determination resides informally in convention, the power of third-party determination is sometimes made explicit, as revealed by legislation, regulation, and judicial judgment. Market transactions take place only with respect to those property rights that are transferable. What is transferable, however, is subject to judgment and revision by third parties. Conflict is a concomitant of the social cooperation achieved through private property and the division of labor, and the resolution of those conflicts and, hence, the particular character of property rights, arises out of third-party resolutions of conflicts.[1]

Human sociability and the problematic of private property

A world of wholly private property is an analytical idealization that provides a framework for analyzing the patterns of social interaction that emerge when people relate to one another within the framework of private property and freedom of contract. The significance of private property is captured by the familiar assertion that good fences make good neighbors. Yet society cannot be organized wholly through private property, because some medium of common property is also necessary. Otherwise, it would be impossible for one person even to approach another person to ask directions, because to do so would require invasion of the other person's field of vision, unless that field was common property. Structured living together requires both private and common property, but this need for mixture both creates potential conflict and is necessary for living well together.

Our natures entail desires for both autonomy and recognition on the one hand, and a desire for solidarity and belonging on the other. Human sociability has two edges. One edge is the pleasant sentiment often ascribed to sociability. This is depicted by friendship and conviviality, and also by gains from trade. The other edge is sharper, and is illustrated by recognition that while we might prefer to perform in some orchestra rather than performing in our rooms, we also typically prefer larger to smaller parts within those orchestras. There will always be conflicts over who will be first violin, so to speak. In actual orchestras, of course, there is a conductor who makes such choices. But orchestras are organizations and not orders. In contrast, societies are orders and not organizations. For the order of society, the symphony is self-organized. As such, there is no person ultimately in charge of society, as against there being numerous different people in charge of various organizations within society.

It would be possible to model this situation as a cooperative game, wherein each party's highest payoff would come from being first violin, with second violin being ranked lower but above the non-cooperative solution where no orchestra forms. In this vein, Peyton Young (1998) expresses his desire to use game theory to deepen and extend insights from Hayek (1945) by using coordination games to illustrate the emergence of institutions that facilitate cooperation. One of those games, the etiquette game, involves two people (M for man and W for woman) meeting at a doorway through which only one person can pass. The options and payoffs Young uses are presented in Table 2.1, where the first entry in each cell pertains to M. This formulation is meant to illustrate the emergence of coordinating patterns of conduct. Each person is better off if one yields to the other, as compared with the stalemate where neither yields. As this is formulated, it is better to go first than second, which is in line with standard presumptions about economic man, as illustrated by a utility function whose value decreases monotonically with the time it takes to arrive at some final destination that lies beyond the doorway.

It is easy enough to construct some model of a person that would fit the payoffs shown above. But would such payoffs really pertain to anyone in actuality? We often observe people holding doors open for others, with the holder going second. Men have often been observed to do this when a woman is close behind, and with the volume of such acts surely rising with the sensed

Table 2.1 Coordination game and emergence of etiquette

	W doesn't yield	*W yields*
M yields	$1, \sqrt{2}$	0, 0
M doesn't yield	0, 0	$\sqrt{2}, 1$

attractiveness of the woman. The etiquette game is portrayed as a general metaphorical summary of the emergence of rules of conduct that facilitate coordination. The point of this illustration is that whether the man or the woman passes first is irrelevant; what is relevant is that they form a common belief about the etiquette of the situation.

It is reasonable to ask whether the etiquette game genuinely illuminates the emergence of patterns of conduct within society. Think about the portrayed payoffs a bit. Each person wants to go first, but each regards a stalemate as the worst possibility. But how is a stalemate truly avoided? The standard response is to invoke randomness. At first, whether M or W goes first may be 50–50. The result of that encounter is then presumed to be public knowledge, somehow, which leads to Bayesian updating that changes the probability away from 50–50. The outcomes of such models can easily lead to the dominance of one rule. In large measure, to assert randomness is surely to parade ignorance as intelligence. We can surely aspire to do better. But how might we go about doing better? It would seem to be necessary to confront head-on the problematic of Hobbes-like reasoning, as did Norbert Elias (1982, 1991) in a different context.

You can start by asking how it came about that two people arrived at the setting described by the etiquette game. The point of the analysis is to use the game as a general metaphor for the emergence of coordinating patterns of conduct that facilitate social interaction. By presumption, then, there was no prior social interaction until those two people met before that doorway. To be sure, this creates a problem in envisioning how that door got there. We might also inquire about the ages of our participants. They clearly must be older than toddlers, and the connotation of the game theoretic formulations is that they are adults.

What this all means is that the civilizing process that yields principles of etiquette as parts of our moral dispositions precedes the arrival of those two people before that doorway, as illustrated by Durkheim (1893) and Elster (1989). Now suppose that we look at the world of actual experience when people meet at doorways. In most cases the encounters are polite, with one deferring to the other. The time involved in deferring, moreover, is surely insignificant and does not lead one to sense having received the short end of the deal. The relationship of precedence and deference, moreover, is complex and variegated. Usually, men defer to women and youth defers to age. But not always by any means. For instance, women have been observed often to hold doors open for men who are heavily laden with packages and who otherwise would have had to turn around and back through the door. Every so often, moreover, one will encounter bad-mannered people, especially young boys, barging through doors, knocking people about as they pass. These people, it is worth noting, actually seem to have payoffs that correspond to those shown in the etiquette game.

Is not the family the crucible within which much of the conduct is learned that the game theorists subsequently work with in their formulations? This recognition points again to the distinction between equilibrium and emergent or generative modes of thinking. For an equilibrium mode, Hobbes-like models that tell stories about adults might seem to do a pretty good job of ordering some observations, even if they also obscure many perplexities in the process. For an emergent or generative mode, however, you need to be able to explain how those people got to that doorway in the first place.

The game theoretic formulation avoids conflict by ignoring it through the interjection of some presumption of randomness that simply selects one of the two to pass first or to be first violin. This approach to explaining cooperation presumes that both parties share a common orientation toward their situation: they both would rather play together than play separately. The interjection of a random procedure for selection is simply a way of closing off what would otherwise be a point of controversy, namely who is actually the better player.

And here there are only two options. One is for third-party selection, as illustrated by the choice by a conductor. Such third-party choice, however, violates the spirit of the coordination game, although a resort to random selection is really a disguised form of third-party selection. The alternative to third-party selection is agreement between the participants over who plays better. For the most part social processes operate to restrain and constrain the conflict that such competition entails, as denoted perhaps by an ethic of sportsmanship. But to constrain such conflict and to civilize it through sportsmanship is not to abolish it. In some historical settings, contests over political succession have been bloody while in others they have been reduced to jousts among highly-paid professionals. How the former patterns of activity give way to the latter is a topic worth examination, as previewed in Elias (1982), but in any case it speaks to the emergence of different processes for the resolution of conflict and not some elimination or even diminution of conflict. However particular patterns of property rights come about, at any particular historical moment they denote zones of temporarily settled conflict.[2]

Property, cooperation, and conflict: the yin-and-yang of social order

The social structure of that temporarily settled conflict is tectonic in character (Young 1991). Cooperation and conflict are nonseparable features of human nature, which are woven throughout and embodied within social processes. Rights of private property denote areas of temporarily settled conflict. Furthermore, the precise character of property rights is continually undergoing change. But property rights do not change by themselves. They change through contestation and disputation. Conflict lies at the core of property rights. At any historical moment there is a good deal of social territory over which property-based relationships are settled, but not all territory has this feature. Nor does settled territory remain settled indefinitely by the mere fact that it is settled today.

Property denotes proper-ness or propriety in conduct. Just what constitutes properness in conduct is determined by other people through the regulative patterns on individual conduct that emerge out of societal processes and configurations, as illustrated by Bruce Benson (1990) and David Friedman (2000). Those processes, moreover, are grounded in conflict that becomes resolved in a way that leads to some redefinition or clarification of the constituents of property. Claims of property arise only in the presence of scarcity; indeed, scarcity is just another name for conflict, regardless of whether that conflict is manifest or suppressed. To hold some property right today is thus no guarantee to hold it tomorrow. You will hold it tomorrow only if no one complains about your holding it today. If someone does complain about your conduct today, whether you continue to hold the right to act in that manner tomorrow will depend on how that conflict is resolved, and with that resolution typically having little to do with your preference in the matter.

For the most part, people accept such regulative patterns as second nature, though not fully and with people differing in the extent of their acceptance. This is hardly surprising, for without contestation there would be stagnation and not development, for conflict is valuable for fomenting societal change, which, of course, is not to claim that conflict is always beneficial (Coser 1964). Property, market, and state all derive from the confrontation between human nature and scarcity. Universal private property is impossible, but so is universal common property. Universal private property would allow no contact between or among people, so markets could never emerge. The emergence of markets requires spheres of commonality, not the least of which is language, the generation of which is not a private activity. Universal commonality would allow no exchange because it would not allow the alienable private property that is necessary for prices to emerge through exchange. Some mixture of private and common property is the only theoretical-historical possibility, which means in turn that markets will have only limited though variable reach within any society.

Property rights draw boundary lines in that proverbial sand. To say this is to induce wonderment at how those lines are established and how they change. Any line in the sand can be contested, and with the extent of contestation varying directly with the value people place on that particular piece of sand. Any line invites a challenge. That challenge will either be rebuffed or will be successful, and with that determination made by other people if the participants cannot resolve the dispute. The relationship of property to conflict is one of yin to yang: they are reciprocal. Historically speaking, any present right of property that is regarded as settled can be traced back to some earlier conflict. We may also be sure that there are instances of what are regarded as settled property rights that will be sources of conflict in the coming years.

Our social nature is surely a source of non-absolute property, as well as a source of continuing contestation in society. References to our social nature are often made in a warm and fuzzy manner, as illustrated by various references to approbation, including Adam Smith throughout the *Theory of*

Moral Sentiments (1759). The claim in this case is that a desire to be well regarded enlists people in the advancement of other people's wants through productive activity, because by doing this they become esteemed. This is surely a reasonable claim, but just as surely there is a dark side to approbation as well, which is explained particularly clearly by Arthur Lovejoy (1961). Approbation entails a desire to rank and compare. This might be done in a friendly manner, as illustrated by respect and admiration. But it can also unfold nastily, as illustrated by envy, jealousy, disparagement, and pugnacity, as examined by Helmut Schoeck (1969). A desire to be feared is cousin to a desire to be esteemed. Both of these sentiments reflect the same desire to rank but operate to different effect. In any case, people have reactions to and preferences about the activities of one another, for good and for bad. Rights of private property denote individual actions that will elicit forbearance from the remainder of society. If such forbearance is not forthcoming, private property is not operative in that instance. What those instances might be will be determined by other people through social processes of some sort, usually judicial or legislative.

Suppose you own a house on a lake, and have a dock at the edge of your property. A storm comes up. A man in a boat tries to tie up to your dock to escape the storm, and you come running out with your rifle, shouting "Leave or die, or else sign over title to your boat." He refuses either to sign or leave, so you shoot him. What will be your fate, reasonably or factually? Probably you will be convicted of murder, probably not first degree. The case law in these matters is pretty clear that your property right in the dock does not extend to your ability to prevent its use by a boater in distress, even though the boater would probably be liable for any damage done to the dock, as illustrated by the well-cited *Ploof v. Putnam*, 81 Vt. 471, 71 A. 188 (1908).

Now change the illustration a bit. Suppose a low-lying area along a river is subject periodically to flooding. The lay of the land is such that flood waters disperse pretty much uniformly throughout the area. It so happens that each of the 100 residents' land-holding includes a section that abuts the river. Some of the residents hatch the idea of raising and strengthening the river bank to reduce the threat from flooding; however, it will not do any good unless everyone participates. All but three people are convinced and agree to participate. If sentiments supported absolute property, a veto by the other three would be accepted, the project would be abandoned, and the water would rise. Far more likely than this outcome, however, is that duress or force will be applied in some manner so as to enable the project to go forward.

Demsetz and property rights in Labrador: variations on a theme

Our sociable natures mean that people have desires, both good and bad, concerning the actions and conduct of other people. Property rights are not absolute, for the range of their reach is limited by the forbearance of others. Property is something that is continually contestable, though the space of contestation during any particular interval of time is but a small portion of the total size of potentially contestable space. While the reach of forbearance is surely captured to a significant extent by the ancient tradition of natural law which to a large extent comes to inform conventional practice, it is also bounded by such formal processes and practices of dispute resolution as courts and parliamentary assemblies.[3]

Harold Demsetz (1967) advanced his well-known claim that private owner-ship replaces common ownership when the change becomes economically efficient. Demsetz illustrated his claim with respect to changes in the owner-ship over animals among Indians living in Labrador. Demsetz's claim, more-over, can be read into Carl Menger's formulation of economizing action. The main storyline is straightforward. As trade in furs expanded, quarrels arose among the Indians as they had to travel longer distances and stay away longer to capture their desired game. By establishing ownership over particular beaver huts, quarrels would be reduced and incentives would be provided to refrain from harvesting overly small and young beavers.

This is a nice story to tell, and it is rendered in comparative static fashion, pretty much in the same fashion as all such analyses of institutional change are rendered, as illustrated by the essays collected in Alston, Eggertsson, and North (1996). These efforts seek to portray change through successive looks through a neo-Walrasian window, as illustrated by Figure 2.1. One view shows fur-bearing animals subject to common ownership. The subsequent view shows those animals subject to private ownership, though it's really not this simple and apparent because you cannot really just look at a snapshot of people and tell whether their relations with one another are governed by private or common property. In any case, both views are presumed to pertain to equilibrated relationships, and yet the views they present differ. That difference must be attributed to some exogenous shock that disturbed the former equilibrium and led to its replacement by the second equilibrium. The analytical challenge is to locate something that can account for this shock. Usually the shock is attributed to technology. In the case of Labrador, it was an expansion in the fur trade, which transformed an abundant supply of animals into a scarce supply.

One notable feature of this approach to the presentation of historical development is that no one is really doing anything in any active voice kind of way. People respond to circumstances that are thrust upon them, but they do not generate those circumstances. In contrast, the same setting would surely play out differently in a number of ways when viewed through the neo-Mengerian window. Those differences, moreover, would speak to the creation of insight into the process by which this transformation occurred. Any such process would start with a complaint, for a complaint is just an expression of felt uneasiness. Beaver are harder to find, and quarrels among hunters are more common, as are such incidents as broken noses and crushed skulls due to growing conflicts among people over who among them will have to travel farther to find game.

What transpires in the society so described? What kinds of history might have transpired if we were to examine a set of parallel worlds? It is certainly easy enough to imagine those complaints being brought before a tribal council, and with some form of property rights to animals being established. Yet it's also easy to imagine other responses to the same initial source of conflict and complaint. For one thing, and closest to what Demsetz describes, licenses could have been issued to particular locations, which is a cousin to private property. Alternatively, the tribal council might have tried to limit the harvest of beaver, perhaps by imposing some kind of tax or by imposing quantitative limits, as do fish and game regulations today. The council might even have undertaken some effort to fashion tastes differently, perhaps by holding opossum festivals to promote the replacement of beaver by opossum in satisfying the sartorial and culinary desires of tribal members.

Furthermore, it's unlikely that once this issue had been resolved, life would proceed in all other respects just as it had before. The complaint over animals set in motion various processes through which people undertake new activities and acquire new capacities. Those new activities and capacities will not generally be forgotten just because people are no longer fighting over beaver. They will surely be put to new uses, promoting emergent changes throughout the society. This, anyway, is how the history would look when examined within the framework of the neo-Mengerian research program. The resolution of those quarrels over beaver will have resulted in the establishment of institutions and precedents that for better or worse provide structure for the resolution of subsequent quarrels. Moreover, quarrels are a permanent feature of society because scarcity and conflict are but two sides of the same human coin.

Habits of heart and mind

Praxeology is silent on the ends people seek, and asserts simply that people seek to be effective in using the means they can secure to attain whatever ends they choose to pursue. Whether Crusoe is alone on his island or is taken as representing any individual in society, praxeology invokes the formal presumption that people use means to attain ends, and in so doing act to replace states or conditions they value less highly with states or conditions they value more highly. For a solitary Crusoe, it is probably pointless to inquire as to whether there is anything further to be said about the ends. For Crusoe in society, however, the matter is not so simple. While a good deal of contemporary discourse invokes a stylized setting whereby interaction among adults generates some form of social order, it is nonetheless the case that adults reach adulthood through being raised in some form of social group.

This process of reaching adulthood was central to the process-based sociology of Norbert Elias (1982, 1991), who noted that the civilizing process entailed the internalization of regulated patterns of conduct that became second nature. It is here where habits of heart and mind are first established. In this respect, the classical orientation toward moral education was that morality was a process of acquisition that began with teaching that, through practice, became so second-nature that it receded into the background of one's bearing. Morality was thus not an object of choice, and was rather a fact of existence that arose out of the particular social setting in which people were raised. To be sure, there are many such social settings in operation within any one society, and so it is surely common to find particularistic differences in the habits of heart and mind in play within a society, even though we would also expect to find a good deal of similarity. Five centuries ago in the West, for instance, it was fine to eat with one's fingers; now it mostly isn't, though there are exceptions. Yet there was never any convention where such a change in custom was articulated and ratified. It just happened through some form of civilizing process at work within a societal catallaxy.

These considerations open an avenue through which the substantive content of ends can be influenced through catallactical processes and formations, as explored to some extent in Wagner (2006b). It should be noted, however, that to speak of a direction of influence over the substantive content of ends does nothing to dispute the universal validity of the means–ends relationship. Individual autonomy prevails at the formal level, but at the substantive level there is a bi-directional flow between individual and society (though taking care not to reify or personalize society, as against treating it as an emergent object). For instance, property and honor are universal categories of human conduct, recognizable even among thieves. That the conduct of thieves toward the property of those outside their band is different is simply a particularistic recognition that the appropriate social grouping for understanding human conduct is substantively variable despite universality for the formal categories, as illustrated by Peter Leeson's (2007) examination of the organization of piratical enterprises.

Most members of a society might accept the limits on their conduct that private property entails. In this case the moral requisites for a market economy will be present. For the most part, it seems plausible to claim that market processes support a form of institutionalized practice that reinforces those initial habits of heart and mind. Of several people who accept a job, most prove to be punctual and dependable, but a couple of them are not and they get fired. This getting fired might be instructional for the unreliable characters, and it is also an instructional reminder for everyone else. In any case, institutionalized practice within the market economy seems often to reinforce the habits of heart and mind on which it is based, similar to Annette Baier's (1997: 34–35) treatment of the inverse relationship between trust and supervision in relationships, as well as Albert Hirschman's (1992) treatment of commercial activity as an instrument for polishing manners.

There are doubtless contrary examples as well. Political processes seem particularly interesting in this respect. Someone owns some marsh land that you happen to think might make a nice bird sanctuary. You could always create an enterprise to do this, possibly by buying that land or perhaps just leasing it. Alternatively, you could petition the legislature to prohibit development of marsh land, thus creating a bird sanctuary by default. If private property maps into the moral injunction to refrain from taking what is not yours, the legislative petition and action maps into a different morality. As such actions are repeated again and again, perhaps the substantive content of those habits of heart and mind undergo some degree of transformation.

Time preference offers a good vehicle for exploring some of these possibilities. Economists typically use rationality in a purely formal manner, viewing it as an attribute that everyone possesses to the same degree, just as they view the ability to breathe (setting aside medical conditions like asthma). It's not at all clear that this is a reasonable presumption. Indeed, across the entire domain of human action, we typically hold that people differ in their interests and talents. If this differentiation holds for the gamut of human activity that comprises life, why doesn't it hold for life itself? As will be explored more fully in Chapter 4, entrepreneurship involves a projection of the self onto the future. This is an act of imagination that can be done with sharper or weaker discernment. Edward Banfield (1958, 1970) argued that poverty was significantly a matter of the way that people project themselves onto the future. Some people do so only weakly, and would be characterized as having relatively high time preferences, perhaps as represented by the first and even the second of the three little pigs in that well-known children's' story, and who were eaten by the wolf after the wolf blew down their hastily-put-together houses. In contrast, the third little pig projected himself into a more distant future and built a brick house.[4]

To the extent the substantive habits of heart and mind are modified through the forms of institutionalized practice that are countenanced within a particular society, it is plausible that there would result some feedback from policy to character, in contrast to the customary direction that runs from character or preference to policy. If people perform better as more is expected of them, the observed standard of performance will be a variable that depends on those expectations. If the content of those expectations differs across institutional settings, societal configurations might be plausibly appraised in terms of the talents and capacities they encourage people to develop, or to abandon.

An old aphorism asserts that "when the going gets tough, the tough get going." This aphorism denotes praxeological action in response to a catallactical situation. But does the aphorism convey the only option? Might social configurations promote other options? Someone who is fired from a job for being late to work too often might be induced to acquire some discipline by setting an alarm clock or refusing to carouse so late into the night. Alternatively, a legal advocate for what some person or organization regards as those who are improperly discharged might advance successfully a class action suit that restrains or eliminates the doctrine of hire-at-will. (Much the same thing, moreover, could be accomplished by legislation.) In this case the resulting generation of social configurations might, among other things, work to weaken the forces of self-discipline by weakening the connection between actions and consequences (Schelling 1984).

Numerous scholars have claimed that the common law tends to promote economic efficiency, as illustrated particularly clearly by application of the Hand Formula to tort cases. According to that formula, expressed verbally by Judge Learned Hand in *United States v. Carroll Towing Co.*, a defendant is negligent only if the expected damage from an accident exceeds the defendant's cost of avoiding the accident.[5] This simple formulation obviously confronts numerous matters of calculation and interpretation. Nonetheless, such scholars as Landes and Posner (1987) and Shavell (1987) claim that the Hand Formula provides a reasonable basis for ordering and understanding actual judgments in tort cases. For Landes and Posner (1987: 1), "the common law of torts is best explained as if the judges who created the law through decisions operating as precedents were trying to promote efficient resource allocation."

Consider a few of the cases Landes and Posner use to articulate their claim, and which are elaborated to different effect in Wagner (1992). In *Hendricks v. Peabody Coal, Co.*, a 16-year-old boy injured himself upon hitting a submerged shelf after diving into an abandoned strip mine that had filled with water.[6] The court ruled for the plaintiff, noting that "the entire body of water could have been closed off with a steel fence for between $12,000 and $14,000. The cost was slight relative to the risk to the children involved." The Court's reasoning clearly proceeds with reference to the categories of the expected loss from an accident and the cost of avoiding the accident.

Landes and Posner used *Adams v. Bullock* to illustrate a contrary ruling.[7] There, a 12-year-old boy was swinging an eight-foot wire while walking along a bridge that crossed the path of an electric trolley. The boy was badly burned when his wire touched the trolley wire. In this case the court ruled that the accident was an "extraordinary casualty, not fairly within the area of ordinary prevision." With respect to the Hand categories, the cost of avoiding the accident will have been higher than it was in *Peabody Coal*.

There is clearly plausibility in the orderings of these cases with respect to the Hand formulation. Yet considerable ambiguity is also present. None of the three arguments that constitute the Hand Formula are externally given magnitudes, but are rather matters of judgment. Moreover, Huber (1988) cites cases where plaintiffs received favorable rulings that do not seem so plausible with respect to the Hand Formula. In one case a man put a 16.5-inch tire on a 16-inch rim; to keep the tire on the rim he inflated the tire to 48 pounds. The tire exploded, the car crashed, and the man was injured, for which he was able to recover because he had not been warned against the possible danger of doing such a stupid thing.

Other cases of similar form could also be cited. Returning, however, to a comparison of *Hendricks* and *Adams*, it is perhaps significant that they were decided 50 years apart, the latter in the carly years of the Progressive era and the former long after the New Deal. An alternative possibility is that the moral sentiments played out differently at the time *Adams* was decided than when *Hendricks* was decided. Whereas the boy in *Hendricks* was left to live with his situation, the boy in *Adams* was compensated, even though each had acted negligently. To what extent and in what direction paths of causation might operate is, of course, an open question. In any case, claims about common law efficiency typically take value and desire as data, and yet there may be causal chains that run in the reverse direction, as considered by Rizzo (1980) and Epstein (1980). Furthermore, Quine (1951) reminds us that such claims necessarily rest upon auxiliary presumptions that could also be challenged.

The material and the moral: a Gordian knot?

Legend tells of a King Gordius who tied such a devilishly gnarled knot that Alexander the Great, so infuriated with his inability to untie it, simply sliced it with his sword. Similar knots abound in human affairs. How is a free-market economy established and maintained? Is this a simple matter of giving instruction in law and economics, or is the matter more complex? And if so, what instruction in particular might be involved? Should a woman who spills coffee while driving feel embarrassed by her clumsiness or should she look for a lawyer to press a claim that the seller should have prevented her from acting so foolishly? What once would have been widely regarded as an act of clumsiness to be hidden from view later became a cause célèbre that returns some modicum of fame and fortune.

A network-based analysis conceptualizes its phenomena in terms of nodes and connections. Network models are typically presented in flat form with a singular connection between nodes. Thus a contract would be portrayed as a connection between two people, with service flowing in one direction and money in the other. An entire economic order could be portrayed in this fashion, as a networked version of an input–output table of relationships among people and enterprises. What is left out of this network picture is any recognition that connections are not singular but entail a structured multiplicity of connections, some surely more foundational than others. This structured multiplicity was implied, for instance, in Emile Durkheim's (1893) objection to Herbert Spencer's (1884) effort to explain the origin of society in contract, whereby Durkheim argued that the ability of people to contract implies some pre-existing domain of commonality that allows the participants to act contractually.

With respect to the material explored in this book, we can think of material, legal, and moral levels of connection, all of which operate jointly in generating observable patterns of societal interaction. By material, I mean the input–output relationships that comprise the material of standard micro theory, and which are the medium though which resources are allocated among activities. To be sure, resources can never allocate themselves, for only people can allocate resources. Moreover, no single person can allocate resources so as to make even a pencil, so resource allocation is a property of the nexus of connections among people. It is necessary to get beneath the resource allocations to understand how those allocations occur and change.

Since only people can allocate resources and can do so only within a nexus of relationships, the nature of those relationships becomes of particular significance. In this respect we can distinguish two conceptually distinct domains of connection among people, one denoted as a legal order and the other denoted as a moral order: these two orders supervene on the economic order, and with all three together constituting the nexus of human relationships that we denote as society. Walter Eucken (1952) notes that a market economy rests upon three legal principles: property, contract, and liability. When personal relationships are governed by these three legal principles, the resulting pattern of interactions constitutes a free-market economy. There is, of course, room for dispute among people as to the precise meaning of these principles in particular instances. Nonetheless, a free-market economy is a meaningful name that can be applied to cases where resource allocations within society emerge when human interaction is framed by the private ordering principles of property, contract, and liability.

But from where comes the legal order that constitutes a market economy? Market economies are not found everywhere, and even when they are found they do not exist in pure form, nor could they. Furthermore, it is apparently not sufficient to export legal code books for people to read as instruction manuals, after which a market economy and its legal order can be put together much as someone might assemble some bookshelves. King Gordius's knot is truly gnarled. The refraction of an economic order through a legal order reveals a moral order of human conduct (Schlicht 1998). The legal principle of private property entails a moral belief that it is wrong to take what is not yours. It also entails a moral belief that private property provides a just basis for ordering human relationships. The legal principle of freedom of contract maps into the moral belief that people should keep their promises or otherwise make good on the damages that result if they do not. It also entails the moral belief that whatever associations and organizations people create are appropriate. The legal principle of liability or tort entails the moral claim of an obligation to redress the wrongs done to others.

This is a pretty severe morality, corresponding to what McCloskey (2006) describes as bourgeois virtues and what Jacobs (1992) describes as the commercial moral syndrome (and which she contrasts with the guardian moral syndrome). Among other things, this morality holds that if you are unsatisfied with any of the many circumstances surrounding your life, you must look to yourself to achieve better circumstances. The exception to this austere remedy for dissatisfaction arises if someone else has violated your right of property, as in stealing your car or watch. As the hold of such moral rectitude weakens, legal interpretation will likewise soften in the direction of weakening the reach of property, contract, and liability. Concomitantly, the extent to which economic relationships are genuinely of the free-market variety will also weaken.

One open question is the extent to which institutionalized practice can influence moral belief and legal principle through its influence on concepts of normativity (and with normativity used in its statistical and not its moral sense). A person could always convert land into a stadium or shopping center by buying it and using it in this manner. An alternative would be to use eminent domain to accomplish the same thing. One thing that surely happens as eminent domain is used, and as its principle is extended through the gamut of legislative activity, is that observed norms about property and property-governed relationships change. If the realm of the moral is purely conventional, notions of normativity can perhaps move anywhere in moral space if institutionalized practice is undertaken with sufficient weight. To the extent morality belongs to the domain of the natural or the real, as illustrated by Budziszewski (2003), there are limits, though perhaps quite elastic ones, to the potential territory open to institutionalized practice.

Collective property

The predominant model of social organization within a framework of private property is an exchange whereby ownership changes hands either indefinitely through sale or temporarily through lease. A market economy could thus be denoted as the total of all such exchanges among economizing entities. Yet private property does not govern all relationships among economizing entities within a society. Political entities, for instance, are characterized by inalienable property, in contrast to the alienability that characterizes private property. Indeed, Murphy and Nagel (2002) argue that collective property and not private property provides a superior point of analytical departure, at least with respect to examinations of distribution and redistribution. Political entities necessarily operate with property and property-governed relationships, but those property rights differ in economically significant respects from private property, as will be explored more fully in Chapter 8.

Markets also facilitate the generation of forms of collective property. Someone who founds a proprietary firm might decide subsequently to convert the firm into a corporation by dividing his interest into 100 shares. What was originally owned by one person is now owned by a collection of people. The theory of agency explains how it is reasonable within the conventions of private property to treat the corporation as acting similarly to a proprietorship, as illustrated by Meckling and Jensen (1976), Fama (1980), Watts and Zimmerman (1983), and Fama and Jensen (1983). What promotes that similarity is the alienability of ownership. Shares of ownership in corporations are acquired voluntarily and they can be sold if someone desires to sever participation in that collective entity.

With political entities, ownership is not alienable so participation cannot be severed and political entities, unlike corporate entities, are not subject to any process of market-based valuation. This difference can inject tectonic sources of turbulence into society, as Chapter 8 will explore. For instance, two corporations might have an intense commercial dispute, for which litigation is one path to resolution. By resolving their dispute without litigation, each corporation can save the expenses of litigation. Within the institutional framework of alienable property, such saving will increase the net income and hence value of the firm. The situation changes if one of the disputants is a political entity because that entity does not operate within a commercial calculus of net worth. In contrast to commercial litigants, an attorney general cannot convert to private use any litigation expenses that were saved through settlement. The attorney general can, however, adapt a litigation strategy to a desire to seek higher political office. In this case, however, litigation expenses are investments in seeking that higher office, even if no political figure would state the matter so baldly (Wagner 1999a).

Within a market setting, relationships are between buyers and sellers and between only them. One party has money to lend; the other party desires to borrow money. There are multiple lenders and borrowers, each of whom is trying to make the best deal they can to advance their plans, and in a setting where not all such plans can be fulfilled in reflection of scarcity as a condition of life. A lender accepts and rejects proffers based on commercial judgment. Borrowers do the same thing. The resulting pattern at any moment is an emergent outcome of this market process that is organized within the framework of private property.

But private property is not the exclusive governing framework within society, as requirements of collective property are also present. With private property, judgments of market participants are final, and market outcomes are unplanned outcomes of multiple interactions among lenders and borrowers. Each exchange relationship is dyadic. Collective property creates a triadic relationship, and this relationship points in a tectonic direction in at least two respects. First, lenders will not be able to reach judgments based exclusively on commercial judgment because they will now have to submit their judgments to audit in a setting where there are expectations about acceptable patterns of lending. Second, the political entity is not operating within an ordinary commercial calculus any more than is an attorney general. In short, actual economic activity within a society characterized by an admixture of private and collective property should be expected to diverge in significant respects from what might have been expected by applying the logic of a pure market economy, as illuminated by Jacobs's (1992) examination of what she called "monstrous moral hybrids."

3 Economizing, calculation, and purposive action

If society is conceptualized in terms of equilibrium states and with any such state reducible to an average or representative individual, it is necessary to work with a deterministic model of individual choice. Within this conceptual framework, a deterministic treatment of individual choice as maximizing utility subject to a budget constraint supports a treatment of society as an equilibrium relationship among individuals. The closed model of utility maximization (U-max) accommodates an analytical emphasis on the prediction of event regularities. The treatment of individual action as closed and mechanistic, moreover, fits comfortably within the neo-Walrasian orientation of society as a closed and mechanistic equilibrium wherein people are whipped into line by the confluence of their utility functions and a market mechanism.

Two main branches of criticism have been raised from within the neo-Walrasian orientation. One branch denies the ubiquity of generalized market clearing and the concomitant presumption in favor of the Pareto efficiency of market-based organization. Various forms of imperfect competition and failures of market clearing are claimed to characterize organized economic activity. The other branch denies the ubiquity of utility maximization, at least in the hyper-rational form in which it is typically presented. In large measure, this growing literature on behavioral economics, which seeks to blend psychology and economics, uses various anomalies associated with U-max to suggest some inadequacies with the standard formulation of U-max. As explored below, many of those anomalies appear as anomalies because human action is viewed through the closed and mechanistic lens provided by the neo-Walrasian window. It is not surprising to find that observations go astray when the real content of human action is neither closed nor mechanistic.

The alternative conception entails individual action that is significantly open, creative, and non-solipsistic. It also entails a societal organism that evolves with varying degrees of turbulence through interactions among individuals. The analytical foreground, moreover, is occupied not by resource allocations but by the generation of moral and institutional arrangements for human self-governance. Human action is not captured adequately by a set of variations on a theme of constrained maximization because the object of analytical interest is development through time and not equilibrium independent of time. This alternative theoretical object requires room both for intentional human action and the emergence of unintentional or spontaneous ordering through interaction among individuals. For Crusoe-in-society, as distinct from Crusoe-as-society, the appropriate theoretical framework is exchange-and-conflict, understood to bear a reciprocal and entangled relationship with one another as illustrated by Boulding (1978) and Buchanan (1964).

The individual participants in any exchange or other form of interaction are treated as economizing individuals. For a theoretical enterprise concerned with understanding the societal resultants of interaction among economizing people, the model of the economizing person provides part of the grammar and syntax through which societal formations are generated, but only part. The purpose of treating Crusoe analytically within a praxeological framework is not to imagine some solitary life outside of society, nor is it to construe society as a large but representative individual, but is to explore some principles of action within the context of society. From one direction individuals pursue plans and societal patterns emerge; from the other direction societal patterns shape and influence individual plans. Those patterns constitute a macro ecology of plans that emerges out of the pursuit of plans by multiple interacting Crusoes. It is, in other words, just as reasonable to speak of macro foundations for micro theory as it is to speak of micro foundations for macro theory. There is bi-directional movement between mind and society, as noted long ago by such seminal thinkers of social-economy as Vilfredo Pareto (1935) and Max Weber (1964), both of whom are examined extensively in Talcott Parsons (1949).

I shall start by exploring some facets of the treatment of human action as closed acts of utility maximization, and with society built up through addition across such acts. The remainder of the chapter will explore various facets of treating human action as involving economizing action that involves measures of openness and creative action. Moreover, the social context of Crusoe within society provides some substantial differences in orientation to that provided by the orientation that treats Crusoe as society or as independent of society. Among other things, a number of the recent claims of behavioral economics that seem to challenge the standard presumptions of utility maximization are not genuinely challenges to economizing action that takes place within a social economy, but rather are intelligible features of such an alternative orientation. Where a theory of choice seeks to explain selection from a basket of given options, a theory of action treats those options not as given but as in part created through imaginative action that imports novelty into society.

Maximization, closure, and hypothesis generation

Constrained maximization is woven tightly into the conceptual organon of the neo-Walrasian orientation. This model pertains just as fully to the profit-maximizing firm as it pertains to the utility-maximizing consumer. The branches of this conceptual organon, moreover, support one another, so that removing or even just weakening one branch threatens the other branches. The corpus of the neo-Walrasian orientation toward economic theory can be reduced to statements of equilibrium conditions in two markets, one for products and one for factors, and with each entailing both supply and demand functions. U-max applied to consumers generates demand in the product market and supply in the factor market. U-max applied to firms generates supply in the product market and demand in the factor market. The entire corpus of economic theory is thus reduced to four variations on a universal theme of utility maximization played in a key of postulated equilibrium.

Many lines of criticism have been advanced against U-max. The literal application of U-max implies that people know the states of all relevant variables and are able to control the use they make of those variables (Morgenstern 1972). A number of scholars have advanced alternative formulations that seek to add realism by limiting the knowledge that individuals possess, usually by formulating some such notion as bounded rationality, as illustrated by Simon (1959, 1978). These formulations appear on the surface to be a movement in the direction of greater realism, though perhaps not. Models are intellectual maps, and all maps reduce the scale of what is observed from that presented by reality. It is no different for the mental maps we call models than it is for road maps. Despite criticism of literal interpretations of U-max, it is undeniable that U-max resonates with an essential and recognizable feature of life: we cannot have all we would like or achieve all the objectives we might desire to achieve, so we must make choices in light of the constraints within which we must live and work.

So a lack of realism cannot be a fatal charge to levy against any such model as U-max. A model is never rejected through remonstrance, and for good reason that relates to the organonic quality of theoretical frameworks. U-max brings analytical closure at the individual level, and this closure is necessary to support the analytical closure that is necessary for the equilibrium that the neo-Walrasian orientation requires. A system of thought that interprets observations as equilibrium states must be based on closed concepts wherein determinate choice at the individual level maps into determinate equilibrium at the societal level. The entire neo-Walrasian edifice fits together, and removal of any one element imperils the remainder of the edifice.

There have, of course, been many critics of U-max, and the growing interest in behavioral economics and the introduction of psychology into economic theory continues and amplifies some of those themes, as illustrated by the essays in Frey and Stutzer (2007). Within the U-max formulation, choice is explained as a meeting between a utility function and the constraints presented by prices and income. Such criticisms as bounded rationality accept those various given conditions, and argue that people have limited capacity to process information. Hence people might not truly maximize utility but will instead attain some lower state of utility. A literal resort to U-max would require that people deliberate over all possible options before making a choice. Doing this would require so much computing time that a consumer could die hungry in a grocery store. The requirement is also incomprehensible if taken literally because the options that are known to a person are typically only a fraction of the options that are truly available. Hence, U-max is not genuinely some approximation to actual conduct or a heuristic that guides it, but rather is a metaphorical description of conventional action.

Furthermore, a formulation that appears to challenge U-max typically can be incorporated into U-max by postulating some cost of searching over options, and perhaps by adding a time constraint to the standard budget constraint. In the presence of such costs of search, utility will still be maximized, only it will be a different maximum than would have resulted if search was unnecessary. At this point, moreover, Ockham's razor comes into play: bounded rationality increases the number of theoretical entities without apparently adding theoretical insight. When economic theory is constructed within an analytical window that uses closed concepts to portray economic phenomena as reflections of static equilibriums, it is hard to see how U-max could be displaced because it is a construction that is perfectly suited for characterizing static relationships among variables: the value of any variable is what it is and not something else because that is where the opposing forces in play neutralize one another; the only question at issue is how to identify and account for those other forces.

U-max is conveyed nicely by formulations involving search. Rather than assuming that people start with full knowledge of their options and the prices of those options, people can be treated as acquiring knowledge of prices by searching for that knowledge, as treated originally in Stigler (1961) and explored thoroughly in Phlips (1988) and High (1990). At a purely formal level, it is plausible to assert that a person will search for prices so long as the expected gain from doing so exceeds the cost. This kind of formulation leads in turn to the generation of hypotheses. An expensive product offers a potentially larger gain from finding a lower price before buying than does a cheap product; a ten percent saving is far more significant when buying a car than when buying a can of baked beans. Thus it is reasonable to expect that people will acquire more information before buying expensive items than before buying cheap items. Vendors of expensive products who offer particularly high prices will thus do less business than similarly situated vendors of cheap products. In consequence of the competitive pressures that the acquisition of knowledge by buyers sets in motion, we should expect to find less variability in the prices of expensive objects than in the prices of cheap objects, and we do. In this way, and in numerous other cases, testable hypotheses can be generated. To point out that the formulation is inadequate or inaccurate as a treatment of how people actually acquire knowledge or make choices is irrelevant, because acquisition speaks to process and is irrelevant to a window through which all observations appear as equilibriums. The analytical task that appears within the neo-Walrasian window is to order various observations consistently with the maintained claim of equilibrium.

For U-max, both utility functions and the set of constraints are given conditions that individuals face. The mental experiment performed by the U-max analytics is to insert an individual into a prefabricated world. The neo-Walrasian window presents the world in terms of static relationships among prices with individual members of society locked into U-max positions. The configurations of reality are in place and the relevant analytical question concerns whether U-max presents a reasonable grammar for appraising that configuration. The elements of that configuration are the goods available on the market and their prices, and also the factor supplies made available and their prices. While the literature on behavioral economics has uncovered a variety of anomalies that arise in using U-max to appraise societal configurations, as illustrated by Camerer and Thaler (1995) and Laibson (1997), it still seems pretty clear that U-max does a good job of ordering *ex post* observations.

The ordering of *ex post* observations is, of course, the only possible analytical task that can be performed while looking through the neo-Walrasian window. For the neo-Walrasian challenge of rendering a consistent account of some given societal configuration, it is surely reasonable to think in terms of averages or representative agents who face given prices and options for choice. After all, at any particular instant the world appears to be prefabricated. And this is as it must be when the theorist stands outside the object of theorization. It is different when the theorist theorizes from inside the object, seeking thus to render social life intelligible in terms of people forming and pursuing plans within a societal ecology. From this alternative orientation, reality is not prefabricated but rather is generated through interactions among people. Different modes of thought are necessary to address the neo-Mengerian challenge, just as Keynes recognized was necessary to face the challenge he thought he was facing. What is at stake, though, is not some kind of essentialist statement about some true theory of individual choice or action; rather what is at stake is consistency between the micro and the macro levels of theorization. Macro-level theories that emphasize the internal generation of change require recourse to individual action that is open and not closed or deterministic.

Economizing action and the generation of societal configurations

For an analytical schema that seeks to explore the continual generation and reformation of societal configurations through interaction among economizing individuals, what we call utility functions are partly genetic and partly acquired by people via feedback from the milieu within which they operate. In this respect, Norbert Elias (1982) explains that people reach adulthood by being raised in social groups within which they acquire orientations toward their actions within the world. Within this alternative orientation, it is not analytically sufficient to treat prices as data because prices emerge and change through interaction among people. Neither are incomes merely data because incomes also are prices and hence emergent phenomena. For a research program concerned with societal qualities that are invariant across time and place, it is surely suitable to treat prices as data. But for a program concerned with the internal generation of continual change in the societal configurations we experience, prices, among other similar phenomena, must be treated as emerging out of societal interaction.

These issues of emergence and the analytical efforts that are required for their illumination, however, cannot be conceptualized by peering through the neo-Walrasian window. The neo-Mengerian window must be used because it presents the world as an unfolding process of emerging and changing relationships among members of society who in turn are to a significant extent engaged in exploration and creative action. An articulation of human action that is suitable for organizing thought when peering through the neo-Mengerian window is simply a different intellectual construct than what is suitable for peering through the neo-Walrasian window.

At first glance, praxeology might appear to be just a variation on U-max. Praxeology construes individual conduct within an economizing logic of choice wherein people apply means to the pursuit of ends. The object of those pursuits is to replace less desired conditions and circumstances with more desired conditions and circumstances. This logic is purely formal and independent of any substantive content concerning the ends that are pursued. It doesn't matter whether someone is seeking to alleviate hunger by sacrificing leisure to find food or to alleviate loneliness by sacrificing autonomy to secure companionship. The formal setting in all cases is that people act to remove uneasiness, which always entails a giving up of something that is valued less to secure something that is valued more, recognizing that mistaken judgments about such matters are always possible. The substantive objects of action can vary hugely within the formal context of economizing action.

To be sure, that variation is limited by our nature, which generates commonality in the objects of action in a formal though not in a substantive sense. For instance, we all need food and water to stay alive, we seek shelter from a multitude of nature's elements ranging from severe storms to threatening animals, we seek companionship and esteem, and we seek meaning and significance outside of ourselves. While such objects of action are common to humanity, this formal commonality is accompanied substantively by both variety in the objects sought and conflict among the seekers: for instance, successful companionship for some can entail loneliness for others. While there is some formal commonality in the objects of human action, it is always acting subjects who pursue those objects. Valuation is the act of a subject in pursuit of an object; it is not a property of the object.

It might seem as though such a praxeological formulation is just a less precise statement of utility maximization. For a scholarly enterprise that seeks to view its analytical object as an equilibrated set of prices, praxeology would surely be sliced away by Ockham's razor just as bounded rationality would be sliced away. But for a scholarly enterprise centered on the continual generation and reformation of social-economic phenomena, it is U-max that would be sliced away because it cannot account adequately for the continual injection of novelty into society. With U-max novelty arises as exogenous shocks and is not an intelligible feature of the social-economic process. It would, of course, be possible to give an inadequate account by positing something like a taste for novelty; this account would be inadequate because novelty is definable only with reference to a process of motion through time.

When people are viewed through the neo-Walrasian window, they appear to be responsive or reactive and not creative or imaginative. Doing such things as maximizing utility or profits is an automatic reflex similar to breathing. We do not truly choose to breathe; we just do it. With breathing, we breathe harder as we move faster; with U-max, we shift baskets as prices change. The people in these models do not create and choose, for these activities inject change into a society. Standard equilibrium models are told in the passive voice and from the point of view of someone standing outside and looking in, much as an entomologist might examine a colony of termites.

The alternative is to construct stories or models in the active voice, wherein people are creating the future through their actions and interactions. To do this requires an analytical point of departure that starts with a formulation of economizing activity that opens naturally into an emergent dynamic orientation toward economic theory. For instance, it is impossible to work with a formulation wherein people generate and reform continually the world they experience and at the same time work with a model of competitive equilibrium where everyone is a price taker (Richardson 1960). These alternative analytical windows are simply incommensurable. In a world of universal price taking, prices can never change nor can new products, services, or enterprises ever be introduced; a prefabricated world holds no place for customized construction.

In this respect, formulations of economizing action cannot be appraised readily against the conventional standard of prediction, because prediction is a standard that is suitable only for formulations based on closed concepts in which nothing emerges. In contrast, any work with emergent phenomena requires the employment of open concepts, wherein what emerges can be rendered intelligible even though its emergence cannot be predicted in advance, as against being rendered sensible *ex post*. The primary theme of such an active-voice effort would perhaps be how pygmies can become giants through property-governed cooperation within society. This would place the principal story on the multiplication of our capabilities through rightly-organized cooperation, which puts the burden on the discovery and articulation of those principles of organization. Neo-Walrasian theorizing is not suitable for doing this because it has no ability to deal with the generation of new configurations out of old configurations. It simply asserts some equilibrium, which is disturbed by exogenous shocks and with some alternative equilibrium subsequently established. The neo-Walrasian framework can be used as a template for social engineering through systems design; however, social engineering is also an object that is subject to explanation as an emergent feature of societal processes.

The challenge is to create a framework of praxeology that is suitable for theorizing about a continually evolving social economy, and to do so in a way that allows societal configurations to be intelligible and even predictable *ex post* and yet never fully determined *ex ante*.[1] This distinction between *ex ante* and *ex post* has, of course, been missing in economic theory for half a century or more, a casualty of the predominant use of the neo-Walrasian window in theorizing about economics where the distinction is irrelevant because it has no analytical work to do.

There would seem to be three significant ways in which praxeology would differ from U-max in theorizing about human action, all of which would operate in the direction of seeking to understand the law-like features of ongoing development within a social economy. First, there is a theory of mind that analogizes mind not to some computer disk which is searched in making choices, but rather analogizes it to a polycentric process of networked connections that is characterized by both reason and passion (Pribram 1971). It is in this regard worth noting that both Vilfredo Pareto and Max Weber, both major contributors to *Sozialökonomik*, distinguished between logical and non-logical action. That distinction corresponds reasonably well to that between the two hemispheres of the brain. It also corresponds to recognition that acts of passion are capable of *ex post* rationalization even though they were not premeditated through processes we would denote as reasoning. To be sure, to make this distinction is not to assert some duality or separability between reason and passion or mind and body. That duality was Descartes' error, as Damasio (1994) explains and as Pinker (1997) and Nussbaum (2001) amplify. It is only to assert a distinction between those actions that are preceded by deliberation and those that are not. This distinction becomes important within a context of monetary calculation, which includes but a subset of economizing action.

Second, with respect to the employment of deliberation and reason the set of options is open and not closed. This is not to deny that people act in large degree out of habit, but is only to assert that they do not act wholly out of habit. They also engage in experimentation and even whimsy. Surely one of the universal qualities of human nature is a dislike of being bored. Within the standard theory of consumer choice, however, a consumer who faces an unchanged set of prices, both product and factor, will never change jobs and will always consume the same basket of goods. In short, that consumer will be terribly bored. Such boredom, however, will not be countenanced. New items will sometimes be bought and tried even if prices haven't changed and even if the qualities of the new products are unknown; new jobs might be pursued, not because they offer more income but because they offer a change.

A desire to avoid boredom is surely an element of our natures, and this quality translates into patterns of individual conduct that can be captured only by working with models of open-ended action.

Third, people differ in how they act with respect to the preceding two features. People are heterogeneous in numerous dimensions that are relevant for the pursuit of an emergent theoretical orientation toward social economy, in which the principal source of energy that propels the emergence is the interaction among different entities, all of whom are acting in praxeologically intelligible fashion. It is widely noted that people differ in the degrees of reason and passion with which they seem to operate. People likewise differ in their thresholds of boredom and their willingness to venture into new situations. They also differ in how they receive and process information and in how they arrive at judgments.

For a research program centered on emergent dynamics and not on comparative statics, these variations among individuals translate into sources of energy that generate new social configurations out of existing configurations. In short, such a research program is predicated upon the belief that societal evolution cannot be reduced to some kind of model of the evolution of a single, representative or average individual. It is rather predicated on a presumption that the characteristic features of some aggregate population are not duplicated within each entity. Hence, societal configurations and their changes can only be rendered genuinely intelligible by a mode of thinking that takes into account an entire population and their relationships and patterns of interaction (Kirman 1992). In other words, outliers matter and do significant work within a theory of societal processes (Gladwell 2008).

Wants, activities, and economizing action

For the most part the treatment of choice by economists has taken consumer choice as the primary object of theorization, with producer choice serving a secondary role. To be sure, genuine choice is absent under either type of formulation. Nonetheless, consumer choice is typically presented first, followed by producer choice. There is a want-driven logic that corresponds to this theoretical order: unfulfilled wants are the point of departure from which productive activity arises. But this logic does not commend the conventional theoretical order by which consumer choice precedes producer choice. This order starts with a consumer choosing among goods, after which the production of those goods is treated. Yet choice among consumer goods can take place only after those goods have been produced, as was recognized by W. S. Jevons (1871).

The logic of action would place production before consumption in two respects. One respect was just noted: the impossibility of consumption until something has first been produced. The other respect, and surely the more significant one, concerns the significance of activity to human nature, as Alfred Marshall (1890) recognized and Talcott Parsons (1931) elaborated in his treatment of wants and activities in Marshall. While the presence of wants inspires activity, the pattern of activity influences the acquisition of knowledge and serves to change the character of wants. For a theoretical effort that seeks to illuminate the emergent dynamics of social interaction, it would seem as though the point of analytical departure should reside with the source of variability, which is activity.

Among other things, activity shapes character and also social relationships, patterns of communication, and associations. The associations that people have and make are based largely on activities. Even a great deal of consumption is based on those activities, as explained by Mary Douglas (1979). Whether people eat dry breakfast cereal or eggs and sausage is not a basis for social activity. Nor is it a basis for the learning that arises through social activity. For a theory centered on emergent dynamics, the central choices involve production and the organization of productive activity. Even a great deal of consumption arises out of productive activity.

For instance, leisure-time activities are treated as consumption and not as production. Yet for most people the use of leisure arises out of productive activities and not out of consumption. How people use their leisure time is significantly governed by their productive activities, both through the knowledge of possibilities that is generated and because of patterns of association and communication that arise within particular contexts of productive activity. For these reasons, production rather than consumption would seem to provide the better framework for theorizing about human action. People will pretty much all consume what they earn, but the particular patterns of consumption will be influenced by production-related patterns of association. For a theory centered on emergent dynamics, the central problem setting for examining human action would bring production-related activities into the analytical foreground and relegate consumption to the background. There still remains the distinction between genuine choice and virtual choice, but that distinction likewise points to differences in the use to which theoretical frameworks are put.

This alternative formulation would reject the conventional formulation of a utility function that is separable in consumption and effort and with consumption entering positively and effort negatively. George Loewenstein (1999) asks why people climb mountains and do similar things. Many explanations could be given, but most of them would point away from a utility function separable in consumption and effort because effort was a simple subtraction from utility. Among other things, such efforts can be sources of meaning, and humans are surely metaphysical creatures who seek meaning. Moreover, a search for meaning will typically involve testing and mastery, which also require effort. After hanging two days on the side of a mountain, a climber sits at home with his companions, feasting and drinking. If utility were separable in consumption and effort, the feasting and drinking would represent consumption purchased through effort; moreover, it would be even better if that consumption could have been secured without first climbing the mountain. Alternatively, the entire duration that runs from climbing through feasting is a single unit of meaningful activity. It is surely reasonable to seek to appraise systems of economic organization with respect to the opportunities they provide for meaningful activity, in contrast to an exclusive concentration on consumption.

From praxeology to catallaxy through social economy

Praxeology and catallaxy are not independent theoretical concepts. They are complementary to one another and describe a bi-directional order of causation. The analytical challenge is not to try to show how praxeology can address standard neo-Walrasian questions, for U-max will always cut more quickly to the chase. The challenge is rather to develop modes of thinking that will convey more fully the evolving, unfolding character of market processes through interaction among participants.

Any reference to an evolving or unfolding process within human societies warrants some words of caution. While evolutionary notions began with the philosophers of the Scottish Enlightenment, evolution has subsequently become the province of biologists. It is this shift in the object of evolutionary thought from human to natural phenomena that calls for some caution. Where the Scottish philosophers started with human intelligence and insight, and explored how such societal configurations as customs and conventions emerged out of interaction among people, the study of natural phenomena inserts randomness in place of intelligence and insight. Evolutionary models typically work in terms of random mutations being thrown into an environment, and with some of those subsequently replicating and expanding, as illustrated long ago in an economic setting by Armen Alchian (1950). This is a fine and even necessary procedure for the natural sciences where we do not have any insight into the objects we are studying. But we do have insight into ourselves. Hence, our injections of something novel into a situation are not adequately conveyed by notions of blind randomness, and have to be addressed instead though notions of intention, foresight, and similar open concepts.

Let me illustrate briefly what I have in mind by considering again the simple model of a consumer searching for prices for some particular commodity. The gain from an additional search is the expected reduction in price that results from the search, and without search there would be no knowledge of prices and no basis for claiming any systematic tendency for prices to be as low as they could be while being consistent with enterprise survival. A difficulty that arises immediately with this formulation is that it is necessary to assume that customers know the probability distribution of prices but not the prices offered at any particular store. If they knew the prices offered by particular stores there would be no need to search for prices. If they didn't know the probability distribution of prices, it would be impossible to construct an expected price reduction from an additional search. The descriptive accuracy of this formulation is surely dubious, but this doesn't matter because what matters is empirical congruence with such observable phenomena as price dispersion across products. Hence, it is possible to treat consumers "as if" they can calculate the requisite statistics: the resulting goodness of fit will tell whether the as-if presumption is sufficient for the job.

The absence of any plausible basis for asserting *a priori* knowledge of such probability distributions causes no analytical problems if someone conducts a large number of searches, for then Bayes' Theorem can be invoked with respect to the *a posteriori* distribution. It can even be invoked in an as-if manner even if it is recognized that it is a rare person who explicitly can make Bayesian calculations. Yet people typically conduct a small number of searches, in which case Bayes' Theorem cannot rescue the procedure because there is no basis for inferring the distribution from the small sample collected even if one is capable of making such calculations.

Yet the search models do yield reasonably accurate results in their ability to map into price dispersions across items. Theorists who work with these types of models do not claim that consumers actually make such calculations, but rather argue that these models do well at ordering various *ex post* observations about prices under the presumption that those observations represent some equilibrium. The analytical apparatus is constructed with closed concepts because closure is a condition required for equilibrium. Among other things, this requires that people be modeled as making probability calculations when uncertainty is present, for an inability to make such calculations would leave the model open and, hence, equilibrium would not exist.

A focus on economizing individuals who operate within an evolving catallaxy, by contrast, requires intelligibility but not predictability, recognizing that what Hayek (1967) characterizes as pattern prediction is what I mean by intelligibility and with genuine predictability speaking to the details that constitute the pattern as a form of prophesy. This alternative orientation shifts the analytical emphasis onto the various societal configurations and conventions that people generate through their economizing actions. Within this alternative orientation, search theory would give reasonable results not because people search and do Bayesian calculations, but because they operate within a catallaxy in which only a few people do such things. In this case, a reasonable account of the phenomena of price dispersion must look to the social processes through which prices emerge, as against looking to individual calculation. To do this requires a form of population-based or ecological thinking, in contrast to reducing a catallaxy to one representative instance of praxeological action. Observed patterns of price dispersion among stores become a feature of social interaction that is not reducible to one prototypical act of individual choice.

In this respect, most people are surely more likely to be able to distinguish low-price from high-price stores without making any explicit effort at search than to be able to specify a probability distribution of prices. These observations, however, speak to processes of social interaction and not to individual search. There will be a societal landscape that emerges in response to the efforts of people to grapple with the challenges presented by the situations that search theory addresses by closed concepts. For one thing, people talk with one another, sharing experiences as they talk, which provides information outside the ambit of search theory.[2] Furthermore, stores advertise and, even more, acquire reputations whereby some stores become known for offering comparatively low prices while other stores become known for offering better customer service and perhaps shopping venues that are more appealing visually. Search theory might map well into some model of price dispersion while remaining silent on the architecture of the various commercial arrangements and organizations within which those prices emerge, for emergence requires open concepts. The picture generated by emergence theorizing would surely be more "realistic" than that created by equilibrium theorizing, in that the main work that is done with respect to price dispersion is surely not accomplished through consumer search because consumers pretty much know these things through different channels. That work is rather accomplished through entrepreneurial actions that do such things as select product attributes and pricing policies, as well as generating market architecture.

U-max can stand alone within the neo-Walrasian framework, for it allows the social level of analysis to be reduced to the choices of a representative individual. Notions of division of labor and division of knowledge are inessential to the neo-Walrasian framework, as these enter only into some such notion as productivity per worker. No work is done by such notions as patterns of distribution of knowledge or talents across people. Since the neo-Walrasian framework supports reduction of society to an individual, theories based on U-max are devices for the generation of what are regarded as social-level hypotheses. Concerns about praxeological action just complicate the analysis without bringing added explanatory power in return.

In contrast to U-max, praxeological action cannot stand by itself. To be sure, a good number of Austrianesque writings seem to verge on saying just this, as illustrated by statements to the effect that nearly the full corpus of economic theory can be derived from the simple notion that individuals act (see Rothbard 1962). Praxeology seeks to articulate individual action that is open, in contrast to the closure postulated by U-max; moreover, it seeks to do so within a social setting where the exact phenomena of praxeological action merge with the empirical-realistic phenomena of catallactical interaction. Where the difference between closed choice and open action leads can be discerned only when many people come together in catallaxy. It is in catallaxy and not in praxeology where the two windows yield more sharply different visualizations of societal phenomena. This is surely as it should be, once we recognize that economics is a social science, and with individual action being just the point of origin from which various societal patterns spring. We start with praxeology, but most interesting economic tales occur within catallaxy and cannot be reduced to praxeology because interaction is not additive and reducible to action. To be sure, neo-Walrasian theorizing typically reduces statements of equilibrium to statements of maximization, but the two are linked tightly by the closed analytical framework that is employed. Within the neo-Mengerian window, however, interaction among acting individuals generates societal formations that are constituted through individual choices and yet cannot be reduced back to individual choices. The two analytical parabolas, X^2 and $-X^2$, come to illuminate the analytical territory differently once their common point of origin is left behind.

Risk, uncertainty, and purposive action

Frank Knight (1921) distinguished between risk, which could be insured against, and uncertainty, which could not because it was not subject to the standard probability calculus. The subsequent years have seen much misplaced and needless controversy over the merits of risk and uncertainty as concepts to bring to bear on topics of analytical interest. For instance, William Fellner (1965) describes Knight's treatment as particularly unfortunate, and seeks instead to use a Bayesian framework to allow probability calculations for all choice situations, through his construction of a semi-probabilistic orientation that he describes as "slanting." Where one side of the controversy seeks to fashion a place for uncertainty, which in turn requires some reduction in the domain to which risk pertains, the other side seeks to eliminate the domain to which uncertainty pertains. This controversy is misplaced and needless because the concepts pertain to non-commensurable domains of human activity, and are not competitive accounts of the same domain of activity.

For the neo-Walrasian orientation, there is no option to the elimination of uncertainty through the probability calculus. One of the hard core claims of this research program is that observations are of equilibrium states. When this observation is combined with the hard core presumption that individuals optimize, theoretical closure requires something like expected utility. People are observed to make choices among options, and it is nonsensical to have them do anything other than maximize expected utility. As an essentialist matter, it might be objected that people might not be aware of all of their options, which would render it impossible literally to apply an expected utility calculus. To raise this kind of issue, however, is to move outside the neo-Walrasian hard core. It's hard if not impossible to give coherent accounts about the choices people might have made had they been aware of such options at the time they made their choices. Expected utility theory fits within the neo-Walrasian hard core and allows theories with empirical content to be developed. Uncertainty must be extinguished within the neo-Walrasian framework.

This doesn't mean that uncertainty is useless for understanding human action and social configurations; it means only that uncertainty can do its work only within the confines of a neo-Mengerian research program because only this type of program seeks to accommodate the open-ended emergence to which uncertainty pertains, as illustrated by Shackle (1961, 1968) and Runde (1996). For analysis based on closed concepts, uncertainty is destructive because it prevents the application of U-max reasoning. U-max requires the ability to construct expected values, while uncertainty denies the possibility of such calculations. For an analytical formulation predicated upon closed concepts and the predictability this yields, uncertainty must be reduced to risk in some fashion. This has nothing to do with truth or falsity in any essentialist sense, and has everything to do with bringing closure to an analytical framework that is predicated upon such closure. A good deal of unnecessary controversy has resulted because of a failure to recognize the non-commensurability of the two analytical windows. To render observed choices explainable and predictable from the perspective of an outside observer, it is necessary to work with closed concepts. Uncertainty is an open concept, risk is a closed concept, and the two pertain to disjunctive analytical frameworks.

Issues concerning the application of probabilistic reasoning to unique economic choices have been both widely employed and yet subject to continual criticism, as explored in Charles McCann (1994) and George Shackle (1972). From within the neo-Walrasian window, such a probabilistic move is a means of bringing closure to an analytical framework that requires such closure. People choose, and from a neo-Walrasian orientation of necessity and explanation, expected value formulations are necessary means of bringing the required analytical closure. An expected value calculus of some type must be postulated to explain choices even when outcomes are uncertain.

For analysis based on open concepts, action can be rendered intelligible but it cannot be truly predicted. If it could be truly predicted, the ability to choose could be taken away from the otherwise choosing person and vested instead in the predictive model. Furthermore, the choosing person would not object to this substitution. Alternatively, if the person were to object, that objection must surely signify that something is missing from the so-called predictive model. What we would have in this case is a situation where the view from the outside looking in is not congruent with the view from the inside looking out. An insurance company can predict that among 10,000 people driving between home and work each week, five of them will have accidents. It is meaningless to construe an individual driver as making a similar prediction. There can be macro-level regularity in the patterned interaction among drivers without there being genuine predictability at the individual level.

Jason Potts (2000: 112–17) contrasts a formulation of *hetero economicus* with the conventional formulation of *homo economicus*. Where *homo economicus* is construed as optimizing over all options contained within the real field, *hetero economicus* is construed as an inquisitive creature who acts both with limited knowledge and with curiosity. *Hetero economicus* acts in an intelligible fashion, which means that he seeks to act effectively in using means to pursue ends. Being an inquisitive creature, however, means that it is possible that the same person would choose differently if placed in the same setting in parallel worlds, whereas the U-max formulation would require the same choice always to be made. People can differ, of course, in just how inquisitive they are. This might simply reflect that some people are more highly spirited than others. From an *ex post* orientation, it is always possible to rationalize an observed choice through an expected value calculation. From an *ex ante* orientation, however, choices can be rendered intelligible without resorting to an expected value calculation.

From the outside looking in, the natural science orientation, the snapshot view from the neo-Walrasian window will offer an *ex post* interpretation based on expected utility maximization. The Ptolemaic maps could always be made to work, after all. From the inside looking out, however, what we have are people acting to attain more desirable circumstances in numerous ways and dimensions, and doing so within a complex environment of interaction where you leave work to head home believing that you will arrive safely, and yet not being able truly to experience your journey before you take it, which means that it isn't genuinely predictable. The outcomes of choices are not genuinely knowable at the time they are made, which is not at all to deny the presence of regular, intelligible patterns within societies.

A 2007 novel by Nicholas Sparks titled *The Choice* illustrates the unknowability of the outcome of choice. In Sparks's story, a man's wife had been in a coma for three months. The husband had an acquaintance who had become increasingly bitter and sad as his wife's coma reached six years. The choice the protagonist faced was whether to execute his wife's living will, which called for her feeding tube to be removed after three months. The story ended with the husband refraining from executing his wife's will and the wife awakening from her coma. At the time of making the choice, the husband could imagine the alternative future experiences but could not choose between them. Moreover, a probability calculus does not apply to such unique settings. One could, of course, apply such a calculus *ex post* and assert that the husband selected the option that he thought offered the higher present value. From the point of view of trying to explain phenomena from the outside looking in, this is perhaps all that can be done. But it is different from the inside looking out. From this alternative vantage point, it is reasonable and intelligible to speak of taking leaps of faith: taking those leaps can be rendered intelligible to third parties even if they cannot be foretold in advance.

To deny genuine predictability or prophesy is not to deny intelligibility, understandability, and the ability to operate effectively in the world. The question at issue is really one of what scope to give for what amount to leaps of faith in human action, as well as how societal configurations might nurture or extinguish such leaps: for instance, perhaps the small, humane scale and highly localized society described by Wilhelm Röpke (1958) might nurture such leaps of faith more fully than the large-scale and highly bureaucratic societies of today and which Röpke criticizes. An expected value calculus does not describe a leap of faith; animal spirits do. A company that insures a large number of drivers against accidents does not experience a leap of faith.

To the contrary, it knows what next year will bring before next year arrives. By contrast, an individual driver makes a leap of faith, one that typically is warranted by subsequent experience but not always. It makes a great deal of sense for an insurance company to assert that 99 percent of its drivers will have no accidents in the coming year. An individual driver, however, will either have an accident during the year or will not.

The appropriate formulation to use will surely depend on the problem setting being examined. One that calls for explanation in terms of equilibrated relationships, perhaps as illustrated by a model that seeks to explain the observed distribution of traffic across different roads, might find some expected utility calculus to be helpful even if it might be acknowledged that it is unlikely that drivers are fully aware of the full range of route options they face. For problems that relate to emergence through time, however, the equivalent of animal spirits or leaps of faith will have more scope for expression, as will be explored particularly in the final four chapters. For instance, entrepreneurial action involves leaps of faith, and in uncertain settings some people seem more ready to take such leaps than other people, as will be examined in the next chapter.

Economizing, computation, and models of mind

Economizing action starts from the presumption that people employ means to attain ends, and do so in a context where not all ends can be attained, which means in turn that choices are necessary both among ends and in the use of means. The conventional way of pursuing the analysis is to postulate fixed ends (Stigler and Becker 1977) that are defined by a utility function. The available means are described by a budget constraint and the expected utility framework assigns means to the service of the various ends. This framework brings the analytical closure that the neo-Walrasian hard core requires. This hard core is directed at rendering sensible a set of contemporaneous observations as consistent reflections of this analytical framework.

What this framework cannot do is generate those observations from some earlier point of departure. It starts at the end of the story, so to speak, and seeks to render it intelligible through expected utility. In contrast, the neo-Mengerian hard core directs the analyst to start at the beginning, so to speak, and to seek to generate those observations through interaction among economizing people. It also works with a texture or pattern to social configurations that contain analytical layers in place of the flat surface of the neo-Walrasian orientation. These layers are the products of the social interaction that generate such emergent phenomena as property rights, contractual entanglements, and money among myriad such products.

Mind is engaged in computation within both research programs, only those programs differ in their conceptualizations of mind. The neo-Walrasian program treats mind as if it were a computer disk or some similar flat-surface object on which computational operations are performed. The given utility function is analogous to read-only memory (ROM), and the utility of various options for choice are calculated swiftly. A utility function evaluates all options by placing them along the real line, which means that all options exist on the same plane; indeed, mind is treated as a plane.

In contrast, the neo-Mengerian program works with an alternative model of mind, one that still calculates, only it does so with a different architecture. That architecture has structure and is not a plane; moreover, it calculates both differently and less quickly, much as the brain calculates less quickly than computers. For instance, computers playing chess calculate over available options before making moves, while humans use a procedure that involves vastly less direct calculation. The number of options to be compared simply overwhelms the computational ability of the human brain, as there are something like 10^{120} options to be explored. This alternative, neo-Mengerian treatment of mind is congruent with much of the contemporary scholarship on brains and minds (Noteboom 2007). Among other things, mind is not some simple computing device as illustrated by a computer, but rather is a system or network of computational organs or mental modules, and which have evolved through natural selection. Pinker (1997: 58) characterizes the operation of the mental modules as "a noisy parliament of competing factions."

Mental life as a network of modules maps well into lexicographic ordering as an alternative to utility functions, though it would also be possible to explore more polycentric arrangements of those mental modules. In this respect, Marvin Minsky (1986) conceptualizes a polycentric mind constituted through a multiplicity of interacting agents, while Daniel Klein (1999) explores some economic-theoretic implications of Minsky's framework. However this alternative structure of mind is conceptualized, mind would have layers of interacting modules.[3] Mental phenomena would thus arise out of the interactions among the modules. In this context, something like an expected utility calculus might operate over a subset of mental activities, mostly those involving habit and familiar situations, such as illustrated by the first few moves of a chess match or driving to work. One way of illustrating such a structural notion of mind, and one that maps as well both into notions of lexicographic ordering and into notions of polycentric minds, is to analogize mind to a tree.

An account of mind and human action that is suitable for carrying forward a neo-Mengerian research program must be able to accommodate at least three significant stylized facts: human nature, moral imagination, and learning through social interaction. Such an account, moreover, must be able to do so in a way that can carry forward the research program in illuminating the emergence of social phenomena through interactions among acting minds, each of which is acting to replace states it values less highly with states it values more highly.

An account of human nature recognizes that there is something common across humanity. Recognition of that commonality, however, must also accommodate recognition of the enormous variability among people in their actions

(Tooby and Cosmides 1990). Albert Schweitzer and Adolf Hitler are both reflections of human nature, to borrow from the title of Arthur Lovejoy's (1961) masterful treatment. The challenge is to develop an economically interesting account of mind that plants both people in some bedrock of human nature while allowing for their starkly different actions in life. The image of the tree provides one such framework, with its taproot denoting human nature.

We all know that trees differ widely despite their identical taproots. Trees, of course, generate a system of roots, and from those roots come the trunk and associated branches. Just as there are numerous possible shapes of trees that can stem from the same taproot, so are there numerous patterns of human action that can stem from the same human nature. For trees, differences would be attributed to such things as differences in soil, rainfall, and the proximity of other trees. For humanity we typically distinguish between genetics and environment, and with it often not being easy to make the relevant distinctions with assurance with present states of knowledge.

The classic approach to morality treated it as habits that were acquired through practice, mostly in childhood, and which were so deeply etched that they were shifted from the domain of conscious thought into that of unconscious action. Morality is not captured usefully by utility functions, for it is not reasonable or plausible to speak of people as choosing morality in the same way that they choose among items in a vending machine. Lexicographic ordering is one way of approaching morality and the moral imagination. In this formulation, the moral imagination (Himmelfarb 1992) would be a mental module that judges and governs the actions being entertained by such other modules within the mind to which we associate the acquisition of utility.

An open question at this point is the extent to which morality is hardwired as part of the taproot of humanity, as against being a variable that is otherwise generated. The former treats morality as genetically governed, as illustrated by Budziszewski (2003); the latter treats it as a variable that can be influenced through practice. While practice is an environmental variable, to claim scope for influence through practice is not to deny a place for genetics. Rather, it is to assert that there is much about these matters that presently we do not understand fully. In any case, it is the domain of practice where scope for social influence resides.

That social influence, moreover, operates in two relatively distinct precincts. One is the family as a source for the cultivation of the moral imagination. Parenting is the province of families, and families differ hugely in how they discharge their parental activities. They also differ in their structure, with one element of that difference being the growth in families without fathers present, some consequences of which have been explored by Charles Murray (1984, 1988). If we conceptualize these parental activities as helping to form the branch roots that also support the human tree, it is easy to see that many different shapes of tree can be generated from the same taproot.

The other precinct of influence is other people. We are pack animals who seek membership in various groups, and these qualities can lead to herding and cascades (Bikhchandaini, Hirshleifer, and Welch 1992). Those qualities can also promote slippery slopes, as explored in Rizzo and Whitman (2003) and Volokoh (2003). The challenge for a model of mind to support a neo-Mengerian program of social economy is to characterize the bi-directional influence between minds and society, as illustrated by the brief discussion of cell phones and email in Chapter 1.

In this vein, Karl Pribram (1971) conceptualizes a holographic mind as a form of polycentric mind with interacting modules. This is a model of an open relationship between mind and environment, with influence running in both directions. In one direction, brain structure influences the actions and experiences of subjects. But in the other direction, the experiences of subjects, immaterial thoughts as well as material sensations, modify brain structure by inducing changes in the relationships and connections among modules. This relationship among modules is expressed well by Arthur Koestler's (1964, 1978) image of holarchy as a hierarchically organized but open system of holons that seem to be self-regulating. Action by the human organism is governed by interaction among layers of holons at lower levels within the organism. It is also governed through interaction at higher levels outside the organism but resident in society.

What is of particular interest for a theory of social economy is how the social-level interactions might influence moral imaginations. Property rights, after all, are reflections of moral imaginations. For instance, the domain for freedom of action varies directly with the willingness and ability of other people to tolerate ambiguity and uncertainty. One direction of influence is that an existing pattern of tolerance governs the domain of liberty. The other possible direction is that the extent of such tolerance might be influenced through socially organized practice. The ability of people freely to create enterprises threatens the security of people who have previously formed enterprises. A program of income insurance might reduce the threat to security but would also reduce the incentive to form enterprises. The theory of the holographic mind holds out the prospect that there is some scope for social configurations to influence those facets of the moral imagination that are represented by tolerance to lesser or greater degrees.

Praxeological reflections on some behavioral challenges to U-max

Recent years have seen a growing number of challenges to the neo-Walrasian standard of rationality and U-max. Among the topics covered in this growing literature are loss aversion, fairness in ultimatum games, nonlinear discounting, and the effect of framing and context on choice. The various behavioral claims are thought to challenge the rational choice form of U-max, though it remains to be seen whether the protective belt of the neo-Walrasian program can dissolve those challenges. These challenges are less significant from a neo-Mengerian orientation. To say this is not, however, to dismiss the material treated by those challenges, for that material is surely to be taken seriously. Those challenges are, however, cast in a different light when they are examined through the neo-Mengerian window.

What is perhaps most notable about the behavioral challenges is that they are posed in terms of representative individuals or group averages, which amounts to the same thing. Consider the various results of ultimatum games surveyed in Camerer and Thaler (1995). In this game between a Proposer and a Responder, Proposer is given a sum of money and offers part of that sum to Responder. Responder can either accept or reject Proposer's offer. If Responder rejects the offer, Proposer also gets nothing. One interpretation of U-max holds that Proposer should offer next to nothing and Responder should accept it because next-to-nothing is more than nothing. The results of multiple experiments, however, find outcomes hovering in the vicinity of even division, and with offers of less than 20 percent being routinely rejected. This has been widely interpreted as an anomaly for U-max.

There has arisen an analytical convention within economic theory by which the starting point for human action is a solitary individual, a Robinson Crusoe. From this point of departure, a good deal of effort has gone into the specification of models through which some version of social order might emerge, as was explored in Chapter 2. The ultimatum game represents a variation on that same framework, for the presumption is that the individuals are narcissistic. In this case, Responder should be willing to take what Proposer offers and Proposer should offer the smallest amount possible above zero. That the experiments do not play out this way clearly brings into question the standard approach that is based on what effectively are narcissistic individuals because the references to self-interest refer to individuals whose objects of interest are contained within themselves and do not reside in the outside world.

It does not seem like such an anomaly for polycentric theories of mind with lexicographic ordering. The problem would seem to reside with the neo-Walrasian interpretation of the economic agent and not with the principle of economizing action. It is rare that encounters at doorways provoke exhibits of rudeness, and the point of departure for explaining how this is so surely resides in processes regarding the acquisition of habits of heart and mind prior to reaching the age where one might pass through a doorway.

The behavioral formulations theorize in terms of isolated individuals, as against theorizing about individual action within some social setting. Those formulations also operate in terms of averages, which also fits the neo-Walrasian motif of reducing observations to surface or planar impressions. In contrast, a neo-Mengerian motif operates with multiple levels, with only the surface subject to direct observation. There are also hidden sources of order that reside beneath the surface. For instance, the permanent income hypothesis is based on maximizing expected utility over a lifetime where future incomes are subject to exponential discounting. In contrast, a good deal of behavioral literature finds support for hyperbolic discounting, thereby generating choices that are inconsistent over time (Laibson 1997). While experiments have found such discounting, they have not found it to be a universal feature of humanity. With respect to the ancient-classical notion of the well-ordered soul, hyperbolic discounting could well be a reflection of disorderliness in the soul. In any case, variability is present in how people act through time, and this variability acquires significance when the analytical focus is placed on the entire population and not just some average character-istic of that population. What would be of particular analytical interest is the forms of interaction among people who acted differently toward the future, along with the organizational and institutional traces those interactions leave behind.

4 Planning, production, and entrepreneurial action

Where Chapter 3 examined in an abstract and general manner praxeological action within society, this chapter explores such action within the specific societal context wherein that action is organized within networks of teams. Ronald Coase (1937) is almost universally regarded as the natural starting point for thinking about team production, as exemplified by Alchian and Demsetz (1972). That starting point is based on the conventional presumption that individuals are independent from society; hence the organization of production into teams involves a trade-off between losses of individual autonomy when activity is organized through teams and gains that team activity offers, as illustrated by lowering transaction costs, spreading risks, and exploiting economies of scale. While I do not dispute the presence of such trade-offs, I would also note that there are other considerations that are surely also present in accounting for patterns of team-based activity. For the most part, these revolve around human nature in some fashion. We aren't solitary creatures, so team production is attractive independently of possible economies of scale or reductions in transaction costs. Yet we also crave accomplishment and glory, which works against the organization of society as a single team, independently of the abolition of prices that would result from such an organizational format.

This chapter starts by reviewing the standard economic theory of the firm within the neo-Walrasian framework wherein the abstract entity we designate as a "market economy" is constituted as an equilibrated set of profit-maximizing firms. Within this prefabricated world, the direction of theoretical movement runs from production to cost and then to market exchange. Production relationships are first established, and with cost emanating from those relationships in light of market-established prices of inputs. This conventional analytical framework is constructed to reveal an underlying consistency in the presumed pattern of equilibrated relationships.

The remainder of the chapter seeks to explore what might be involved in theorizing about ongoing processes of continual fabrication, wherein the appearance of prefabrication is but an imaginary state that pertains to a static society and not to real society. Within this alternative formulation, cost is borne before and not after production. Choices to bear cost in advance of production are the province of entrepreneurship which seeks to attain some projected future state. Such entrepreneurial action, moreover, occurs within a networked ecology of enterprises of various forms, and with those particular forms also being established through entrepreneurial action.

Among other things, I do not distinguish between economic, political, and civic domains with respect to team-based activity, at least in any sense of analytical independence. As a matter of accounting, it is possible to distinguish among such different types of enterprise and to develop measures of their volumes of activity. From the point of view of social-economic theorizing, however, all such enterprises and their activities emerge through interaction among the individuals who comprise a society. All such enterprises, therefore, arise out of the efforts of people to secure more highly desired circumstances, recognizing that both the objects to which those desires are associated and their beliefs about the causal connections between those desires and the available means varies across people. For instance, profit-seeking, non-profit, and state-based enterprises all emerge out of the same bedding ground (Wagner 2007). What results is an emergent ecology of enterprises of various organizational formats. The central point of this alternative conceptual effort is to characterize the internally-generated character of societal transformation. At any historical instant, a particular enterprise map can be explained as a result of interaction among economizing agents who (1) are alike in their universal striving to reduce uneasiness by employing means to seek ends and (2) differ from one another in the means they can obtain, in the particular ends they pursue, and in their understanding of or knowledge about the causal connection between those means and ends. That historical instant, however, is only a snapshot of a society in motion, for it is this same process of interaction within society that generates continual transformation in enterprise maps through time.

Cost, production, and the theory of the firm

The theory of production and the firm is what it is and remains what it is because, without it, the coherence of the theory of static equilibrium would dissolve. The logical order of that theory moves from production to cost, although the theory is presented as a simultaneously determined set of prices and quantities, and not as some sequential relationship. The theory starts with a characterization of production as a relationship between inputs and output. This has the appearance of a recipe without any of the reality, in that it provides no instruction by which someone could combine inputs and subsequently generate output. Indeed, the application of inputs and the appearance of output are simultaneous, which might seem truly astounding were it not for the assumption that economic relationships are in steady state or frozen condition.

Rather than writing a general production relationship, suppose we work with the Cobb-Douglas relationship where $X = L^a K^{1-a}$, where L and K denote inputs of labor and capital. The simultaneous relationship between inputs and output is viewed as reasonable because of the assumption of a steady state. Suppose X denotes furniture of various types that are made from wood. As for how a single variable X can plausibly denote all kinds of wood-based furniture, this also is rendered sensible by the presumption of steady stateness. Furniture output may contain a long vector of particular products, illustrated by various types of chairs, tables, chests of drawers, and the like, but with steady-state equilibrium all of this can be transformed hedonically into a scalar measure of some standardized glob of output. To be sure, trees take some years to grow. Perhaps you plant a tree now and harvest it 20 years later. But this causes no problem for simultaneity, for you simply assume that you have stands of trees of each age, and when you harvest mature trees you replace them with new ones. Envisioning life as steady-state equilibrium allows one to achieve enormous economies of simplification.

In the actual harvesting of trees and making of furniture, a huge variety of equipment and skills are brought to bear, but these can be collapsed hedonically to K and L by virtue of the steady-state presumption. The production recipe says nothing about how actually to combine those ingredients, leaving these matters for the troops on the ground to resolve. Here, it is assumed that those troops select those combinations so as to minimize the cost of producing any level of output, and selecting among possible levels to maximize a firm's net worth. Starting from the Cobb-Douglas recipe, firms are assumed to purchase inputs in competitive factor markets at prices P_K and P_L. Cost is defined as $C = LP_L + KP_K$. From here, you construct the input demand functions $L = \alpha C/P_L$ and $K = (1-\alpha)C/P_K$. Substituting these input demand functions into the cost function gives the standard functional relationship between cost and output, $C = \beta X$, where β denotes a complicated ratio of prices and exponents.

The central point of this review is that the theoretical effort must run from production to cost. Even though the object of the theorizing effort is a simultaneously equilibrated system of relationships, the production component is regarded as the foundational component: you derive cost functions from production functions; you do not derive production functions from cost functions. In contrast, cost must precede production within the neo-Mengerian window because a decision to undertake an activity must precede any ascertainment of the outcome of that activity. Also at issue here is whether value is governed by one principle or by two. The neo-Walrasian window appears to show two independent principles of value: utility and cost. From utility you get demand and from cost you get supply, only to get supply you must first pass through production. In contrast, the neo-Mengerian window would show all action originating in human efforts to use means to attain ends, which leaves utility as the only principle of value. Production is as much an effort to remove uneasiness as is sleeping. Perhaps Crusoe starts the day with a little water, some remnants of dry wood, and a half-eaten rabbit. He will not spend the day lounging around daydreaming about yachts coming to take him away, because his thought of the nearness of thirst and hunger wakes him from his lethargy. Crusoe likes lounging around, but he also likes to eat and drink. To achieve a more desired state down the road, he needs to gather wood, collect water, and find some animals to kill. How Crusoe divides his time between lounging around and gathering objects of sustenance is governed by a single principle and not by two independent principles.

If we look at the logical order of Crusoe's conduct, cost precedes production. Crusoe decides in light of his uneasiness (including the present anticipation of uneasiness that is looming) to engage in productive activity. In the decision to stop daydreaming and to start looking for food and drink, Crusoe bears the cost of productive activity, as explained lucidly in Buchanan (1969) and amplified by the essays collected in Buchanan and Thirlby (1973). Instead of daydreaming, Crusoe is now scrambling over rocks and through brush, looking for objects of sustenance. How much sustenance Crusoe actually captures and how long it will last him will be revealed in due course. The yield from productive activity comes subsequent to the decision to bear the cost of engaging in productive activity.

If cost precedes production and if price is governed solely by utility and not by two independent principles, utility and cost (production), the conventional formulation of demand-and-supply does not crumble but it does require a different articulation. Demand still reflects consumer utility, but so does supply. At the most elemental level, how much effort Crusoe devotes to looking for food depends on his desire for food. The cost of looking for food is the value Crusoe places on whatever else he might have accomplished in place of looking for food. Demand and supply bear a reciprocal relationship to one another, in modern social economies as well as for Crusoe, as Philip Wicksteed (1914) explains. Supply and demand are images of the same principle of action.

While the preceding illustration with respect to Crusoe illustrates that cost precedes production, it can also meld quickly into representative agent forms of modeling by treating society as just an aggregate of Crusoes. Whether *n* Crusoes will operate as *n* independent firms or whether they will combine into some smaller number of firms is generally treated in terms of the trade-offs noted above. Within this Coase-like formulation, homogeneous individuals will combine into production teams when savings in transaction costs exceed the agency costs of organization. While I have no objection to such formulations as part of the story, they do comprise only part of the story regarding the ecological organization of team activity within societies. Any plan for production involves an imaginative projection from present to future. In a world of significant heterogeneity, people can differ in how they arrive at such projections and in the opportunities they believe the future to contain. It's surely reasonable to think that people who have particularly sharp or acute images of future possibilities will take a leading role in trying to seize those future opportunities.

Any production plan must involve some means of getting from here to there. It is here where capital comes into play (Lachmann 1956, Lewin 1999). Cost is borne in advance of production, and it is only subsequent to production that revenue can be derived from that production. Capital provides the means of bridging the gap in time between the bearing of cost and the receipt of revenue. The neo-Mengerian window shows clearly that an economy is a constellation of intersecting production plans all moving through time. By taking a slice through some instant of time, the neo-Walrasian window obscures the sequential nature of the economic process by making it appear as if it was simultaneous.

Production plans have been treated here as the province of some individual owner or entrepreneur. This treatment maintains a similarity of outlook with the purposeful individual action that is the subject of praxeology. Any enterprise will generate returns in future years, possibly negative in some cases but never intentionally so. While these returns might accrue to an individual and will do so for a proprietorship, in the contemporary world those returns are often divided among large numbers of individuals through various patterns of ownership arrangements. These governance arrangements are themselves forms of constitutions that people create to promote their joint interests in the corporate enterprise (Vanberg 1992). It is perhaps worth noting in this respect that there is a good deal of similarity between corporate forms of commercial enterprise and cities, and a similarity that goes far beyond the reference to cities as being municipal corporations (Foldvary 1994, MacCallum 1970). Among other things, both forms of enterprise involve a diffuse set of suppliers of equity, the value of which is governed by decisions made by a relatively small set of managers. In both cases there are also procedures by which challenges can be made to current management, as will be explored in Chapter 8.

Production plans within an evolving nexus

A recipe is a fine way to think about production, even if the standard representations are inadequate for generating insight into the coordinating properties of emergent patterns of economic organization (as against yielding statements of some aggregate patterns of necessary conditions for postulated equilibrium relationships). Production is reasonably characterized as a relationship between inputs and output, only some interval of time must separate the application of inputs and the generation of output, and no presumption of equilibrium will serve to erase this consideration because the object of interest is coordinating processes and not conditions of a coordinated equilibrium.

When the object of interest is placed on processes through which coordinated patterns of activity are generated, as against being placed on necessary conditions for hypothesized equilibrium, the putty-like characterization of inputs must give way to some alternative characterization that makes closer contact with the world we experience. To designate inputs as labor and capital is to give them no specific form and to treat them instead just as generalized productive power. Actual inputs, however, have specific form, some of which are provided by nature but most of which are formed through conscious choice for specific purposes, or at least are applicable to only a subset of all extant production activities. Among other things, this means that the specific character of inputs is itself largely the result of economizing activity.

Moreover, this holds as much for those human capacities we designate as human capital as it holds for various physical goods and intellectual capital. People do not just create knowledge. They acquire specific forms of knowledge. Some people learn foreign languages, some learn how to write instructions for computers, and some learn how to treat sick dogs. Just as beer barrels and blast furnaces are distinct items (Lachmann 1956), so are aircraft pilots (and pilots trained for different aircraft as well) and fork-lift operators distinct forms of human capital. The particular forms all of those various types of capital take emerge out of entrepreneurial plans and actions.

Recall Leonard Read's (1958) essay, *I, Pencil*, in conjunction with Oskar Morgenstern's (1972) objection to maximization on the grounds that most of the variables of relevance are not under an individual's control (though the presumption of universal price taking gives the illusion of being under individual control). Read's claim is that the ability to produce even such a simple item as a pencil is not within any person's competence. You might think of yourself as a producer of pencils, and in doing so you combine numerous inputs assembled from around the world. But it is not you alone sitting in your shop thinking of all the ingredients you have to assemble, and then assembling them to produce pencils. The ability to produce pencils is itself an emergent quality of the *nexus* of social interaction. To place the emphasis on nexus brings to the foreground the ability of institutions to promote or impede beneficial social interaction (Buchanan 2002).

We can accept the centrality of nexus, and yet examine individual plans for production within that nexus. At the same time, though, the centrality of nexus is revealed in such things as observations of the fortunes of immigrants as between their loci of origination and their places of destination. Typically, they fare better in their places of destination, not because they have acquired new talents but because the nexus into which they have moved provides more and better opportunities for the talents they already possess.

Any plan for production can be denoted by a sequence of nodes and connections. It would even be possible to model a single household as a miniature evenly rotating economy in this regard. That household might have several production plans, each of which can be represented by nodes and connections pointing forward. All of these would illustrate recipes. For instance, potato seeds might be planted in spring and subsequently harvested, and with some of those harvested potatoes used to create seed for the next planting. Some pigs might be kept to help reduce the garbage, and with intervals of breeding and slaughtering taking place. You can easily imagine the use of a directed graph to illustrate this formal portrayal of plans.

We can denote a plan as a directed graph extending into the future from some point of origin. Figure 4.1 illustrates what I have in mind. The line designated "Actor's Plan" shows four nodes connected by intervals. This description in terms of nodes and intervals is intended to represent several relevant features concerning plans and their execution. One is that they extend from the present into the future. Hence, entrepreneurial action involves a projection from present onto future. Another feature is a distinction between plans and the execution of plans. Plans have a point of initial formulation, and can also be subject to amendment or revision. Amendment, however, is not something continuous. It is discrete. The first node in the actor's plan portrayed by Figure 4.1 denotes the initial formulation. The first line segment denotes a period of subsequent execution in light of the original plan. The second node denotes a point of revision based on knowledge acquired since the initial formulation. The second interval denotes the enterprise's execution after revision, and with the third node denoting another point of revision.

Also denoted in Figure 4.1 is the insertion of substitute and complementary plans into the society's ecology of plans, and with these appearing at various times after the actor's plan has been created or revised. Substitute plans are those that would reduce the value of the actor's plan while complementary plans would increase that value. There is no pre-coordination among plans. It is the insertion of other plans that leads possibly to revision of the original plan. It is also, of course, recognition of the possibility of such insertions that leads to flexibility, with assessment and revision being parts of any plan. In the temporal sense depicted in Figure 4.1, the line segments between nodes constitute a type of short run where a plan is operated on a type of automatic pilot, so to speak, until judgments have been made to revise the plan. The long run in this conceptualization constitutes some planning horizon that provides navigational guidance, as represented by the final node in Figure 4.1.

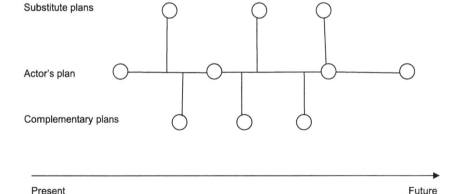

Figure 4.1 Entrepreneurial plans as directed graphs.

A distinction between short run and long run is a staple distinction in economic analysis. At the micro level we distinguish between a short run where firms can vary their mix of inputs but not their scale of output and a long run where everything is variable. At the macro level, such a distinction finds expression in such notions as that a Phillips curve might exist in the short run due to monetary surprises but in the long run it cannot exist because the one-time surprise will have become common knowledge. This distinction between short run and long run, it should be noted, is a sensible construction from within the neo-Walrasian window. The neo-Walrasian window allows the viewing of equilibrated snapshots. Each such snapshot corresponds to sets of data that are assumed to undergird the particular equilibrium snapshot that is being viewed.

In contrast, no such distinction appears at the societal level from within the neo-Mengerian window, even though it appears at the individual level. The distinction does not denote a reference to calendar time, but rather is the result of a thought experiment concerning what is thought to be the ability of people to adjust to new data. Starting from some initial equilibrium, some exogenous shock is introduced that will require a new long-run equilibrium. The short run thus corresponds to some position prior to the attainment of that new equilibrium. With respect to Phillips-curve illustrations, that equilibrium is invariant to the rate of inflation in many models. Some of those models, however, allow people to experience a period during which they are confused between relative and absolute price changes, which results in a negative Phillips relationship appearing for some interval.

Notice, however, that this use of short run and long run is based on all participants being pre-coordinated like a parade, and then experiencing the same exogenous shock at the same time. The scene appears differently when viewed through the neo-Mengerian window, and in two significant respects: (1) the distinction is real or historical and not conceptual or analytical and (2) the distinction pertains to individuals but not to societies. To speak of a long run for a society, however, is to invoke a concept that is illusory. The distinction between short run and long run is a reasonable distinction for rendering individual action intelligible, but it has no referent when it is applied to society because there is no sentient creature who acts by creating and revising plans. At any date on a calendar, there will be some entrepreneurs who are initiating plans, there will be other entrepreneurs who are letting their plans operate, and there will be yet other entrepreneurs who are revising plans.

Entrepreneurship, time, and the projected future

It is easy enough to imagine two snapshot representations of a society taken at different times. A comparison of those snapshots would offer two possibilities. One is that they would appear identical, in which case we would describe the society as static and it would be portrayed accurately by a model of static equilibrium. The other is that they would be different in a number of respects. There are many forms those differences could take, depending on the level of detail that was brought into play. It is easy enough to account for a static society, for people simply repeat their preceding activities. To account for changing patterns of activity requires agents for change who operate within the society. Entrepreneurship is the source of such change, as it is through entrepreneurship that tomorrow's snapshot will appear differently from today's.

There will always be a bridge in society between today and tomorrow. That bridge could be fabricated wholly from convention, in which case the society will be in stasis because tomorrow will be just like today. To escape stasis requires entrepreneurial actions that attempt to build different bridges between today and tomorrow. All entrepreneurial activity involves action set in motion today so as to realize a vision projected onto some tomorrow. Entrepreneurial plans assemble resources to provide services that will become available at some future date. The value of those entrepreneurial plans will not be revealed until that future date arrives. To bridge the gap between present and future, the entrepreneur must contract with various suppliers of inputs. The value of those inputs will depend on the eventual valuations customers place upon those services once they are offered for sale, but entrepreneurial contracts will be based in the meanwhile on the entrepreneur's projection of that future moment onto the present and with capital serving as the instrument to bridge present and future (Casson 1982, Kirzner 1985, Loasby 1982, Sautet 2000, Schmitz 2004).

Any entrepreneurial plan entails decisions to commit resources in advance of production and before any market valuation of that subsequent production can be revealed. By choosing to pursue one production plan rather than another, entrepreneurs are bearing cost in advance of production, as explained in Buchanan (1969). The organization of production is subsequent to the bearing of cost, and so in no way are cost functions derived from production functions. As a matter of accounting, the expenses reflected in accounting statements are trails left by production plans. But in terms of rendering economic activity intelligible in terms of people conceiving and implementing plans, the decision to bear cost is made in advance of production, and with the market valuation of that decision not revealed until some time in the future.

John Maynard Keynes was playing in the right ballpark when he characterized entrepreneurship in terms of animal spirits, and averred that they can wax and wane. The waxing and waning of spirit is surely something that everyone has experienced at some time. Entrepreneurship involves a foray into territory that is not yet charted and so represents a type of exploration. At any moment, the number of explorers can vary, as Keynes suggested by his allusion to the waxing and waning of animal spirits. Yet Keynes was surely also off the mark in his reference to animal spirits, for this suggests something non-rational or even irrational about entrepreneurship, and which Marchionatti (1999) seeks to rescue from claims of irrationality.

Entrepreneurship is assimilated to some image of venturing into truly uncharted territory with no idea of what will be encountered. In this setting there is no plausible basis for forming expectations, and so all we can say is that there are some venturesome souls who are moved by the animal spirits stirring within them.

Entrepreneurship clearly involves some move into uncharted territory, but never is that territory wholly uncharted (Butos and Koppl 1993, Demmert and Klein 2003). There are clues that can help provide navigational guidance. As David Harper (1996) notes, entrepreneurship has the same structure as the scientific testing of hypotheses. Something new is being explored, but the territory also has a lot of familiar elements. There is no way to know whether a hypothesis will work out until it is tested, but yet the scientist is acting on informed hunches and not non-rational animal spirits of some variable degree of exuberance.

Combinatorics perhaps provides a helpful illustration. Suppose you have 52 ingredients available to you as a chef, and for some reason the meals you will assemble must each contain 13 ingredients. You want to combine your available ingredients into meals so as to receive the highest return from customers from your effort. There are over 635 billion ways of selecting 13 ingredients out of 52 possibilities. If you offered a different dish each evening for 50 years, you would have tried only 18,250 of those possibilities, and in no way would you have obtained any kind of statistically useful information. Of those who are seized by their animal spirits to plunge blindly into this combinatorial world, some might make lucky guesses and fare well while others do not and fail (Alchian 1950). Yet the unfolding of social life is not reasonably reduced wholly to random selection among combinatorial options.

While natural evolution might be characterized in such combinatorial terms, social evolution is different because of our knowledge of ourselves and one another, as well as because we never venture wholly into unknown territory. There is no blind plunge into a combinatorial world, even if there is no recipe that guarantees success either. Garlic might be one available ingredient, bread another, and ice cream yet a third. Our knowledge of ourselves generalized outward and projected onto others rejects many possible combinations while embracing other combinations as possible. Thus garlic might be combined with bread, but it will not be shaved and spread over ice cream. Invention is not about venturing wholly into unexplored combinatorial territory, but is about tweaking combinations as aided by beliefs about plausibility that are afforded by our ability to view the social world from the inside looking out. Thus one might plausibly offer a wheat-based breakfast cereal laced with chocolate, but not one littered with crabmeat particles.

For the most part, what we call invention is a recombination of the familiar. For instance, people once rode around in carriages pulled by horses. People also used motors in factories. Someone subsequently put a motor on a carriage and the automobile was born. Alternatively, new cookbooks are continually being published and these offer many new recipes. Yet the list of available ingredients remains pretty much unchanged. Culinary creativity occurs in combinatorial space where familiar ingredients are combined in different ways. For yet a different illustration, science fiction entails much employment of the writer's imagination. Yet science fiction likewise engages in recombining what is familiar in ways that are unfamiliar, for otherwise the work would be unintelligible. For instance, the example from *Star Trek* of being beamed up to a waiting spaceship is a work of science fiction, and yet it is assembled by combining familiar elements in a different way: we have notions of particles of light, we know of particle accelerators, and we have notions of assembly and disassembly; it is thus imaginative but not unintelligible to envision beaming people into waiting spaceships. Entrepreneurial invention takes the typical form of making different patterns of connection in combinatorial space, most of which has been previously explored even if not in those particular patterns. While the entrepreneurial journey enters new territory, it also brings a good deal of familiar territory in its train.

While entrepreneurial action directed at the future is the province of praxeology, it nonetheless occurs within a social context. That context might support such activity, but then again it might not. Just as people might differ among themselves when arrayed along some spectrum running from conventionality to idiosyncrasy, so might societies. A highly conventional society might snuff out individual idiosyncrasy, either directly through martial force or indirectly through various forms of shunning. Alternatively, an idiosyncratic individual might set in motion processes that loosen what had been a highly conventional society. These are topics worthy of both conceptual and historical examination.

Entrepreneurial imagination within the ecology of enterprises

At any moment we would expect some enterprises within a society's ecology of enterprises to be at nodal positions where they are either creating or revising entrepreneurial plans, but we would expect the preponderance of enterprises to be operating somewhere along the execution interval of those plans. Suppose that 95 percent of enterprises are operating within their execution phases, leaving five percent of enterprises at nodal positions where they are either creating or revising plans. This kind of situation would generate observations that would fit with the reasonably predictive properties of models of static equilibrium. An established furniture manufacturer that also owned its forests would confront the world in pretty much simultaneous fashion. During any year, or other time span, it would be planting trees, harvesting trees, buying and repairing equipment, and making furniture, all of it appearing to be simultaneous. In large measure, the firm would be flying on automatic pilot, so to speak. The firm would operate with established supplier relationships and distributor relationships, and prices this year could be represented as relatively simple revisions to prices last year. The operation of such an established firm could be modeled as an application of hysteresis, which means that the present value of a variable is to a significant degree explained by its recent history; hysteresis would not seem to go too far wrong much of the time, at least so long as the time interval was kept appropriately short, whatever appropriate means in this case.

All such established firms are located within a nexus of established firms, and their actions could be described with reasonable accuracy as practicing a form of commercial stasis. The empirical success of static equilibrium modeling surely fits this claim. A scientific procedure that considers explanatory success in terms of averages, moreover, will be forced into making such a conclusion. To avoid such a conclusion, it is necessary to consider the entire population of enterprises and plans, and with especial attention given to outliers, and outliers of two forms. One form is the incipient enterprise that is just entering the enterprise ecology. The other form is the presence of creativity and plan revision within established enterprises, for we should never think that creativity comes only from new enterprises. The point is rather that in terms of a dichotomy between creative and routine, the preponderance of activity is routine and not creative. Indeed, the very notion of a plan as involving some duration of time between initiation and completion requires such preponderance. Furthermore, the observation that the world confronts us mostly as familiar from day to day is congruent with this preponderance as well.

Yet there is surely a link between incipient creativity and static continuation, in that those static enterprises that do not respond to relevant developments within the nexus will lose standing and become candidates for death, whether through dissolution or takeover. What this suggests is that the appropriate grammar to apply to the nexus is the grammar that is appropriate to incipient enterprises (including the creative margins of established enterprises). In this respect, there would seem to be a reasonable distinction between the initial entrepreneurial act whereby a new plan of production is set in motion and subsequent acts whereby ongoing plans are revised and amended.

It is with respect to the initial entrepreneurial act that we experience the clearest connection with the sequential, time-using character of production plans. A decision is made today to undertake a production plan that will not yield a commercial product for five years. A simple illustration might be someone harvesting grapes to make wine. To make the wine available in five years, inputs must be hired at various dates during the preceding interval. There is no way truly to establish the actual value of those inputs, though, of course, it is usually possible to make relatively informed guesses. The true value, however, will appear only after five years, when consumers reveal their willingness to buy the product; furthermore, this willingness will also be influenced by entrepreneurial judgments about pricing, which is ignored by usual presumptions about prices as given data and which will be considered in the next section. For the most part, however, the owners of those inputs will demand current payment, which they will obtain in a competitive environment. The fundamental entrepreneurial action involves assembling and hiring resources today based on a belief or hypothesis about the subsequent market value of the product when it is made available, as illustrated by David Harper's (1996) treatment of the similarities between entrepreneurial action and scientific exploration, as suggested also by Israel Kirzner (1979).

It is, of course, always imaginable that the enterprise could be operated as a cooperative. In this case input suppliers would not receive current payment but would invest in the firm for five years, and with the value of that investment determined after the wine is subsequently sold. There are cooperative enterprises in which people make in-kind investments, but this is a rare situation. To a large extent this is surely due to differences in temperament among people, but it is surely also due to problems of valuation and calculation in the absence of actual market transactions. Consider the valuation of capital contributions when those contributions do not result through normal commercial transactions. Equilibrium thinking makes it seem that this could be overcome, but this is not so apparent otherwise. One investor makes and supplies 100 oak barrels. What capital claim does this give on the enterprise and its future revenues? If you call around, you might find that such barrels range from $700 to $900. If you ask the investor, he is likely to assert that his barrels are truly superb, perhaps even better than anything now on the market, which will provide added finesse to the wine when it is ready for the market, so his investment is properly valued at $1,000 per barrel. The only way to resolve any such controversy is to take it to the open market, but then you would lose the in-kind investment that the cooperative enterprise requires. So the enterprise is not organized cooperatively, but with investors to provide the means to hire inputs today when the value of those inputs will not be determined for at least five years. The act of entrepreneurship is thus a conjecture about both the ability of the enterprise to produce its product successfully and about reception that consumers give to the product once it is made available.

Within static equilibrium theory, money occupies a peculiar position whose significance is somewhere between small and null. The theory of equilibrium takes no recourse to money, as equilibrium conditions are stated in real and not nominal magnitudes. Money is thus a veil, the thickness of which governs the extent to which money obscures the underlying reality. What we thus get from standard equilibrium theorizing is that money is a negative element in society, and with the only question being just how strongly negative. The strength of that negativity depends on the thickness of money's veiled quality, and the central claim in support of central banking or other forms of state domination over monetary processes is that such collective action can limit the damage from monetary obfuscation.

If money is a veil, no matter how thin a veil, it might seem to be a good idea to try to get rid of it. But this would transform economic relationships into barter relationships, and no one is so foolish as to support this. Money must thus be something far more significant than a veil. And it is, for it is the primary language of commercial calculation and conduct. The order of commercial action surely runs from nominal to real and not from real to nominal. In the aforementioned illustration of planning to produce wine, the commercial plan will involve projections of such things as how much money will be tied up in land, vines, barrels, labor, and so on. These projections will be combined with projections about volumes of production and beliefs about market prices when the product is available for the market. Such commercial planning entails much detailed knowledge about many things: for instance, the effects of different cooperage, of different types of blends of varieties, and of different types of marketing channels. In all such respects and in the many other relevant respects, projected results will be expressed in money, the lingua franca of commercial action. Money is not a veil but is the universal language of commercial action.

Pricing and entrepreneurship

Microeconomic theory is commonly described as "price theory" or "market theory." Chapter 5 explains that neo-Walrasian-style theory entails a restricted and limited theory of markets because its formulation in terms of market structure and equilibrium sets aside considerations of emergent dynamics, through which market configurations are being continually revised through profit-seeking activities. Something similar can be said about pricing. For the most part, prices are what they are because they eliminate excess demands under some postulated set of initial conditions. Prices in these theoretical constructions do not emerge out of entrepreneurial action and interaction, but rather are data required by imposing market clearing upon a set of presumed initial conditions.

Think of how pricing is presented. A firm hires inputs to produce an output. If the industry is competitive in the standard fashion, the firm accepts the industry price, however this might have been established (a point that accentuates that the neo-Walrasian theory is about mutual consistency and not about development or emergence). So you have a market for bread, eggs, or whatever product is being considered, and with competitive equilibrium being denoted by the condition P=MC. Now ask yourself the last time you saw a single-product firm. Take bread, baked by a baker. You do not go to a bakery and ask for bread. You have to be more specific than that. Moreover, the baker carries more than just bread. You can get cakes, rolls, muffins, pies, among other items. The bakery is a multi-product firm. All firms are multi-product firms. Yet economic theory is not conveyed in terms of multi-product firms. Doing so would destroy the simplicity of the comparisons and analyses summarized by P=MC because multi-product firms are ensnared in common costs and joint costs, and this ensnarement renders problematic the commonly made claims about the welfare properties of P=MC.

What is the marginal cost of a roll sitting on a baker's shelf? The answer, of course, is that it is zero because it has already been baked (McKean and Minasian 1966, Brancato and Wagner 2004). If we go back to the start, we can imagine a baker deciding about the mix of products to create: how many of which types of bread, and similarly for the other products. There will be some ingredients that have the property that if they are used in one product, they are not available for use in some other product. Such ingredients as flour, butter, and eggs have this property. But there are many elements of the baker's operation for which this is not true: among these are heat for the ovens and premises, lighting, furniture and fixtures, and so on. The marginal cost of a loaf of a particular kind of bread thus involves a significant dose of arbitrariness, even if you follow the conventional standards of the cost accountants.

A bakery, moreover, is one of the simplest of enterprises to operate, at least small-scale bakeries that cater only to walk-in customers. It's a different matter when you get to commercial bakeries, different again for the operation of such print media as newspapers and magazines, and different yet again for pricing of the gamut of digitally supplied media. These are all cases where any measure of the outlays directly attributable to a particular product multiplied by the number of such products produced, will fall far short of making production commercially feasible. Yet such products do get produced, not through uniform pricing, though, but through complex pricing arrangements that are themselves an important determinant of the success of a commercial venture. Price formation is a topic that comes into the analytical foreground of a neo-Mengerian focus on emergent dynamics.

Think about the price of such a simple product as a magazine. An economic model might well speak of the price of a magazine, but what is that price and how does it support entrepreneurial action? One thing that is apparent from the start is that not all copies of the same magazine sell for the same price. The price on the newsstand is different from the price by subscription. Moreover, subscription prices are not uniform to all subscribers, and not just because of differences in the length of subscription. They also vary through special offers and deals, and even on how close to expiration a current subscription is. More than this, subscriptions are not the sole source of revenue to a magazine. Advertising provides substantial revenue, and the ability to attract advertising depends not only on the volume of distribution but also on various demographic characteristics of readership. Even in the simple case of a magazine, price formation involves a vector of elements and not a scalar magnitude, and with the commercial success of the enterprise depending partly on entrepreneurial choices regarding those elements. Pricing is an object of entrepreneurial choice and not a piece of data.

The so-called law of one price is one of the necessary conditions for competitive equilibrium: all products of the same type sell for the same price. It is not at all clear what to make of this so-called law. It is a necessary condition for equilibrium. But it's also easy to observe that the same object sells for multiple prices in the same vicinity. So what might be made of this observation? One possibility is that such contrary observations can be used as affirmation that our observations do not pertain to equilibrium states. Such an affirmation, however, would clash with the hard core of the neo-Walrasian research program. To maintain that program, it is necessary to protect its hard core against contrary observations. There are several ways this protection might be achieved.

For instance, it could be argued that the observed price differentials are only apparent and not real. An item might carry a lower price in one store than in another without violating the law of one price, provided only that the object is bundled with something else that varies between the locations. One store might offer pleasant and spacious surroundings with easy parking and plenty of checkout counters. The other store, which carries the item at a lower price, might offer spartan and crowded surroundings, with congested parking and with long waits to check out.

There are numerous other ways in which observed price differences could be reconciled with the law of one price. A good deal of empirical work within any particular research program entails efforts to reconcile some presumptions of the hard core with empirical observations that appear to contradict that hard core. For the neo-Walrasian hard core and the uses to which it is put, price cannot serve as an emergent phenomenon because the analytical framework is concerned with rendering statements that are valid outside of time and place. At the same time, however, a theoretical framework that seeks to account for the emergent dynamics of societal change must allow pricing to be an object of action, in which prices at one level of analysis emerge through interaction, even if at another level of analysis they are data most of the time for most people. Within an emergent ecology of enterprises, it is reasonable simultaneously to recognize that most people take most prices as data most of the time, while at the same time recognizing that not all people can take all prices as data all of the time. Furthermore, the source of the motion that propels change through time resides in the points where the data is emerging and not where it is given, for through emergence what was previously taken as given will subsequently change. It is the five percent of enterprises not in stasis at any particular instant that are eroding the static reposes of the other enterprises; once again, outliers do significant work in a theory of social economy.

Turbulence within the ecology of plans

Births and deaths will be a natural feature of any ecology of enterprises. During any interval, some plans will be abandoned and new ones will be created. To use the same distribution used earlier, suppose that 95 percent of plans remain in place throughout any interval. This situation might be said, econometrically speaking, to mean that the hypothesis of static equilibrium cannot be rejected at the five percent level of significance. The view through the neo-Walrasian window would seem to receive empirical support.

Methods of observation, which are the only methods we have for the natural world, can lead us astray when applied to human populations, despite the goodness of fit they might give.

This point gets into the distinction between thinking in terms of averages, or other measures of central tendency, and thinking in terms of the entire population. This distinction becomes particularly important in cases where important work is done by the structure of relationships, which is abolished through averaging, just as hedonics abolishes structure. A population where everyone follows fixed routines might be inert. Perhaps the propulsive energy comes from those who do not, and who, through their efforts, impart motion and direction to society. In *Theory of Economic Development* (1912) Joseph Schumpeter described entrepreneurs as providing leadership within a capitalist society. In the capitalist society that Schumpeter had in mind, entrepreneurs occupied the foreground of the stage and politicians worked in the background as stagehands. As we have evolved over the near-century since Schumpeter wrote, the stagehands have moved onto center stage, though not dominating it, but certainly securing prominence. In any case, the births and deaths of enterprises are likely to be of far greater significance than measures based on averages would convey, for such measures could well make it seem that static equilibrium is a reasonably accurate presumption. In this regard, it is perhaps important to distinguish between incipient and established enterprises because it is the incipient enterprises that inject change into society.

With the births and deaths that occur through time, changes are made in the patterns of connections among plans at any instance of time. What these changes imply and how they work themselves out depend on the relationship between the changing connections that accompany the births and deaths and remaining nexus of plans and connections. What seems clear is that the result will be a further unsettling of existing plans that will hasten further deaths and births down the road. In some cases, old plans will become less valuable because the new plans offer superior options to customers. In other cases, old plans will become more valuable. Perhaps more significantly, the new plans will set in motion new combinatorial-type explorations that inspire the formation of additional new plans.

Such formation, moreover, will surely provide information to other people that might well encourage them to form yet additional enterprises. One person's act of commercial illumination can lead other people to see opportunities that the original illuminator did not see. In this case, one person's exploration of combinatorial territory leads other people to see connections that appear useful to them even if not to the original explorer. For instance, one person's development of insulated storage bags might have led someone else to think how such materials might be used to expand the geographic range over which pizza could be delivered to homes. Alertness to opportunities surely follows a combinatorial pattern in that it involves combining a subset of elements from among a larger set of possible elements. To some extent, some of that assembly might have been created for other purposes by other enterprises, and then carried forward with suitable modification to the new enterprise. In this fashion, entrepreneurial energy may have aggregate properties that resemble increasing returns (Buchanan and Yoon 1994), only it is not really a matter that the application of additional doses of input leads to increasing additions to output.

Placidity, turbulence, and institutional arrangement

Entrepreneurial projections onto the future can go wrong, and in two directions. That future might prove better than the entrepreneur's projection, which returns profit to the entrepreneur. But it might also prove inferior, in which case the entrepreneur incurs losses. Entrepreneurial action, moreover, is not isolated action but rather occurs within a nexus of relationships. One entrepreneur's actions can thus affect the value of other entrepreneurial plans within that nexus. Moreover, the value of any particular entrepreneurial plan can be affected by actions undertaken elsewhere within that nexus. An entrepreneur might incur a loss because another entrepreneur subsequently developed a plan that diverted business to this other entrepreneur. Alternatively, an entrepreneur might receive profit because some subsequent entrepreneurial plan increased the value customers placed on his own product. The profit or loss associated with entrepreneurial plans is not fully under the control of the entrepreneur because it arises out of a continually changing nexus of relationships.

Flexibility is an important element of entrepreneurial action because unforeseeable and unforeseen events will continually buffet entrepreneurial plans, sometimes severely. An important part of that flexibility is achieved through institutionally mediated relationships (Lachmann 1971). It is strange in this respect to observe the recourse in macro theorizing to claims about price inflexibility as explanations for what is presumed to be macro disequilibrium. A stylized model might say that long-term contracting injects inflexibility into the economic nexus, with it then being argued that macro policy, usually of an inflationist variety, might be needed to offset that inflexibility.

Yet long-term contracts are often renegotiated or even breached. If breached, the basic remedy is that the breaching party is liable for lost profits from the breach, but nothing more. With this principle as background, moreover, most changes in commercial expectations lead to renegotiation of contracts rather than breaches. In either case, the nexus of enterprises exhibits far more flexibility in the presence of changing circumstances than a literal reading of long-term contracts would imply. To be sure, there are islands of inflexibility within that nexus of commercial flexibility. For the most part, however, that inflexibility arises in the vicinity of state-sponsored enterprises. Moreover, that inflexibility can arise both through requirements that state-based enterprises impose on market-based enterprises within their zone of interest, as explained by Epstein (1993), and though independent actions by state-based enterprises.

One significant source of the imposition of inflexibility by state-based enterprises onto market-based enterprises arises through labor legislation. An airline orders 80 aircraft from a manufacturer, based on its projections about demand for its services over the next several years. For whatever reason, air travel decreases and the airline breaches its contract (though renegotiation would be more plausible). What the airline cannot do, however, is breach its contract for labor services. American labor legislation prevents this, which leaves bankruptcy as the only way to breach labor contracts in the face of changes in commercial circumstances, which illustrates the institutional incongruity that Lachmann (1971) described.

Another source of inflexibility arises through the Big Player status of state-based enterprises, a theme developed with particular clarity by Roger Koppl (2002). A Big Player is an entity that operates under different principles of action than ordinary people, in part because of its size but even more so because it is not a residual claimant to the difference between earnings and expenses. For instance, consider a trade dispute between two entrepreneurs. The entrepreneurs will have strong incentives to settle their dispute rather than litigate it because they can save the various expenses of litigation, thereby expanding the residual that they can claim. Indeed, most disputes are settled without trial.

The situation is different if a Big Player is a party to the suit. The Big Player can claim no residual. Indeed, litigation expenses can sometimes serve as investments in future political activity. In the tobacco settlement from 1998, for instance, state attorneys general often hired private firms to pursue litigation against the major tobacco companies on behalf of the state, as against using attorneys from the Attorney General's office. Some of those attorneys general subsequently ran for higher office and received campaign contributions from the law firms that were awarded contracts to pursue the litigation (Wagner 1999a). In yet other cases, the continuation of a dispute can be a strategy of rent extraction (McChesney 1997). Relationships among market-based firms proceed differently, more smoothly and concordantly, than do those commercial relationships involving both market-based and state-based enterprises, and for reasons grounded fundamentally in institutional congruity or its absence.

Constitutional frameworks for the organization of production

Many strands of thought have sought to address why production is organized in business firms and not wholly in proprietorships. Organization in proprietorships might seem to be the initial point of departure for a theory that starts from individual action and builds up to macro-level observations regarding the organization of production. Numerous efforts have been advanced to reconcile this proprietary point of departure with our observation that much activity is organized through firms in which many people participate and in different capacities.

Ronald Coase (1937) presented the well-received formulation that a world of proprietorships would entail significant transaction costs that might be lowered through incorporating many of those transactions into a firm. In this way, all of the participants within a firm could potentially fare better than they would fare as individual proprietors. As for the proprietary form in particular, in contrast to cooperative forms, Armen Alchian and Harold Demsetz (1972) explained that the proprietary form would combat shirking through the status of residual claimacy, because the residual claimant would gain directly to the extent that he was able to reduce shirking through his actions. In a related vein, Oliver Williamson (1996) treats opportunism as a significant threat within firms, and uses the control of opportunism to explain significant features of the organization of business firms. Nicholai Foss (1993) and Brian Loasby (1998) examine how the operation of firms depends on how the firm is able to combine disparate talents and competencies, which is to a large extent a matter of achieving a constitutive pattern of relationships (Vanberg 1992) that makes good use of those disparate talents and competencies. Edith Penrose (1959) presents a wide-ranging treatment of many relevant matters.

There is surely also a sense in which productive organizations are natural, just as society is natural and not an object to be explained though some explicit deliberative process, just as Durkheim (1893) treated society as natural and not as constructed through contract. As social creatures, participation in joint projects can often be rewarding in their own right. In some cases working together can offer returns that would not accrue while working alone and meeting others only for market exchange. To posit this is not to deny problems of opportunism or shirking, but is only to assert that the organization of people into teams may to a significant extent be part of human nature as against being a matter wholly of explicit contract. Even if so, the constitutional organization of those teams would still be an issue to be settled, as noted by Viktor Vanberg (1992) and as examined in particular with respect to the organization of automobile production by Gail Heffernan (2003). Another aspect of team production, also grounded in human nature, concerns variability in entrepreneurial vision, or in the strength of animal spirits. Some people are simply more venturesome or more daring in adventuring into uncharted territory that comes with entrepreneurial activity. To the extent an entrepreneurial vision calls for team production, the entrepreneur will need to enlist other participants, and in doing so will create a constitutional framework that will govern relationships among the participants.

Overwhelmingly, economic theory has explained how private property provides a framework for the creation of market-based organizations. Yet much of the productive work of societies is accomplished through politically-established organizations, as will be explored more fully in Chapter 8. While political entities are constituted within a different governing framework than commercial entities, there are also a number of similarities. A good deal of that similarity is captured by the description of cities as municipal corporations. Cities are corporate bodies that contain many particular enterprises. As with commercial enterprises, municipal enterprises are managed by a relative handful of people as compared with the far larger number of people who supply capital to and receive service from those enterprises. The same settings of potential shirking and opportunism that arise with commercial enterprises arise as well with political enterprises, save that it is easier for someone to avoid a commercial enterprise than a political enterprise. Political enterprises can have forced investors and forced consumers, where such categories do not apply to commercial enterprises. Regardless of how these differences might play out, the organization of production within a society occurs within both types of enterprises, and with those enterprises often being knottedly entangled with one another, some effects of which will be examined in Chapter 8 and which has been explored in preliminary fashion in Wagner (2007).

Expected value, animal spirits, and informed guesses

Starting from a presumption of general equilibrium, models of individual choice must support that equilibrium presumption. To explain choice through the maximization of expected utility allows this to be done. The neo-Walrasian orientation thus requires something like the maximization of expected utility to maintain the integrity of its hard core. Such a formulation also appears sensible from the outside looking in. Recalling the Nicholas Sparks story *The Choice*, what other option is there to explain why the husband disobeyed his wife's request to remove the feeding tubes? A reasonable answer from the outside looking in is surely that the husband expected to receive higher utility from this choice than from the alternative, for otherwise he would have chosen differently.

From the inside looking out, however, the situation appears differently. From this alternative orientation, the theoretical challenge is to render the world intelligible in terms of people forming and pursuing plans and dreams. We know from the story that the protagonist had thought about the various options, and yet the choice represented a kind of leap of faith, or a reflection of an animal spirit, realizing that the passing of time dictates the making of some choice in any event. Indeed, in many cases it is the passing of time that makes choices necessary, because life cannot effectively go on until a choice is made. At some point evidence will no longer be accumulated or deliberated over because there are other things that require attention. At this point a choice will be made. This choice could be explained retrodictively as the maximization of expected utility, though there is no reason for it to be so. Indeed, there is good reason to wonder just why it is thought necessary to have a predictive theory of choice. Within the neo-Walrasian hard core, this is a necessary ingredient. The theory starts with a presumption of general equilibrium, which in turn entails the presumption that the aggregate of individual choices is consistent with the postulated initial conditions.

For the neo-Mengerian hard core, however, such individual determinism is unnecessary because at the societal level there is turbulence and not equilibrium. The macro ecology of plans is generally but not wholly coordinated. Furthermore, new entrepreneurial plans are continually being injected into the societal nexus, and with these new plans reinforcing some existing plans and undermining others, and creating turbulence in either case. This is not to deny that there is a lot of habitual action within everyone. It's only that life cannot be reduced wholly to habit, and must to some extent be open to creative experiment and the exploration of novelty. The assuredness of expected utility maximization might be reasonably operative over 95 percent of the population 95 percent of the time, which is surely a fine basis for seeking to explain contemporaneous observations. But contemporaneous observation provides no bridge from today to tomorrow, let alone to the day after tomorrow. This bridge, moreover, must be based on creation and experimentation, and with the products of that creation and experimentation leading to revisions in the actions of the other 95 percent of participants within the human ecology.

In this respect, Snowdon, Vane, and Wynarczyk (1994: 382) close their treatment of post-Keynesian economics with this bit of highly relevant dialog from J. K. Galbraith's *A Tenured Professor* (1990):

> *Professor Grierson*: A good model has predictive value.
> *Professor McCrimmon*: If predictions aren't reliable, of what value are they?
> *Professor Grierson*: To put it simply, the American businessman, in his business planning, has to have something better than a guess.
> *Professor McCrimmon*: So a wrong prediction is better than a guess?
> *Professor Grierson*: A prediction is something to go on. It narrows the range of uncertainty for the business firm.
> *Professor McCrimmon*: You're saying that uncertainty is reduced by a wrong prediction but increased by a wrong guess?

5 Markets and prices as emergent patterns of human interaction

A timeless logic of equilibrium patterns of resource allocation must take prices and markets as data. The object of explanation is an allocation of resources that is accompanied by a consistent set of market prices. This analytical framework requires the analyst to postulate the existence of some set of markets along with prices that are consistent with clearing those markets in light of consumer preferences. If two snapshots taken at different times are compared, each will show resource allocations in conjunction with a supporting set of market clearing prices. Within this comparative-static framework, prices, markets, and allocations are universal features of social life, the formal equilibrium quality of which holds invariably across time and place.

To describe each observation as pertaining to equilibrium relationships, while at the same time recognizing that the substance of those relationships varies across time and place, is to hide from view any account of the transformation across sets of equilibrium observations. Recognition of this substantive variability speaks to an emergent-dynamic process of internally-generated momentum by which the first snapshot is transformed into the second. Generation describes a process that operates through time, and through which a state that exists at one moment is transformed into some alternative state at a later moment. Generation must be explored within a temporal logic, as illustrated by Allen *et al.* (1991). Within this emergent-dynamic framework, prices and markets are social configurations that people generate through their interactions with one another as they act to remove uneasiness by exploiting perceived opportunities for gain. These changes through time speak to generation and generative processes, and these are the objects of interest in this chapter. What is taken as given for an a-temporal theory about resource allocation cannot be taken as given for a temporally-based theory of the continual generation of market configuration. Neither prices nor market configurations are data within a neo-Mengerian orientation because these are emergent products of human interaction. People do not just act within the context of market data, although such action is also part of life. That market data and the associated market configurations are continually changing through interaction among economizing individuals. Market configurations and the prices they entail are what they are today because they have emerged out of previous interaction; moreover, interaction underway today will generate changes to tomorrow's market configurations.

From ordinal valuation to cardinal prices through social interaction

Praxeology treats discrete actions that involve choice-and-renunciation based on projections onto some future, in some cases a future that will arrive momentarily, while in other cases a future that lies far ahead. If we were to shadow Robinson Crusoe, we would observe him making and undertaking a continuing sequence of actions and associated choices. At any particular instant, Crusoe faces options. Perhaps he chooses to pick blueberries when he could have chosen to trap a rabbit or perhaps even taken a nap. We necessarily would say that Crusoe valued blueberries at that instant more highly than he valued a rabbit or a nap because it would make no sense to assert otherwise. By chasing after blueberries, Crusoe is renouncing the possibility of catching a rabbit; at that instant he values a harvest of blueberries more highly than a rabbit. The cost of those blueberries is the value that Crusoe placed on the renounced rabbit. The cost of choosing one option is the value that is placed on the option not chosen. Value and cost are not independent of each other, because each pertains to the same act of choice-and-renunciation: value pertains to the object chosen while cost pertains to the object not chosen. Crusoe's world is distinctly ordinal, and in this world it is easy to see that value and cost are just reciprocal features of any choice.

When the setting changes to a social economy, transactions with other people replace Crusoe's transactions with nature. Those transactions could be isolated instances of occasional barter, or at least we are capable of imagining such instances. The world of contemporary experience, however, presents transactions as mostly numerous and regular. When transactions are numerous among interacting people and not rare among isolated people, the resulting scope for comparisons of terms across transactions leads to the emergence of market prices. It is easy enough to see how prices can arise through exchanges within a social economy as the density of transactions increases. The formation of prices and the concomitant emergence of money is illustrated nicely by Howitt and Clower (2000). They start with a simple model of barter where a set of shops each carries two goods. Customers have goods they seek to barter for the goods carried by the shops. If a shop has a good the customer wants and is willing to accept the other good the consumer holds, a trade takes place. Within their computational model, the shops begin by carrying different combinations of goods; however, the profit-seeking incentives of the shops leads them all eventually to carry one good in common with the other shops, with that common good being what we mean by money. Howitt and Clower present a computational rendition of Menger's (1892) explanation for the emergence of money out of barter, with money being simply the most saleable of the various commodities.

Within a framework of motion through time, it is not sufficient to treat prices as data that are given prior to market transactions because those prices emerge through a sufficiently dense network of transactions among participants. Yet within an ongoing social economy, prices also appear as data to most people most of the time. But prices cannot be data to everyone, or else they could never change. It is possible for most people to take prices as data because some people are acting to create the prices that other people accept. The emergence of prices must be understood ecologically in terms of an interacting population of agents, because such a process of emergence cannot be reduced to action by a representative agent.

A similar situation exists with respect to language. At one analytical level, people use dictionaries to discern proper spelling and usage. At a different analytical level, lexicographers compile reports on how people use language. Yet the dictionaries are continually changing, which means that people continually are generating new usages that previously were not in the dictionaries. Thinking in terms of emergent phenomena requires recognition that phenomena can exist at different analytical levels, as illustrated earlier by the distinction between a traffic jam and the individual cars that constitute the jam. There is no inconsistency in thinking in terms of analytical levels, though such a framework could not sensibly be applied to a representative agent. Within an ecological setting, however, what we observe is a temporal process of interaction within an open-ended setting of human action where novelty is continually being injected into the catallaxy.

Transactions are based on ordinal valuations and comparisons, as represented by the sentiment of valuing the option selected more highly than the option renounced. The emergence of market prices gives a cardinal veneer to an ordinal reality. One consequence of this cardinal veneer is that prices appear to represent a disjunction between value and cost. This disjunction is represented by the notion of the Marshallian cross, where market price is explained as a confluence of the demand-side forces of consumer valuation and the supply-side forces of producer cost. This disjunction would appear to mean that market price is governed by interaction between two opposing forces: consumer valuation on the one hand and producer cost on the other.

This appearance of a confluence between opposing forces, however, is an illusion created by the emergence of objective prices out of interaction among intersecting subjective valuations. The distinction between subjective and objective is a source of much confusion and needless controversy in economic discourse, and it is perhaps worth pausing momentarily to offer a brief clarification. Subjective and objective are simply adjectives that correspond to the nouns, subject and object. There is a subject who acts and there is an object toward which the subject acts. It is, of course, possible for the object of a subject's action to be another acting subject, as examined in Martin Buber (1958). Still, the distinction is clear. Valuations are properties of acting subjects, so can only be subjective. Prices are properties of objects toward which subjects act, so can only be objective.

Much of the confusion probably arises through a failure to recognize that prices are emergent phenomena that supervene on transactions among acting subjects. This relationship of supervention means that it is not accurate to speak of prices as existing on the same level of reality as valuations. This relationship of supervention was central to Carl Menger's original formulation but is set aside in the neo-Walrasian formulations where prices are treated as data that exist prior to market transactions. Prices and transactions are treated as simultaneous within the neo-Walrasian logic, as everything must be when the central vision is one of instantaneousness and not one of time-dependence. The confluence of independent forces of demand and supply, however, is a surface appearance created by the neo-Walrasian presumption that economic phenomena are instantaneous and not sequential and time-dependent. Once the sequential relationships are brought forward and the supervention of prices on valuations is recognized, it becomes clear that value and cost are not two independent principles that govern price, but rather are images of one another, and with prices emerging through interactions among acting subjects and their valuations.

The emergence of prices provides a cardinality that is absent when Crusoe is alone. This cardinality invites the separation of price formation into two components, one corresponding to the buyer's valuation of the good and the other corresponding to the seller's cost of producing the good. Price thus comes to be interpreted as indicating both value and cost, and as serving as measures of both. A transaction involves two parties, and it is conventional to designate one party the buyer and the other the seller, and with value pertaining to the buyer and cost to the seller. Hence, the two independent principles that are said to govern price correspond to the two sides of any transaction. Yet only one principle is at work in any transaction, and this is the effort of each party to replace a less-valued with a more-valued option. In exchanging money for a good (or a rabbit for a bag of shrimp), a buyer is declaring the item sought to be more valuable than the item offered. The seller is making the same declaration, only the items are reversed in the seller's scale of value. Both parties are able to achieve higher valued situations through trade.

Transactions and their terms are governed by the valuations of participants, with cost-of-production being just another word for valuation and not an independent influence over transactions. Suppose it becomes necessary to travel longer distances to harvest shrimp. By Marshallian convention this would be described as an increase in the cost of producing shrimp, so the labor time spent traveling would exert an independent influence over price. It's easy enough to understand that the shrimper would like to receive more rabbits in exchange for shrimp in compensation for the greater effort devoted to harvesting shrimp. Nonetheless, the willingness of the shrimper to travel the longer distance is governed by the desires of customers for shrimp and not by the desire of the shrimper to be compensated for the longer time spent traveling. Under these circumstances, we would expect fewer shrimp to be harvested and the price of shrimp to rise. All of this, however, is governed by consumer valuation.

Actions are the observable consequences of choices among options. Any choice involves embracing one option and rejecting some alternative. To the option chosen we normally ascribe the term value or utility, while to the option rejected we normally ascribe the term cost. Both of those terms, however, reflect valuations by the chooser (Buchanan 1969). These valuations are ordinal, standing in a relation of higher and lower to one another. Within a social setting of market exchange, prices emerge as a phenomenon that Crusoe would never face on his own even though he would continually face choices. Prices are cardinal superventions on the underlying ordinal valuations, but in no way does this cardinal property give scope for cost of production to act as an independent determinant of price. Prices are reflections of valuation, and with expensive items fetching a high price not because they are costly to produce but because they are valued highly by consumers, which in turn makes producers willing to undertake great effort to make those items available.

Exchange theory and market theory: what are the objects?

What is commonly called the theory of markets is actually a theory of exchange and not a theory of markets. The object of analytical interest in neo-Walrasian expositions of market theory is the equilibrium price of some product or service, and with markets and their characteristic features treated as data. The relationship is dyadic in character with a set of individual buyers confronting one or more producers. The central analytical issue concerns the equilibrium price of various products, with such constructions as asymmetric information being used as vehicles to move price in some particular direction as compared with what it would have been under some postulated condition of symmetrical information.

The Edgeworth-Bowley portrayal in Figure 5.1 shows the point. As between the two parties shown there, one price might yield position A while another price might yield position C. For instance, A might be an outcome with asymmetric information while C is an outcome with symmetric information. Furthermore, intermediate positions along B are also possible. There is no need to review the theory of exchange here. The central point is simply that the material that is examined under the heading of a theory of markets can be captured readily by the Edgeworth-Bowley construction as a matter of the distribution of gains from trade under various presumed conditions. The object of the conventional theory of markets is some equilibrium price, and price is the consequent of exchange. To be sure, the theory of price is pretty rudimentary, due at least in part to its adoption of the single-product firm as its archetype. Still, price and exchange are aspects of the same phenomena, and both can be illustrated by the same dyadic treatment.

There is, however, nothing dyadic about markets. Within a regime of

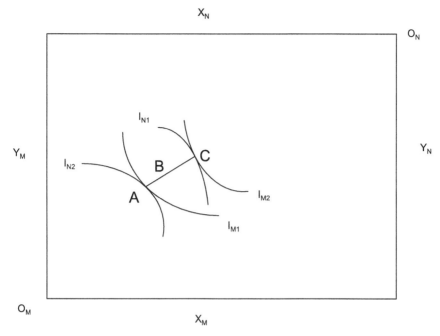

Figure 5.1 Theory of exchange (static).

private and alienable property, a market is an open-access commons. According to the principles of property and contract, everyone is free to establish commercial enterprises, and those enterprises will be successful only to the extent that entrepreneurs convince various kinds of people to support the activities of the enterprise. Access to the market is open to all, and the resulting interaction among participants will generate emergent social configurations that constitute the structure that encases market phenomena.

While trade and price can arise in a dyadic relationship, a market is not a simple addition across a set of such dyadic relationships. This, anyway, is the theme that underlies my claim that economics operates with a theory of exchange but not a generative theory of market configuration. The conventional focus on static equilibrium prevents a theory of markets from even appearing on the analytical agenda, as against offering categories of stipulated market types. Figure 5.2 illustrates this claim. The two panels A and B refer to different periods, both with 11 enterprises located within some enterprise space. Each panel shows connections among the 11 nodes, and with the pattern of connections changing between the panels, and with some of those enterprises changing commercial location as well.

An abstract comparison of the two panels illustrates what would be the object of a theory of markets, and which will be explored more fully below. Each panel could be described in terms of an equilibrium theory. But how would you then explain the transformation of the first panel into the second?

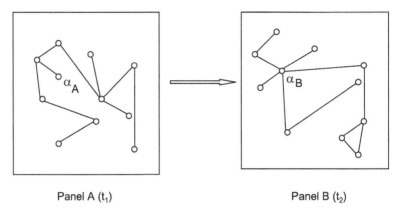

Panel A (t₁)   Panel B (t₂)

Figure 5.2 Theory of markets (emergent dynamics).

You cannot, of course. That transformation just happens, which is economic theory pursued in the passive voice. The active voice alternative would have Panel B emerge out of Panel A, only this cannot be done in continuous time so it must be analyzed in discrete, snapshot fashion. These two panels are meant to illustrate this developmental process.

How might we characterize or explain the emergence of the second panel out of the first? Look at the nodes labeled α_A and α_B. These are meant to pertain to the same enterprise. In Panel A the enterprise denoted by α is connected directly with only one node. In Panel B, α is directly connected with five nodes. In a commercial setting, this should translate into increased success and value. But how did this happen? There are many stories that might be told, but they would all revolve around trying to fashion connections with other people and enterprises. The development of technology offers one such avenue while the offering of new types of service is another. For instance, a retail grocery store might respond to technological developments by allowing people to order groceries online and then delivering them by appointment. A mapping of commercial relationships would show the entrepreneurial development of new patterns of connection and activity. In both cases, people might refer generically to the retail grocery market.

What is particularly notable, however, is the continuing transformation that is occurring in the actual features of this market. This transformation has several dimensions: new vendors are entering the market, old vendors are leaving, new types of products are being offered, and old products are being reconfigured or even abandoned. As a neo-Walrasian abstraction, "market" is a timeless and universal category without particular substantive content. As a neo-Mengerian reality, markets are substantive configurations within society. They are emergent, spontaneously-generated by-products of human interaction among economizing individuals.

If you look further at Figure 5.2, you will also see a southeasterly drift by some nodes, which can indicate a kind of commercial relocation, as illustrated by the development of new products and services. This figure places emphasis, very abstractly, on *location* and *connection*. Location refers to some notion of the attributes of a product. If wire-based phones were assigned one location in this abstract commodity space, cell phones would occupy a different location. Connection refers to whatever brings value to some commercial location. A cell phone that allows a caller to speak to someone entails less connection than one that allows a caller to also read news and take and send photos.

Within this analytical framework, firms are competing in trying to develop connections to bring value to their entrepreneurial plans, and possibly shifting their locations in an abstract product space. As time passes, the graphical mapping of the enterprise space changes in several ways: firms are born and die, firms develop new connections or lose old ones, and firms move to new locations in enterprise space. In consequence, the mapping of enterprise space is transformed through the continuing search for gain that we denote as competition. It is this continual transformation that is the object of a theory of markets. Market theory treats the continual change in the social organization of economic activity that emerges within a society, and presumably emerges differently under alternative institutional configurations.

Figure 5.3 can be used to illustrate the same point in a different manner, as well as to illustrate the point that the neo-Walrasian and the neo-Mengerian frameworks do not seek to offer contrary explanations for the same phenomena but rather seek to explain different phenomena. Within a neo-Walrasian framework, Figure 5.3 illustrates the standard comparative statics of alternative equilibrium positions in light of differences in postulated data. As compared with point A in the two panels, point B pertains to a stronger preference to X relative to Y. In Panel A this appears as an increase in demand for X; in Panel B it appears as a shift to an alternative position on the production-possibility frontier. Figure 5.3 illustrates a response to a "what if" type of question. It answers that the structure of production would differ if

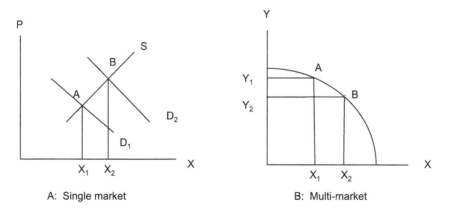

A: Single market   B: Multi-market

Figure 5.3 Statics, dynamics, and market theory.

preferences were those described by A than if they were those described by B. In other words, Figure 5.3 pertains to the timeless world of logic.

What is absent from this portrayal is any examination of how the transformation depicted by Figure 5.3 might actually take place. To be sure, Paul Samuelson (1947) advanced his correspondence principle to connect statics and dynamics. Samuelson's notion of dynamics, however, was purely notional and did not deal genuinely with action through time. A central feature of action through time is learning. With learning comes the creation of new enterprises and revisions to the operation of old enterprises. Learning also brings changes in consumer valuations in its train as people gain new insight into the relation between means and ends, as well as perhaps new insight into their ends. When time is allowed to pass, it is impossible for such points as A and B in Figure 5.3 to refer to anything other than the logic of relationships outside of time. If time is allowed to pass, knowledge must be allowed to change, and once this happens the standard "given" conditions of comparative statics cannot be taken as given for genuine historical dynamics.

It is no wonder that the passing of time has caused such consternation for economic theorists as to lead them to write such works as *Economics and the Antagonism of Time* (Vickers 1994) and *Wrestling with Time* (Currie and Steedman 1990). However antagonistic time might appear to theoretical efforts and no matter how much wrestling it might provoke, a neo-Mengerian research program must address phenomena that emerge through interaction over time among economizing individuals. Figure 5.3 can thus be understood differently, as a summarization of some stylized facts that pertain to distinct points in time. In this alternative, historical setting, the comparative output vectors (X_1, Y_1) and (X_2, Y_2) would be directly observable, and with the shift in preferences and demands denoted by $D_1 \rightarrow D_2$ being an interpretative hypothesis to help give an account of the historical observation.

Where Figure 5.3 denotes sufficient information to give an account of the comparative statics, it is not sufficient to relate the historical dynamics by which the market configuration was transformed over the time period being considered. "Market" is an abstract noun that pertains to what is generally an open-access commons. People are free to choose whether to participate as producers in the market, and are free also to choose the extent of their participation. The comparative statics of Figure 5.3 would assert that if all firms face identical U-shaped cost functions, the increased production of X would be provided wholly by new firms. This condition is necessitated by the logic of the problem setting. Historical experience, however, is different. Among other things, there is nothing corresponding to any announcement of an increase in demand for X. This statement might correspond to a theoretical logic but it does not correspond to any practical logic.

Absent some articulation of new demand conditions prior to any action to engage in production, production decisions are made by entrepreneurs who act on beliefs about future market opportunities within their field of vision and who act now to capture those opportunities when they arrive.

Furthermore, there is no process of assignment that assures that just the right capacity will be added. Figure 5.3 might correspond to five additional firms producing X. But ten firms might seek to enter the market, in which case some entrepreneurial plans will fail and will be revised or even abandoned. Among other things, this means that conflicts will arise among firms, and also that social processes and procedures will arise to settle such conflicts as those that arise through bankruptcy and insolvency. Within the neo-Mengerian orientation, the generation of such market formations would occupy the foreground of analytical attention. Those formations, moreover, are largely emergent products of interaction and not direct objects of choice and most certainly are not data.

Lemons and asymmetric information

George Akerlof's (1970) widely-cited paper on used cars is perhaps the quintessential contemporary illustration of asymmetric information. Akerlof's model begins with a textbook formulation of perfect competition, asserts asymmetrical information wherein sellers know more about the condition of their cars than do buyers, and concludes that a market for used cars would collapse. Used cars are categorized as being either good or bad. Owners are presumed to know which type of car they own, but buyers are presumed to have no ability to distinguish between good and bad cars. Information is held asymmetrically between buyers and sellers. Consequently, bad cars dominate the market because sellers remove their good cars from the market when all they can obtain is what they could have obtained from selling a bad car. In consequence, a market for used cars would collapse as lemons drive good cars from the market.

The world Akerlof depicts clearly does not describe reality, even though some buyers of used cars quickly become unhappy with their purchases. The lack of close contact between the model and reality was recognized by Akerlof when he closed his paper with two or three paragraphs about how institutions might mitigate some of the forces of market failure that the bulk of his paper described. Several things are notable about this common analytical procedure. One is that those mitigating institutions are simply assumed as exogenous features outside the model. The model itself is one of market failure when compared against the conventional model of perfect competition, due to the posited asymmetrical information. While those exogenous institutions might thus serve to mitigate some market failure, mitigation is not elimination, so failures are presumed to remain, which in turn means that markets are capable of yet more perfection.

But from where comes that perfection, it might be asked? The only possible answer is that it must come from some source outside the model because the model itself entails no such source of mitigating activity. Within conventional theorizing, moreover, the state is the only locus of action outside the market, so continued correction resides within the domain of state, due to the structure of the analytical window through which the phenomena at hand are viewed. An equilibrium model as portrayed in the standard formulations of perfect competition will suffocate exchanges when asymmetric information is introduced. Yet exchanges do occur despite the pure form of the lemons model, and which Akerlof seeks to explain through his peroration about institutions. In doing this, he sticks with a theory of exchange and avoids theorizing about markets.

A genuine market-based theory would give some explanation of how the emergence of networks tends to generate symmetry out of asymmetry. Two people face one another in a trading situation, where one party knows something that the other party doesn't know. This approach treats each instance of trade as independent of all other trades, with market outcomes being a simple addition across those trades. There is no genuine interaction of any sort taking place. In contrast, interaction combined with entrepreneurship generates organizations and networks connecting organizations and people. One party does not come to a trade naked and alone, but brings along a variety of instruments of assistance.

Akerlof's illustration makes sense only in a setting where you meet someone along a roadway somewhere, and you hand over cash and take away the car. That setting fits the lemons problem. Only it doesn't exist for cars, and probably never has, and, moreover, that non-existence can be attributed mostly to network-generated or market-generated relationships that lie beyond the purview of dyadic exchange. Indeed, matters start to change as soon as sales take place at residences and not alongside some sparsely traveled highway. An unhappy buyer has self-help remedies to call upon, which a seller of a lemon might wish to avoid facing. The buyer might be meaner and carry a bigger gun than the seller. Alternatively, payment might have been made in check for which payment can be stopped. Yet again, payment could have been made by credit, and thus bring other resources to bear on that particular trade. Also, cars are registered, have certificates of title, and so on, which brings still further resources to bear on particular trades.

Economists treat markets in very austere fashion as represented by supply and demand functions, which is really no theory of markets at all but rather is a theory of the terms of trade. The presence of lemons shrinks the extent of the market. This shrinkage is what Akerlof describes. At the same time, however, there are profits to be made by developing some new node and set of connections that would enable those trades to take place and thereby allow the extent of the market to expand, as illustrated by Figure 5.2. It is meaningful to speak of a market for used cars today just as it was meaningful to speak of one 50 years ago; however, the substantive features of those two markets differ enormously and in many dimensions. What accounts for those differences in substantive features, moreover, are the continual efforts of people to find and exploit new profit opportunities by developing new organizational arrangements and contractual forms, as well as by technological innovations. This process of continuing market evolution involves the continuing collection of $100 bills waiting to be discovered, in reference to Mancur Olson (1996).

The market for used cars has evolved along numerous lines. Suppose you look at those two panels of Figure 5.2 as denoting some abstract rendition of the used car market separated by some sufficient period of time to allow the relevant commercial maps to undergo some interesting transformation. At the technological level cars have improved greatly in reliability; enterprises that work to advance such technology participate in the generation of new substantive configurations for what we denote abstractly as the market for used cars. There have been great advances in the technology of detecting the condition of cars, which likewise leads to changes in market configurations. These advances have also reversed the standard presumption that asymmetric information works to the advantage of sellers because it is now easy for third parties to determine the condition of used cars. There are even firms that specialize in offering reconditioned used cars along with warranties, something that was unheard of not too many years ago. It is all these kinds of transformations, and numerous other sources of transformation, that would comprise the objects of interest for a theory of markets, in distinction to a theory of exchange.

In its most generic meaning, a lemon is an obstacle to trade. Since any trade implies gain, potential gains will exist from removing obstacles. These removals of obstacles do not, however, have to emerge somehow from inside of any particular exchange. Outsiders can participate in a large number of ways in developing technologies, contractual forms, and commercial configurations that reduce the obstacles to trade. In a comparison of the two panels of Figure 5.2, the most significant storylines would be told in terms of people trying to create and promote those new technologies, commercial formations, and contractual provisions that would transform the substantive character of what we would continue to call the market for used cars, recognizing that the universal entity we mean by a market for used cars refers to a wide variety of particular species of such a market. Moreover, the replacement of one species with another would be rendered intelligible through entrepreneurial action injected into a catallactical arena. Praxeology would illuminate the catallactical transformation that we call progress or substantive market evolution.

We return to the views provided by our two distinct conceptual windows onto the world. The neo-Walrasian window places resource allocations in the analytical foreground, while locating such things as technologies, preferences, and institutions in some background set of data. Starting from the reasonable presumption of asymmetric information, a presumption that could be avoided only by assuming that everyone knows everything, the extent of the market is less than it would have been with symmetric information. Various institutional arrangements might mitigate this restriction of the extent of the market, but restriction there will always be. Intervention from outside the market is the only source of change to expand the extent of the market. The primary outside source is the state, though technological change is also typically viewed as data and so is also outside the market.

A different scene appears through the neo-Mengerian window. People are universally acting to remove uneasiness. Some people will be uneasy because they would like to acquire a used car. Other people will be uneasy because they own a car that they would like to convert to cash that they can put to other uses. To posit a lemons-like situation is not to end the story at a destination called Market Failure. It is rather to set in motion various types of invention and experimentation that will expand the extent of the market. Some of that effort will go into inventing technologies that make cars more reliable in the first place. Other effort will go into developing equipment that will increase the ability of third parties to determine the condition of particular cars. Yet other effort will go into developing reputational capital and commercial goodwill through the cultivation of satisfied customers. A prime feature of the view through the neo-Mengerian window is the continual change in market architecture that accompanies the efforts of participants to remove sensed uneasiness, as explored in Klein (1997, 2000), and with the consequence being an expansion in the extent of the market.

Credit markets: still more lemons

With respect to the participants in particular exchanges, symmetrical information is surely a rarity. Life proceeds through a division of knowledge where each of us knows a lot about a little and a little about a lot. The standard presumption should surely be asymmetrical information. But exchanges do not occur in isolation but rather occur within market configurations that contain many participants and commercial practices that have emerged through prior commercial interaction. Individual instances of exchange thus occur within some particular market context. While that context will always reflect the universal search for mutual gain, it will also reflect particular institutional and organizational details that vary across specific settings for interaction.

Consider claims about credit rationing as an alternative instance of the ubiquitous claim about lemons. In this case, the claim is made that borrowers know whether they are good or bad risks but lenders do not. Hence, the situational setting is presumptively the same as that for used cars. What results is a market dominated by high-risk borrowers who are willing to pay higher interest than low-risk borrowers, and who would thus drive the low-risk borrowers out of the market if credit were auctioned off to bidders. With a competitive market thus analogized to an auction market, it is credit rationing that allows low-risk bidders to obtain credit. Credit rationing is thus regarded as a sign of market imperfection because buyers do not face some set price at which they can select their preferred amounts of credit. Hence, the market for credit is described as being imperfect, and with such designated imperfection commonly regarded as possibly providing scope for state regulation to improve matters.

To be sure, credit does not constitute some kind of shrinking or collapsing market, as many people seem continually to receive unsolicited offers of credit. Yet it is undeniably true that the market for credit operates differently than the market for green beans. The same universal principles are at work in both markets, but these principles unfold in different specific ways. Yet those differences are fully intelligible as reflections of the search for mutual gain under circumstances that differ across the different markets.

For green beans, vendors post prices in their stores and individual buyers select however many beans they want at that price. Credit isn't supplied in this manner, but this doesn't mean that credit is rationed in the same sense that beans could be subject to rationing under a regime of price controls. Someone who buys too many green beans will have a hard time reversing that transaction. The beans are an asset that cannot be readily transferred into some other asset. One thing this low liquidity accomplishes is that it gives people an incentive to economize on their original purchases, because if they purchase more than they can profitably use they are stuck with the remainder and suffer the capital loss that this implies.

The situation is different with credit. Credit is readily transferable into other assets of roughly equivalent value. Moreover, credit transactions are not transfers of ownership. They are rental contracts. With green beans there is a transfer of ownership, but with credit a lender leases assets to the borrower. Rental contracts differ from sales contracts in numerous ways, none of which leads to any suggestion that so-called credit rationing is some sign of market imperfection, as against reflecting emergent institutional relationships that expand the extent of the market. All rental contracts present problems that are absent with sales contracts. Some of those problems arise from concerns about liability for damage to the asset. It is easy enough formally to state that the borrower should be liable for damage to the asset beyond normal wear. To be able actually to implement such a formal provision involves more than mere blackboard arithmetic, particularly as the stakes involved in any potential dispute rise. Other problems arise from concerns about repossessing the asset at the expiration of the contract. Objects that occupy fixed locations, like buildings, entail different problems than mobile objects like cars. Moreover, mobile objects that are bulky and subject to registration, like cars, entail different problems from mobile objects that are small and not subject to registration, like uncut diamonds.

All rental contracts face agency-like problems regarding the potential for conversion of the asset, either in whole or in part, from the owner's account to the tenant's account. Sometimes this prospect is incorporated relatively easily into contractual terms, as illustrated by contracts to lease automobiles. In contrast, a market for leasing jewelry is tiny and a market for leasing uncut diamonds is even smaller. The leasing of credit faces similar problems and situations. The value of a credit contract to a lender will not be determined until after the asset has been returned, in sharp contrast to the value of a sales contract. When seen in this light, it is easy to understand how the institutional architecture of market arrangements regarding credit would entail such varied practices as collateral, reputation, and limits on amount of credit extended to any particular borrower as a form of portfolio balancing across borrowers.

Credit transactions also typically involve heavy doses of political participation beyond what appears in most other market settings. Credit relationships are rarely between borrower and lender alone. If they were, lenders would apply ordinary commercial calculations to select among borrowers, and this would be the end of the story, unless issues subsequently arose about asset conversion through a failure of the borrower to pay back the loan. Actual credit relationships involve considerable political participation at several levels, eliminating both the dyadic relationship and the simple application of economic calculation. Credit transactions are almost never between borrower and lender alone. A lender's decision to reject a borrower's request for credit does not end the matter because the borrower must also demonstrate a pattern of lending that is acceptable to the relevant political officials. Credit transactions are rarely organized through the dyadic transactions sketched by the conventional theory of market exchange and rather are ensnared in political calculation, as will be considered in Chapter 8.

Market transformation in retailing

The preceding treatments of used car markets and credit markets can potentially be extended to a variety of topics concerning the emergence and transformation of market formations. Something like Figure 5.2 can be used to illuminate how the entrepreneurial search for gain transforms the substantive structure of commercial relationships. These transformations occur before our very eyes, so to speak, and are recognizable only after they have occurred. For instance, grocery stores today are dramatically different from what they were 50 years ago, and in numerous dimensions and with no singular point of origin for that transformation. Similar transformations have occurred throughout retailing. Those transformations start with individual entrepreneurial actions in one small portion of the retail world, and subsequently spread and transmute throughout some nexus of retail relationships, and with that transformation continually underway.

In most cases it is now relatively easy to exchange merchandise bought from retail stores. Many stores now have specialists who deal with returns, and do so generally with minimal hassle. It was not always this way. It seems rather obvious that a store wouldn't want unhappy customers, but it hasn't always been the case that it was easy to return merchandise. What has changed is the ability of retail stores to deal with returned merchandise. A store that makes it easier to return merchandise will increase consumer satisfaction, though at a cost. A spontaneous order story of transformation would explain transformation through interaction among multiple market participants, each of whom is acting in some relatively local manner. It would thus be off-base to postulate something like a technological or organizational innovation as a macro-like entity that lowered the cost of accepting returned merchandise. Instead, the story would unfold through interaction among multiple participants, each of whom was responding to local situations and opportunities, and with the aggregate result of new commercial patterns being emergent and not chosen.

For instance, part of the story might reside in changes in inventory management that computerization and bar coding has made possible. Previously, returns had to be accompanied by paper forms, and the difference between filling in a form and then sending it somewhere to be filed and simply swiping a bar code is far larger than it might seem at first glance. Specialist firms might also arise as intermediaries between the primary vendors who accepted the returned merchandise and the ultimate disposal of those items. There is no doubt that the world of retailing and retail enterprise has undergone extensive and continuing transformation. The analytical challenge is to capture this transformation as an emergent result of localized instances of profit-seeking activity: some nexus of relationships is taken as given and some participants seek to exploit opportunities they perceive within that nexus. Such efforts, however, stimulate similar actions elsewhere in that nexus, and the interaction among such actions generates transformation in the architectural patterns that pertain to that nexus.

This analysis of transformation would run in terms of a number of actions that together make a significant difference, rather than there being one magical or unique action. It would not be that someone just decided to become more accommodating on returns. Instead, it would be developed in more of a nexus-like framework of connections coming together (though, of course, someone would have to recognize that they came together): someone develops bar coding, then someone links bar coding to changes in inventory management, followed by someone thinking that some of the saving in inventory expenses could be invested in consumer goodwill through an altered attitude toward returns (with perhaps specialist firms then developing later).[1] In any case, retailing provides a rich vein that could be mined with respect to the interplay between praxeological action and catallactic transformation.

One notable feature of retailing is its ecology, which contains the full gamut of sizes of enterprise, ranging from gigantic chains to small proprietorships. This variation in sizes might seem to call to mind the oft-repeated distinction between personal and impersonal exchange. If exchanges are thought to be isolated and unconnected events, the dichotomy between personal and impersonal exchanges might seem relatively straightforward. Once we start to pursue a genuine theory of markets, however, the dichotomy between personal and impersonal exchange starts to dissolve. Exchanges are no longer isolated from one another, but are neighbors in many ways through the networked market nexus that market participants generate.

The common distinction between personal and impersonal exchange is represented by the assimilation of impersonal exchange to notions of mass society. Yet people do not encounter the social world in some massed form. Mass society is an objectification that, with an exception to be noted momentarily, stands outside of much if not most personal experience. People do not encounter society as a unitary mass but in bits and pieces through individual interactions that mostly entail I–Thou relationships (Buber 1958). Relationships that are developed through markets, including the associated arrangements that we denote as Civil Society, can transform what might otherwise be an impersonal world into more of a personal world. For instance, relationships between corporations are only derivatively between corporations, for they are first of all between individual representatives of those corporations. Those connections are established and maintained through interaction among particular individuals associated with those enterprises.

What would seem to emerge is a variation on the small world theme developed by Duncan Watts (1999). Watts' primary theme is that there typically are only about five degrees of separation between any two people within a society. If society is viewed as an aggregate it has the appearance of a mass. But when viewed as a networked pattern of relationships, individuals exist within networked patterns of relationships of variable density. To assert this small world or personalistic character of market-based relationships is not to assimilate the market to some warm and fuzzy object. It is only to move some distance in that direction. Suppose we look at synonyms. Cold and indifferent would seem to be reasonable synonyms for impersonal. Friendly and supportive would seem to be reasonable synonyms for personal. Perhaps one of the underplayed virtues of the market ordering of human relationships is the ability of such a process to replace the coldness of impersonal exchange with the warmth of personal exchange, creating a friendlier world in the process, or to transform I–It relationships into I–Thou relationships. In related fashion, the claim that commerce can be a civilizing force goes back at least to the Scottish Enlightenment, as is surveyed by Hirschman (1977, 1992).

If you ask where the relationships of impersonal exchange seem to be most prevalent, the answer would surely be to locate such impersonality within the precincts of state-based arenas. About all one has to do in this respect is to compare the reception received when buying a pair of shoes with the reception received when applying for a dog license or renewing a driver's license. Personal exchange entails relationships among equals and a probing for mutual gains from trade. These are I–Thou relationships for the most part. When state-based arenas operate in the vicinity of market-based enterprises, the I–It character of impersonal relationships seems to come into play. State-based enterprises typically are not engaged in probing for mutual gains with potential contractual partners. They are rather engaged in enforcing rules without regard to mutual gain, and with the other parties serving as objects that they need to put into proper order so that they can file reports that will place them in a fine light with respect to the interests of their political sponsors and inquisitors. In this respect, Buber's (1958) distinction between

I–Thou and I–It relationships maps pretty directly into Jacobs's (1992) distinction between the commercial and the guardian moral syndromes.

Prices as sufficient statistics?

In two widely cited papers, Sanford Grossman and Joseph Stiglitz (1976, 1980) asked whether market prices were sufficient statistics for achieving a Pareto-efficient allocation of resources.[2] They gave a negative answer, arguing instead that prices would be informationally inefficient. If everyone acted on the basis of market prices alone, Pareto inefficiency would characterize the resulting resource allocation. Among other things, knowledge is a public good that will be under-supplied according to standard expositions. Hence, Hayek's (1945) argument of the coordinative properties of market prices is rejected. This rejection, however, does not so much address the claims Hayek advanced as it shows the non-commensurability of the neo-Walrasian and neo-Mengerian research programs.

The concern with sufficient statistics was framed by Grossman and Stiglitz within the context of the neo-Walrasian program. The existence of general equilibrium concerns the existence of a set of prices that will lead to zero excess demands for all commodities under the postulated initial conditions. The question of sufficient statistics concerns whether individuals will have appropriate incentives to acquire enough price information to support a Pareto-efficient allocation. Information will always be incomplete, and the question is whether the amount of information possessed by people is sufficient to sustain a Pareto-efficient allocation. To the extent information is a public good, there are reasons to think that people will refrain from acquiring information and rely instead upon existing market prices. To the extent this happens, information will be acquired to an extent that is inadequate for sustaining a Pareto-efficient allocation.

The non-commensurability between programs arises because Pareto efficiency is an alien concept to the neo-Mengerian program (Wagner 2007: 179–203). Pareto efficiency applies to an end-of-history construction, for a Pareto-efficient state is one in which exchange would cease. But exchange never ceases, and there are always gains from trade that people are seeking to exploit. Efficiency is an empty concept for the neo-Mengerian program. Among other things, any state that is described as Pareto inefficient within a neo-Walrasian framework is one that entails profit opportunities. Within the neo-Mengerian framework, people are continually searching for such opportunities and creating enterprises and contractual forms to make possible their exploitation. Furthermore, efficiency is a sensible concept to apply to an organization but not to an order because an organization aims to achieve ends but an order does not.

Within a neo-Mengerian framework there is no presumption that prices are sufficient statistics. Even Hayek (1945) claims only that most people can rely on price information in most situations. He does not claim that everyone can do so or does do so. Most people do not need to know why the price of pencils has risen. Whatever the reason for the rise in price, we may be sure that most people will make more intense use of their pencils as the price rises. For some people, however, prudent conduct requires additional information. For an owner of a stationery store who has problems of allocating shelf space and cultivating relationships with suppliers, it might be desirable to determine whether the rise in price is temporary or longer-lived.

From the outside looking in, there is no adequate way to say how much information is enough. It is probably reasonable to think that academics are biased toward claims of there being insufficient information. At the same time, however, market processes both use and generate a great deal of information. It is easy to think that we are drowning in information if this topic is approached from the inside looking out, for which Bowden (1989) is relevant for its treatment of statistics from the inside looking out. An alternative question might be the extent to which that information contributes genuinely to knowledge. This addresses the relation between knowledge and information, for which different treatments are possible (Boettke 2002). One distinction is a type of stock-flow distinction. Thus knowledge would be a stock while information would be a flow. A related distinction is between theory and observation. This distinction springs from recognition that observations become meaningful only as they are organized through theoretical or conceptual frameworks. This hearkens back to Hayek's (1952) treatment of the mind as a classification system. Theories provide the basis for classification of observations. Information arises in observational bits, the meaning of which depends on the conceptual or theoretical basis of knowledge that is necessary to render the observations meaningful.

While prices are surely necessary statistics for economic calculation, they are not sufficient for such calculation. Prices do not reflect some equilibrium position, so any calculation of future circumstances cannot be based on a presumption that those prices will carry forward to the relevant future moment. Economic calculation requires more than prices, for prices are simply a device for summarizing the anticipated consequences of plans. Commercial judgment is also necessary for economic calculation, though good judgment wouldn't get very far without prices to guide calculation. This theme about economic calculation and the necessity of alienable private property and the prices that are thereby generated was central to the treatment of collectivist planning, as illustrated by the essays in Hayek (1935) and given a contemporary restatement in Boettke (2001).

Competition: static state vs. dynamic process

A theory of markets, as distinct from a theory of exchange, would have as its object an explanation of the continual reformation of commercial formations and practices through the competitive search for profit opportunities. This conceptualization entails a different notion of competition from what is typically invoked by economists, as will be explored more fully in Chapter 6. Unlike trees and sand, competition and monopoly are not phenomena that appear directly to our senses. They are products of the mental maps we construct to make sense of our observations. We are all necessarily captives of our mental maps. There is nothing wrong with this because there is no option. Competition has been used in divergent ways within the history of economics, as Paul McNulty (1968) explains with particular clarity. One orientation is static, with competition being a form of descriptive adjective that has nothing to do with competition in the ordinary sense of the verb, to compete. The other orientation is dynamic, in that competition is treated as an activity, a verb.

Starting late in the nineteenth century, economic theory became dominated by a conceptual framework and orientation that looked to nineteenth-century physics models of static, mechanistic equilibrium for inspiration (Mirowski 1989). What is most notable about competition within this conceptual orientation is that it does not refer to any kind of activity that people mean when they speak of competing or of being competitive, and refers rather to some descriptive features of some hypothesized equilibrium. Within this conceptual framework, products are produced with known technologies that themselves do not change (technically, they are exogenous to the model). The concept of equilibrium that is central to this conceptual orientation is the equilibrium that results, as a matter of logic and not of actual experience, if each seller provides such a small part of an industry's output that it could exert no perceptible influence over industry output and the resulting product price.

Within the context of static equilibrium, each firm is conceptualized as continuing indefinitely to do what it is doing today, for in doing this the conditions of equilibrium are maintained. The reference to competition being static means that technology is frozen in time, and is not an object of competitive activity. Firms do not compete by trying to develop new technologies or products. Competition is only about price in the static approach. This notion of competition is useful for some pedagogic purposes because of its lucid simplicity. It leads to an idealized notion of competition where there are so many firms that none of them can exert any influence over market price, and rather must take the market price as something that is given to them and beyond their influence. Within this static framework, established products are produced within the context of clearly defined markets. There would be no ambiguity about the respective offerings of a phone company, a television company, and a computer company. The conceptual framework of the static approach to competition is simple and free from ambiguity.

With the boundaries of different products and markets clearly defined and distinct, the only question to be determined is how many producers will engage in producing that product. When there are many producers, the market is described as being competitive. When there is one producer, it is described as monopolistic. The territory in-between is ambiguous, and has been variously described as oligopolistic and as monopolistically competitive. What is most characteristic of this approach to competition is the complete absence of anything resembling genuine competition, as in competing for the patronage of customers. The only way a firm can gain significant influence over price is by attaining a monopoly, or something in the vicinity of monopoly, as perhaps illustrated by an 80 percent share of some market.

The alternative approach treats competition as an activity, a verb. Where the static treatment freezes technology and product development, the dynamic treatment regards the development of technologies and new products as the central feature of market-based competition. This second, dynamic way of treating competition, moreover, brings into the analytical foreground questions that are of more relevance for human flourishing than does the first, static way, for the road to flourishing runs through the development of new services and not through the indefinite continuation of old ones. Once rivalry is introduced, competition becomes an activity and not some static state of affairs. This shift in mental map brings invention and innovation into the foreground, for a significant part of the competitive process involves firms in trying to develop offerings that customers value more highly than the offerings of other competitors.

Competition is the normal activity of commercial entities seeking to expand their presence within the commercial marketplace; it is a rivalrous process that requires firms to pay continual attention to the ability of their products and services to meet customer requirements. A firm that would seek simply to hold onto its current market share by standing pat with its present offerings will lose out to more vigorous competitors that develop superior products and services. There is no equilibrium position of rest for competitors, within the context of a dynamic approach to competition. Rather what exists is a continual need to be creative and innovative, for otherwise you will lose even your previous customers due to the creative and innovative efforts of your competitors.

The dynamic approach to competition is fundamentally about invention and innovation, and in several dimensions. New technologies can be invented, as when sound was added to motion pictures, when television came to be delivered through cable, or when telephones were given the capacity to identify incoming callers. New technologies can also bring about significant changes in the commercial landscape, as when the washing machine replaced the scrub board, bringing forth new companies in the process. Or as an alternative illustration, when improvements in automobile travel after World War II led to more people taking longer trips to unfamiliar places. This led, in turn, to a desire for some greater degree of familiarity in the places people stayed and ate while they were away from home. In response, there was a growth of franchise and chain store operations in the provision of food and lodging, as entrepreneurs undertook new patterns of commercial activity so as to bring increased familiarity to an increasingly mobile population.

The static approach to competition places its analytical focus on the division of a market among providers, as illustrated by Herfindahl indexes of concentration. The dynamic treatment of competition does not deny the arithmetic accuracy of measures of static concentration, but rather disputes their significance because the central feature of competition is that the world looks different now than it looked 20 years ago, and this difference is due to the operation of competition. Twenty years ago, telephones were tethered to walls; moreover, if you wanted to make local phone calls you had to use equipment and lines owned by a Baby Bell. Ownership of copper wire connections had a vastly different significance then than it does now. Then, a caller's voice could travel nowhere without a copper wire connection. Now, such a connection is unnecessary, and in several respects, all of which have come into play through competition. For one thing, there are wireless technologies available, many of them. Moreover, cable TV now offers phone services. Phone companies, moreover, are now offering a television service. Indeed, the long-standing distinction among telephone, television, and computer is vanishing through the spread of digitalization. Even electric power companies are able to carry broadband over power lines, though there is some question of commercial feasibility in light of the intensely competitive nature of telecom today. The commercial map is being reformed dramatically through competition, and perhaps the prime accomplishment of state regulation is to slow the speed of reformation.

State enterprises and the search for sustainable rents

Successful entrepreneurial discovery yields rents. How long those rents can be obtained depends on how quickly they are eroded through competitive responses. The relative length of time, moreover, does not need to be terribly long to be economically significant. At a ten percent rate of discount, a rent that lasts for seven years is about half as valuable as one that would last forever. Joseph Schumpeter (1934) construed competition as a process by which incipient enterprises replaced established enterprises. The more openly competitive markets are, the quicker this replacement will occur. In the presence of incipient competition, however, it would be unreasonable to expect those established enterprises to go gently into that dark night of commercial has-beens. The traits that brought initial success will not allow them to leave the commercial stage without a fight. This fight might be conducted through commercial channels. But it can also be conducted through political channels. The creation of a regulatory process changes the rules by which competition proceeds, which has nothing to do with the so-called policing of competition that is standard fare in the typical discussions of the topic.

Part of the commercial strategy of many enterprises will involve the use of regulatory proceedings to increase the durability of entrepreneurial rents and to redistribute such rents. These activities are exemplified nicely in the continuing controversies over telecom regulation. A merger, for instance, is never a simple commercial transaction. Various regulatory permissions must be obtained. The granting of those permissions, moreover, emerges through a process where many competitors participate in trying to influence the terms on which permission is granted, and in some cases even trying to prevent the merger or acquisition. There would seem to be good reason to believe that in these processes the advantage will generally belong to established over incipient enterprises. This is not just because of the accumulated wealth possessed by the established enterprises. It is also because of the stronger network of connections that establishment brings.

Competition is commonly defined in terms of some notion of objective products or services. An alternative approach to competition would look to plans and their formation. The central feature of a market economy is that any entrepreneurial plan can go forward without securing permission from any particular person. A successful enterprise will, of course, require permission from many people, including financiers, vendors, workers, and customers. However, there will be no particular person whose permission is required. In network terms, competition entails degeneracy.[3]

A plan, whether possessed by an enterprise or by a consumer, can be conceptualized as a directed graph pointing forward through time, as Figure 4.1 illustrated. That plan will pass through various nodes, and with those nodes denoting various points of participation that will be necessary for a successful plan. For a consumer, nodes might correspond to airlines and hotels as components of a vacation plan. For a business, nodes might correspond to input suppliers and customers. Degeneracy means that the removal of any particular node does not destroy the plan or ensure its failure because other paths can be constructed: the graph of the plan entails degeneracy. State regulation, however, can eliminate degeneracy by requiring entrepreneurial plans to pass through particular nodes, and in this sense is perhaps about the only meaningful notion of monopoly that is reasonably sensible, in contrast to conventional antitrust actions that seek not to promote degeneracy but to transfer wealth among enterprises.

6 Competition and its social organization

Equilibrium-based theorizing treats competition as a structure or pattern of observations at some instant, as illustrated by the discussion at the end of Chapter 5. Competition is a structural feature whose intensity is a function of the number of firms who are judged to be competitors in what is judged to be an industry. The object of such a theory of competition is to establish a relationship between market price and market structure, and with market structure denoted by the number of competitors in some objectively defined industry. Without doubt, this approach to competition operates through anti-trust law and procedures to increase the demand for economists to testify as to the intensity of competition associated with particular industry structures or firm practices.

The intellectual cogency of the approach, however, is disputable. This structural approach to competition arose late in the nineteenth century, as a product of the effort of some economists to set forth a set of sufficient conditions under which the law of one price would have to hold, as explored by George Stigler (1957), and with the transformation in the meaning of competition away from an active process into a static structure portrayed by Frank Machovec (1995). The inspiration for the structural approach was Antoine Cournot (1838), who derived a mechanical relationship between price and the number of sellers of an identical product. Competition was thus a state whose intensity varies directly with the number of sellers. Anything that reduces the number of sellers or creates differences among formerly identical products is a reduction in the intensity of competition. By this approach, the world became less competitive when Henry Ford abandoned his requirement that all Fords be painted black and allowed buyers to choose among other colors.

The emergent-dynamic orientation provides a sharply different orientation. Competition is no longer a structural relationship among firms in what is defined as an industry. It is not a state whose intensity varies with some notion of market structure. There is no sense in which state policy can increase or decrease competition because competition is a ubiquitous and ineradicable feature of social life. State policy might change the particular forms that competition takes, but it cannot influence the fact of competition;

indeed, state policy is as much a feature of competition within society as are what are considered as more typical economic activities. Competition is grounded in human nature, wherein we regard ourselves as organisms distinct from the other human organisms in a society. The form of competition can be influenced within a society, but the fact of competition is invariant to social organization. Even in communist systems which were predicated upon a denial of competition, there was intense competition to secure positions of power and privilege.

The most that can be achieved with respect to competition is that it be channeled in ways that promote societal flourishing, as against being channeled in destructive ways. In a somewhat paradoxical use of language, the theory of a free-market economy explains how competition operates to secure social cooperation on a gigantic scale by transforming a society into a web of mutually supportive relationships that allow people to flourish relative to how they would fare on their own. For instance, the ability of people to use pencils is a product of the cooperative activity that emerges through competitively-organized relationships wherein no one person is able to do everything necessary to make a pencil. Competition is a natural consequent of people being free to assign themselves to particular activities within a society, as against being assigned to activities by some external authority; even in the latter case, moreover, there will be competition among people to secure positions of power to assign other people.

Competition, moreover, is not just something that takes place among commercial enterprises. Most fundamentally, competition takes place among individuals, and from this individual-centered point of departure competition extends to the enterprises into which those people cluster. Even within this setting of enterprises, competition among individuals continues unabated. Hence, those who participate within any particular enterprise are also in competition with one another, even while they act cooperatively with one another. For instance, a violinist might accept the award of first violin to someone else and yet harbor hope of taking that first seat at some later date or in a different orchestra. This competition, moreover, extends to politically-organized enterprises. Those enterprises compete among themselves as well as with market-based enterprises, but this competition among enterprises emerges out of competition among the individual participants within those enterprises.

This chapter concentrates on three features of competition as the foundation for the generation of social cooperation. One, the process of generating cooperation through competition inherently involves conflict among people, which places great significance on processes and procedures for containing and resolving conflict. Two, the institutional arrangements through which such conflict is resolved, or at least contained, can influence the character of a society in numerous ways. Three, what we call progress, at least in its material if not in its moral facets, is a consequent of the social arrangements for the resolution of conflict and the organization of competition.

Innovation and conflict resolution

Innovations of whatever form, whether in language, manners, or commerce, always originate at some particular node in a societal nexus. The subsequent spread of any innovation depends (1) on the receptivity to that innovation at other nodes, (2) the resistance to it at yet other nodes, and (3) the differential ability of some nodes to overcome resistance. Any innovation will upset previously formed plans. The idealized theory of an unhampered market economy envisions people at other nodes as simply allowing the innovation to enter, and adjusting their own plans as best they can. Yet there is no reason to think that people will actually act in this manner. And with the social-theoretic orientation pursued here, it is necessary to take all such possibilities into account, and not just possibilities that maintain a pervasive harmony among people through mutual forbearance.

To describe a society in terms of nodes and connections leaves open the properties of those connections and the principles on which they are formed. In a pure market relationship, all connections are formed and severed voluntarily according to the principles of private property and freedom of contract. This is not the same thing as saying that all relationships are genuinely voluntary, for a good deal of duress can be present in social relationships. Within an ideal-typical market system, the insertion and spread of innovations is governed by the beliefs about profitable action at each node of the nexus. All action starts with a sense of uneasiness and is carried forward through some plan of action to remove that uneasiness. Within an idealized market economy, that uneasiness can be removed only by offering services of value to other participants within that nexus and at terms on which those other participants are willing to accept.

Any innovative effort will disrupt plans elsewhere in the societal nexus. There are many responses possible in the presence of such disruption, only some of which will involve forbearance to that disruption elsewhere in the societal nexus. Responses grounded in forbearance will require a reformation in commercial plans and activities elsewhere in the nexus so as to meet the challenge presented by the competing innovator. But forbearance is a choice and not a necessity. In place of forbearance, other competitors might support the construction of regulatory barriers to commercial introduction of the innovation, as explored by Stigler (1975). To the extent such barriers result, such regulation would slow down the spread of innovations through the nexus as well as possibly lowering the volume of innovative effort and surely influencing the direction of such effort.

Ludwig Lachmann (1971) notes that the institutional order of a society has a hierarchical character, where some institutions rest upon other, more foundational institutions. Property rights and freedom of contract, for instance, provide a foundation upon which various forms of commercial enterprise can be established. Property and contract are higher-order institutions on which rest lower-order arrangements for bankruptcy and insolvency. Lachmann notes that the full set of institutions might operate together in congruent or concordant fashion. He also notes that those institutions can clash. It is surely plausible to think that as such clashing becomes more severe, innovative efforts are reduced as well as redirected. It is worth noting in this respect that conflict is largely a concomitant of innovation. In a stationary society there is little scope for conflict, as conflict would be attributed largely to incomplete socialization in the ways of the tribe or clan or however the relevant group is designated.

But it is in the injection of novelty where opportunities for conflict especially arise. Novelty unsettles existing relationships, which invariably works to the disadvantages of some while working to the advantage of others. And to recognize that innovation will generate increases in well-being for most people is not sufficient in itself to dissolve the potential conflict. Status and standing also matter to people. Someone might be the CEO of a prominent firm and enjoy the social prominence that comes with that position. An innovation that would undermine the prominence of that firm might be regarded as threatening even if that CEO could obtain employment elsewhere.

Let me weave a brief tale around spilt coffee to illustrate possible institutional incongruity. A woman buys coffee from the drive-thru window of a fast-food vendor. While driving she spills coffee on herself, and in her painful distraction crashes into the car traveling in the next lane. What is she to do? What is the other driver to do? To start, it could be thought that the woman had no business drinking while driving, and so by drinking was *ipso facto* negligent. The woman might even think something similar herself. The story might end with this recognition by the woman, but perhaps not.

Elsewhere, a creative attorney hears of the coffee-connected accident, and thinks that possibly there is a case waiting to be made. And why wouldn't she think this? After all, Guy de Maupassant wrote a well-received story about what is surely an improbable object, a piece of string. If a creative writer can fashion an interesting story around a piece of string, a creative attorney should be able to fashion a plausible cause of action around a cup of coffee. The lawyer is an entrepreneur who is alert to new opportunities (Kirzner 1979), and thinks that this case might offer such an opportunity. So she approaches the woman and offers to take her case on contingency. This is an ordinary contractual arrangement within the market framework. The attorney secures a court date and obtains a jury trial. What happens next? What kind of institution is the jury and court?

The jury can judge for the woman or against her. We typically conceptualize juries and courts as disinterested truth-seekers, but there is no compelling reason to do this once we explore the setting from the inside looking out. The woman is not wealthy and her insurance coverage is modest. In contrast, medical claims are high, much of it due to the damage to the other car and driver. To rule for the woman brings the resources of the vendor to bear on covering the claims that the woman cannot cover. To rule against her is either to throw the matter into bankruptcy or onto some state office as the woman now becomes eligible for public relief of various forms. Suppose that jurors posses reasonable intuitions about double-entry accounting. To rule against the woman thus means either that their tax bills will be nudged higher or that the playground children use on weekends, holidays, and vacations will now be open for fewer hours because of budget cuts made necessary by rising medical expenses.

I spin this tale not to advance substantive claims about the actions of jurors but to illustrate in a substantive way Lachmann's abstract claim about possible institutional incongruity. Market-based arrangements generally feature people who occupy positions of residual claimacy with respect to their actions. The attorney who takes a case on contingency is in such a position. In my tale, the hypothesized reasoning of jurors is likewise based on residual claimacy, only that residual position is filtered through a state-operated program that operates differently, and so hours of operation are based on budgets and not directly on revenue derived from playground admissions. To rule against the plaintiff is thus to rule for increased claims for the plaintiff's victim through public support, which in turn means some combination of higher taxes and lower spending on other public services.

With respect to innovation, state enterprises would seem to exert largely a conserving influence on the pace by which innovations spread within a social nexus. Within a regime of private ordering, the pace at which an innovation flows through a nexus depends on the willingness exhibited at individual nodes to embrace that innovation. No particular node is able to block that innovation, though any node can choose to ignore it. It is unlikely, moreover, that genuine innovations will be taken first to state-based nodes because of the difficulty in appropriating profit through such nodes, along with the necessity to convince a greater number of people to participate in the innovative enterprise. Regulation, for instance, is to a significant degree a vehicle for slowing down the pace of transformation within the nexus of relationships, thereby conserving the wealth of otherwise threatened enterprises, as will be explored below. Where some regulations conserve endangered species, others conserve endangered enterprises. So long as the volume of market-based enterprises and connections is large relative to those that run through state-based enterprises, however, state action might exert relatively aggregate small effect on slowing innovation-induced transformation, mostly because political entities are typically sluggish relative to private entities due to different arrangement of property rights within the different types of enterprise.

Universal competition, particular manifestations

Competition is a universal, non-eradicable feature of social life. There is no position in society that is free from contestation, nor is there any individual who is free from competitive activity. There can never be any choice to abolish competition. Even a hermit who wants only to live alone in some beautiful and verdant environment will face competition from other people who discover that place. Even someone who renounces material wealth and comfort to serve the poor will face competition from competing claimants for aid, and so will end up having to choose among those competing claimants.

The universality of competition can play out in many particular ways, and with differing social consequences arising out of such differences. Any competitive process can be described in terms of some set of rules that govern and guide the actions of participants. Those rules, however, are not wide open to conscious choice, though there can be margins open to choice (Leeson 2006). For the most part those rules reside within the moral sentiments, as illustrated by notions of just action and fair play. In saying this, however, it should not be thought that what constitutes just action and fair play is identically and commonly held by all participants, for to do this would be to bring in a presumption of harmony through the analytical back door.

Private property depicts one particular institutional framework through which competition secures social cooperation. While private property is often assimilated to the notion of liberty, it is actually a denial of or restriction on liberty of action: the transformation of common property into private property, for instance, restricts freedom of action while also restraining conflict. An established appliance store might carry a large but still limited number of items, and at the same time offer a good deal of information to customers about those appliances when they ask for it. A larger appliance store opens in the region; it carries lower prices but offers little to no information about the products it carries. A number of buyers obtain information about the products from the smaller store and then buy at lower price from the larger store.

What does private property require in this instance? The answer, of course, depends on just what it is that various interested parties are willing to do in this situation. One possible meaning of private property resides in forbearance, in which case the smaller store would have to do the best it could in the presence of competition from the larger store, thereby accepting that it would lose business to the larger store and perhaps go out of business itself. Alternatively, the smaller store might pursue legal action, perhaps by claiming that the larger store is gaining some unjust enrichment because the smaller store provides information to the benefit of the larger store, but receives no payment in return. If such action is successful, some of the sticks within the bundle of property rights will have been rearranged as a large vendor's prices become subject to some measure of control by smaller vendors. In this case the meaning of private property as it pertains to this type of situation will have been changed, just as private property in a dock means something different in stormy weather than in calm weather.

This complaint could also be taken to a legislative forum, perhaps leading to the establishment of minimum retail prices for appliances, and possibly also the prohibition of retail enterprises beyond some stipulated size, perhaps stated in square footage.[1] Both the legal and the political efforts at competition involve contestations over established patterns of property rights and seek to establish different patterns. Other forms of competition are also possible, though these are often thought of as occupying some illegitimate underworld of competition. Gossip and rumors could be spread to the detriment of the larger store. Vandalism could be undertaken. A police chief whose brother owns a small appliance store might probe those acts of vandalism with only perfunctory energy. In any case, the institutional framework through which competition organizes social cooperation is complementary to the institutional framework though which conflicts among people are settled or suppressed, or fester and simmer.

It is easy enough to see that some forms of competition are destructive relative to other forms. While competition is inherent in human societies, it is reasonable to think of seeking to control what are thought to be relatively harmful forms of competition. To a significant extent this control becomes the province of the policing activities of governments. Some of this goes under the heading of the protection of person and property. But a great deal of it concerns types of conduct that benefit some people while harming others, as illustrated by commercial competition where losing competitors seek protection in the face of the competitive activity of other enterprises.

It can be granted that some forms of competition are generally beneficial and others harmful without there being any easy way to make that distinction in particular cases, at least in a way that would command general agreement. For the most part, the making of this kind of distinction is the province of political and legal institutions and processes. Private property exists to the extent that third parties forbear from disputing an owner's use of property. A small company might develop a new line of cereal products and seek to get them placed in grocery stores. One response to getting rebuffed by those stores is to give up on the idea, and either liquidate the enterprise or pursue some effort at marketing the cereal directly by mail. To do the latter would, of course, require an added infusion of capital, which might be difficult to obtain. Pursuing either of these responses would illustrate forbearance from contesting the use of property rights by the stores that refused to carry the cereals.

There is, however, no assurance or necessity that forbearance will be practiced. The company might pursue legal or political channels, either of which will involve contestation over the right of property. In either forum, such contestation would involve a claim that existing stores do not have absolute rights to the use of shelves in their stores because they owe some duty to incipient vendors to carry their merchandise, at least for some trial period. If that contestation is successful, property rights will have been changed, with market processes then coming to operate under a different framework of governing rules.

Competition denotes freedom of action under some set of rules. But different sets of rules are possible, as are different institutional processes for establishing and amending those rules. At the most generic level, all such contestation starts with a complaint regarding the use of what the antagonist regards as a proper use of a right of property. Coase (1960) shows that such disputes can often be settled within the framework of private property. The owners of established stores might think that the new cereal will reduce their net income from their cereal shelves while the incipient producer believes the contrary. There are two approaches to pursuing this dispute about divergent beliefs about future circumstances. One approach is friendly in that the dispute is contained among the disputants; the other is hostile in that the dispute is extended to third parties.

The friendly approach follows the template outlined by Coase (1960). There are numerous particular ways the incipient vendor might try to do this, and the range of those ways is probably limited only by the range of the commercial imagination. Guarantees about sales could be offered and bonds posted, and with the bond defaulting to the store if the guarantee had not been met within the stipulated time. The store might require terms that the incipient producer is not willing to accept. This rejection could end the matter, but there is no necessity that it would do so. It's imaginable that the dispute could be taken to the Board of Directors or, alternatively, to shareholders, perhaps through a proxy fight over membership on the Board of Directors. Either of these alternative stages in this conflict would still be friendly, in that they confined the conflict to the two parties to the dispute.

These alternative stages would also be relatively expensive as compared with directly hostile approaches that called in third parties. Under normal circumstances, legal or regulatory complaint would surely involve less capital outlay than would efforts to take over the firm. Or at least the required capital outlay of different approaches would be a relevant consideration. These alternative approaches are openly hostile in that they bring third parties into the dispute. In taking this step, the incipient producer is contesting the ability of the store to exercise full control over the use of shelves in the store. If the incipient producer's claim is granted, the store will no longer have full control over the use of shelf space because there will now exist some right of incipient producers to obtain a presence in those shelves, or at least there will come to exist some judicial or regulatory proceeding by which incipient producers can petition to gain access to shelves.

The postulated dispute involves conflicting claims over the ability of the new cereal to contribute to the net worth of the store, with hostile approaches turning to third parties for settlement of the dispute. Jerzy Neyman (1950) presents an instructive discussion of a similar controversy, where a lady claimed that she could distinguish between two methods for making a cup of tea: one method entailed adding milk to tea while the other method entailed adding tea to milk. Most of Neyman's discussion concerns different experimental designs and the ability of those designs to offer a discriminating judgment about the lady's claim, recognizing that perfection was impossible in any case, and so there was an unavoidable trade-off between granting the lady's claim when she really couldn't discriminate and failing to grant it when she really could discriminate. Neyman also gave some attention to the mental outlook of the judge who was conducting the experiment and offering the judgment. Among other things, he was described as both "very strict" and "very benevolent" (p. 274). This mental outlook was an assumption made to convey a theme about the statistical testing of hypotheses. How well that outlook carries forward to legal and political processes is an open question.

There are plausible grounds for thinking that this outlook toward judging does not carry forward readily or smoothly to political and regulatory processes. Commercial disputes between two parties leave the participants as residual claimants to their actions. This position of residual claimacy gives the disputants good reason to settle their dispute because they can convert what would otherwise be legal expenses to net worth. The incentive to settle varies inversely with the divergence of belief held by the disputants about the likely outcome of a trial. Such legal processes as discovery and deposition serve to narrow the range of outlook in this case because each side learns of the theories and evidence held by the other side. In this respect, well over 90 percent of commercial disputes seem to be settled without trial.

The injection of political participants into this process of dispute settlement replaces a relatively smooth process with something that is more discordant and tectonic, by creating a type of cultural clash between institutional arrangements, which again recurs to Lachmann's (1971) claim about possible incongruity among institutions. When a political officer stands on one side of a dispute, as against mediating a dispute between private parties, the referee becomes a player. Moreover, the political player represents what can only be described as a different culture, much as Jane Jacobs (1992) captures by her distinction between two moral syndromes, the commercial and the guardian. While both syndromes are necessary for a society to operate, they can also conflict as they become commingled. A political participant in a dispute with a commercial enterprise does not operate according to the same principles of residual claimacy. Political calculation replaces economic calculation, as will be examined further in Chapter 8. How that calculation might work out depends on the plans held by that political officer. Those plans might include seeking higher office, in which case the selection of cases and the expenditure in pursuit of litigation can serve as investments in seeking higher office. For a political official, settlement of a case does not offer any direct increase in net worth, in contrast to the situation faced by a private disputant. Indeed, settlement might remove from public attention what could be a valuable form of directing attention to the aspirant for higher office.

Institutional competition

It is conventional to describe competition as occurring within some particular institutional framework that governs societal interaction. Competition can also in principle occur among institutional frameworks, particularly once it is recognized that people can differ in their evaluation of those frameworks. An institutional framework governs the nexus of relationships that constitute a particular social economy. Within one such framework people might be able to establish commercial enterprises by mutual agreement among voluntary participants, and with that ability extending to the ability subsequently to sell that enterprise either in whole or in part. Within another institutional framework, the formation of commercial enterprises beyond a certain asset size might also require some regulatory approval. Furthermore, the sale of enterprises, either in whole or in part, might likewise require regulatory approval.

Competition is typically portrayed as a process that takes place within some particular set of rules that governs interaction among the participants. An idealized market economy describes one set of such rules, although, of course, many particular specifications of rights of private property are possible within the generic framework denoted by private property. Thus there can be a family of rules denoted by private property. For any particular set of rules, the ordinary theory of a market economy seeks to explore how competition within that framework of rules creates a self-organized pattern of economic activity. Competition is the somewhat paradoxical name given to the process by which social cooperation is attained without any person or office being charged with securing that cooperation.

While it is useful for some purposes to treat those rules as data, those rules also change through time. The content of private property changes over time through social processes that also involve competition. At one time a person who wanted to sell a business could sell it to any willing buyer. Now the set of eligible buyers might be restricted by antitrust agencies and some of the terms of sale might be restricted by securities regulation. The rules governing human interaction can also serve as objects of competitive advantage. In line with the oft-noted claim about building that proverbial better mousetrap, a firm can try to gain a competitive advantage by building a better mousetrap or by building a better network for getting mousetraps placed in retail outlets. This situation would represent competition within the framework of market-friendly rules.

Perhaps a competitor offers a less expensive mousetrap built of flimsier wood that sometimes shatters upon trapping a mouse. Judging from its success with customers, many people judge the lower price to be sufficient compensation for living with the prospect that every so often a mousetrap will shatter. The producer of the costlier mousetrap might compete within the framework of market rules by perhaps developing an adhesive compound that would allow sawdust to be fashioned into mousetraps and yet not shatter, with this leading to a competitive mousetrap. Another option for competition is to change the rules by which market competition occurs. This change in rules could occur through either legal, regulatory, or legislative processes, in which case the object of competition would be the rules that govern relationship among market participants.

As a legal illustration, an attorney might file a class action suit on behalf of buyers of shattered mousetraps. Some customers could surely be found who received cuts from the shattered wood fragments, and who subsequently had to be treated for infected fingers due to mouse debris that contaminated the wood that pricked their fingers. A successful suit could well remove that type of product from the market because the expected damage from liability would not allow that mousetrap to remain competitive with what formerly had been the more expensive mousetrap.

As a regulatory illustration, a petition could be filed with a safety commission to set standards for mousetraps. This proceeding could have pretty much the same effect as a successful lawsuit. Legislation could likewise come into play to change the institutional framework to the same effect. For instance, the wood for the inexpensive mousetraps could have been produced by people who work at home on a piece-rate basis. Legislation could be enacted that incorporated such work into minimum wage requirements, which in turn reduced the competitive price advantage held by that mousetrap.

In principle, variation in institutional frameworks can serve as a form of competition that generates information about the properties of different frameworks, as explored by the essays collected in Bergh and Höijer (2008). In practice, there typically are many forms of institutional differences in play, which reduces the clarity of any association that might be inferred between institutions and performance. In one area the organization and reorganization of commercial enterprises might be wholly a matter of private law. In another area such commercial activities are subject to public law, as illustrated by various statutes regarding monopoly. If all other institutional arrangements were the same between the two places and if this social experiment were to play out for several years, information about the comparative properties of these two frameworks could plausibly be secured.

Such claims on behalf of institutional competition are never as clear as this simple comparison would suggest, and for two distinct reasons. For one thing, the *ceteris paribus* condition will rarely if ever obtain. Commercial organization might be subject only to private law in one area and public law in another, but this single dichotomy might not capture fully or accurately the relevant differences. For instance, in some places private law might be articulated through market-based processes of dispute resolution while in other places it is articulated through state-supplied courts. Similarly, a public law of antitrust might be instantiated in numerous different ways, and with the consequent performance properties differing among those ways.

Furthermore, institutional frameworks are emergent features of social interaction and are subject to ongoing change. The conditions of an experimental laboratory typically are not met because the framework is continually changing, particularly with respect to public law. For instance, one year rules governing mergers might change, in another year there might be changes in occupational healthy and safety, and so on. So the simple conditions for a laboratory experiment where institutional frameworks are the same except for one particular element, and where this difference persists for several years, are not found in reality. All the same, the differences in institutional arrangements that are made possible by relatively decentralized systems of governance provide some semblance of laboratory experimentation even if they cannot provide a genuine laboratory.

Competition and the constitution of dispute resolution

Competition will always appear in societies, and at the same time, rightly ordered cooperation allows us to live more commodiously than would otherwise be possible. From this, we can reasonably conclude that some forms of competition among people are generally more conducive to human flourishing than other forms, though to say this does not imply that everyone would or should hold the same ranking of different forms of competition. From this conclusion about flourishing, it is a short step to think of constituting some agency or creating some process that would operate to suppress the undesired forms of competition so that the desired forms can expand. And, indeed, societies have many such resources allocated to such activities.

Some difficult problems arise all the same with respect to such activities and efforts. Free commercial competition surely unleashes innovative forces to a larger extent perhaps than any other framework of social organization. Yet the very presence of such an openly competitive form of social organization generates problems that threaten to undermine those social arrangements. People seem particularly averse to losses for the most part, at least based on some forms of experimental evidence, as presented in Kahneman, Knetsch and Thaler (1990), and Tversky and Kahneman (1991). The progressive character of a system of free competition, however, would involve significant losses along with its gains. As a theoretical and arithmetical proposition, the expanding wealth that arises out of the progressive character of an openly competitive society will potentially leave everyone better off.

This statement of potential is a simple matter of arithmetic: with growing wealth there is no reason grounded in arithmetic that any person should necessarily experience declining wealth. Yet the progressive character of freely competitive societies means that some enterprises and occupations will be dying just as others are flourishing. Though the gain in value to the expanding enterprises exceeds the loss in value to the contracting enterprises, the gains from progress will be unevenly distributed throughout the society, and typically with a good number of people being on the losing end, at least for a while.

With respect to matters of moral rectitude, one imaginable position is that those who experience such losses as failing businesses or vanishing jobs will reinvent themselves and reposition their activities. And there is plenty of reason for advising this kind of response. After all, the society is getting wealthier in the aggregate, and this growth in aggregate wealth expands the commercial opportunities of those who have recently been on the losing end of commercial competition. By getting back in the game, so to speak, a momentary loss can be recovered, and with plenty of interest. This type of response is encapsulated in the aphorism that when the going gets tough, the tough get going.

But it's not the only possible response, nor is it a widely prevalent response. These days, the most common form of political activity is providing what are called "constituent services." Many of these services involve helping constituents negotiate their way through various bureaucratic and regulatory mazes. Another form of constituent service can reside in helping people deal with threatening competition and the capital losses that are looming. To be sure, there are different forms that such service can take, ranging from direct aid to threatened enterprises and activities to insurance-type programs.

If at some moment there is one set of enterprises that are expanding and another that are contracting, the latter set of enterprises and the various input suppliers associated with them would tend to have some proclivity to support restrictions on competition to reduce or offset the losses. It might be objected that doing this would be a short-term resolution, which is true. Yet we should remember that at a ten percent rate of discount, seven years is roughly equivalent to half of forever. So we should expect that to some extent a system based on free and open competition will generate cleavages between expanding and contracting enterprises, and with those cleavages generating support for political sources of income to replace the commercial sources that were not secured because they were secured by competitors instead.

The basic framework of private ordering reflects the presumption that competition is not a tort or offense. A losing competitor cannot claim damages against a superior competitor. But how is that superior quality recognized? All such claims could be settled through private resolution. The alternative is public resolution. But what to do about such cases as spilled coffee? Judges and juries operate with their various moral sentiments as these apply to the case at hand, but they are rendering third-party judgments in any case. To the extent conflicts are not resolved directly by the participants, they will be resolved instead by third parties, and with adjudication and regulation serving as the two most significant forms of third-party resolution.

Regulation and competition

All economic activity is regulated. An unregulated economy cannot truly exist. Private property regulates competitive activity, as commercial activity must conform to the rules of private property. A product that consumers do not care to buy will regulate the producer's continued production of that product. A working environment that is not attractive will require firms to pay higher wages than otherwise would be necessary. In these and many other ways, economic activity is regulated through private ordering. With private ordering, regulatory authority is dispersed throughout the society. It's not necessary that everyone like a producer's offering. What is necessary is only that a sufficient number of people like that offering so that the producer chooses to continue producing the product.

Perhaps more significantly, there is no one person's displeasure with a producer's offering that can prevent the product from being produced. A successful commercial plan requires support from many people if it is to be successful. It is all of these other people who serve collectively to regulate the producer's conduct. At the same time, however, there is no one person who has the ability to prevent a commercial plan from being pursued. There is no position of monopoly under private ordering because there are always alternative inputs available for the pursuit of commercial plans. The rules of private property assure that all inputs are assembled voluntarily. If monopoly has any meaning in a world of ubiquitous competition, it takes the form of a nodal point through which a commercial plan must pass, and with a commercial plan being treated as a directed graph that passes through an array of nodes where inputs are obtained on its way to final evaluation by a consumer.

The rules of private property do not provide veto points over someone else's commercial plans, for those rules operate only to prevent conscription into the service of someone else's commercial plans. In contrast, regulation through public ordering creates nodal points through which commercial plans must pass if they are to go forward. Such regulatory nodes are almost the exclusive source of monopoly in society because there is no way that a commercial plan can contract around that node. Perhaps one of the most egregious uses of regulatory power in this manner was the refusal of the Civil Aeronautics Board to license a single new airline over its entire period of existence from 1938 to 1979, despite the phenomenal growth in air travel that took place, as well as the proliferation of carriers that occurred after the demise of the CAB.

The ability of such regulatory monopoly to influence the value of commercial plans will elicit commercial efforts to secure favorable regulatory treatment. This use of power to extract payments from commercial enterprises has been labeled rent extraction by Fred McChesney (1997). Rent extraction is to be distinguished from its more familiar cousin, rent seeking, articulated initially by Tullock (1967), elaborated on and actually named by Kruger (1974), surveyed in Tollison (1982), and with a good deal of the literature collected in Rowley, Tollison, and Tullock (1988). Rent seeking and rent extraction are to politics what bribery and extortion are to ordinary people. Rent seeking describes what people have in mind by lobbying. It refers to the payments people make to secure political favors. A sports magnate would like to secure special tax treatment for a stadium under construction. The magnate might lobby to get this enacted, or, more likely, retain someone else to do this for him, possibly an ex-legislator. In this regard, it is noteworthy that few defeated or retired legislators return to their home districts. Most of them stay close to politics, in reflection of changes their legislative experience made in their human capital.

But rent seeking is only part of the story of money and politics, and perhaps only the minor part. Rent extraction may be even more significant. It refers to the payments people make to avoid being victimized by politically harmful measures. If rent seeking would be called bribery if it occurred between private persons, rent extraction would be called extortion. There is one vital difference between rent seeking and rent extraction that should not be ignored, and which may explain why the former has received more attention than the latter. With rent seeking, politicians are portrayed as relatively passive victims. They are deluged by lobbyists, and on occasion capitulate to those interests. The politician is caught in a squeeze between the intensity of special interests and the quietude of the public interest. With rent extraction, politicians are in the forefront of the action. They are the active initiators who continually look for targets. Those targets have a choice. They can ignore the politicians and lose a lot of their wealth. Or they can participate politically, thereby softening their losses.

Regulation transforms dyadic commercial relationships into triadic relationships, creating a form of mixed economy (Ikeda 1997). Regulation is not about making economic processes more competitive. This is impossible because economic processes are always maximally competitive as an implication of human nature. All that can be accomplished through public ordering is changing the forms that competition takes. Many regulations seek to control prices. With respect to the Civil Aeronautics Board in the US, air fares were controlled along with the prohibition of new carriers. The fares that were charged did conform to the regulatory requirements. Carriers thus could not compete by offering lower prices, so they competed along other margins. Planes were less crowded, meals were served, and service was plentiful and helpful, and with what otherwise would have been profits being transformed into consumer amenities through the competitive search for patronage.

Regulation is not about making life more or less competitive, and is rather about shifting the course of the competition that is inextinguishable as a feature of human nature. Thus regulation is mainly about the creation of alliances within a network of relationships, wherein some nodal positions gain advantage relative to other positions. For instance, Anderson, Shughart, and Tollison (1983) show that what has been widely described as a mistake by the Federal Reserve in allowing the money supply to contract during the early stages of the Great Depression also worked to the advantage of member banks as most of the banking failures occurred among non-member banks. The general point behind this particular claim is that regulation through public ordering is an arrangement that gives competitive advantage to some competitors relative to others. Regulation can channel the competitive process in a different direction from what otherwise would have resulted, but it cannot make the economic process more competitive than it will naturally be anyway.

Progress as continuing societal transformation

It is possible to imagine an inert society where a succession of snapshots taken as time passes would show no changes other than the changing of faces as people are born, age, and die. There are also societies and historical epochs that seem to mirror this image of inertness. Stone Age societies would seem to fit this image, as would the Yanomami of today who live in the Amazon rainforest. Indeed, it is only over the past two centuries or so that improvement in material conditions has become a regular feature of life (Mokyr 1990, Aghion and Howitt 1992, Easterlin 2000).

We now experience transformation as a continuing and not a sporadic process, though we also recognize that the pace of transformation varies within and across nexuses. All transformation starts at some node and spreads. In some cases the spread is rapid and wide, while in other cases it is slow and narrow. In any case, transformation begins with some particular person doing something differently than before. The effect of this difference upon the overall societal nexus subsequently depends on the adjustments that are set in motion elsewhere within that nexus. All societal transformation has this structural property of something new being inserted at one node within a nexus. What happens subsequently depends on the character of the connections and relationships among nodes. Some nodes invariably are more influential than other nodes.

The theory of an unhampered market economy is one where all connections are crafted voluntarily within the framework established by private property and freedom of contract and association. Someone who develops a new technique for mining coal would be able to put it to use at that node, and other nodes would adjust and adapt as those who operated those nodes thought best. Along the way, there might be various contracts that would have to be renegotiated or breached, and some mergers and acquisitions could well occur. But all of these adjustments would be regulated by the simple private law framework of property and contract (Epstein 1995).

The nexus evolves differently once state-based enterprises and public law enter the nexus. If coal mining is unionized, the new technology might not be able to be employed. Or perhaps it could be employed, only without any change in the number of miners employed. In this instance, public ordering prevents the renegotiation or breach of contracts when labor unions are involved. Public ordering also often involves restrictions or prohibitions on mergers and acquisitions that might be set in motion by new ideas originating somewhere in the nexus. The owner of a family-based business that owns a handful of grocery stores might be prevented by antitrust from selling those stores to the highest bidder, as illustrated by *US v. Vons* where antitrust was used to prevent the sale of a family-owned set of grocery stores to a larger chain of stores.[2]

It's not just regulation that creates obstacles within the nexus when public ordering is present. When public and private ordering are brought together, as they must, the resulting institutional incongruity can create obstacles to the spread of progressive innovation, though often only as a minor nuisance rather than a major retardant. Consider an ordinary commercial illustration. An innovation introduced at one node, perhaps the addition of a home delivery service to a grocery store, leads to an increased demand for land and preferably next to the current premises. A furniture store stands adjacent to the grocery store. Private ordering provides a simple framework by which the two parties can come to an agreement over whether the adjacent land is more valuable as a furniture store or as an annex to the grocery store. If the grocery store is able to buy the premises, the owner of the furniture store is agreeing that that land is more valuable as an annex to the grocery store. The furniture store will have to bear some expense in relocating and getting re-established in that new location, but it has concluded that the offer from the grocery store makes relocation worthwhile.

Alternatively, suppose the adjacent land is owned by the state and houses executives from the Board of Education. There can be no direct test of valuations through bids and offers because state property, while alienable, is held in common. People who make decisions have no residual claimant position that attaches to the land. The executives who work at the Board are residual claimants in such things as their commuting times and in whatever other adjustments might be required by a move to a new location. Those executives might face a longer commute and they will certainly face some costs of relocation, possibly even having to work a weekend or two to get settled. They will not, however, be able to claim any residual value from any real estate transaction.[3] While these kinds of transactions do happen, they proceed differently than they would within a nexus that was ordered wholly privately. The spread of innovations and their effect on the overall societal nexus of relationships will be influenced by differential receptivity across the different nodes of a nexus.

The centrality of nexus to growth

It is common to think about growth by referring to an aggregate production function and its postulated arguments. By invoking the neo-Walrasian presumption of equilibrium, the multiplicity of goods and services actually produced can be reduced to a single good designated simply as output. An economy surely cannot get any simpler than its representation through an aggregate production function: one type of output is produced by combining two inputs. Hedonic transformation, moreover, makes it possible to apply any particular designation to that output if it is desired to sound concrete and not wholly abstract. If a box of toothpicks sells for $1 and a box of mushrooms sells for $4, it is possible to describe whatever mix of output is actually produced either in toothpick-equivalents or mushroom-equivalents. In making this hedonic reduction, of course, output is actually being reduced to dollars (or whatever other monetary unit is in use).

Such aggregative reductions recall Leonard Read's (1958) essay on pencils where he explained that no one truly knows how to make a pencil, or even to describe fully how to make pencils. By this, Read meant that no one could prepare a recipe that someone else could follow and produce pencils. To be sure, Read listed a good number of components of the process of producing pencils to illustrate his theme. For instance, he mentioned harvesting cedar trees and milling the logs to produce slats to hold the lead which, Read also noted, contain no lead. But Read's description was only the proverbial tip of the iceberg. A full recipe would involve instructions to millions of people throughout the globe extending back dozens of years, in order to describe the coordinated actions that would be necessary to make a simple pencil available today.

It is fully within the spirit of aggregate growth theory to model growth in a pencil economy, recognizing that other products could be reduced to pencil equivalents through hedonic transformation. Once we do this, however, we confront the problem Read identified. At this point we come to a fork in the road. The commonly taken fork, the one that dominates macro growth theory, simply ignores Read's point about complexity. This theory doesn't claim to offer insight into the production of pencils or anything else, but rather simply observes that they are produced, and wraps an equilibrium-based vocabulary around that observation, thus wrapping a linguistic cocoon around a mystery.

The other fork would seek truly to illuminate some of the contours of that mystery so as to better understand how pencils emerge through catallactic interaction, and also how growth occurs. By bringing catallactic interaction to the foreground, the centrality of nexus becomes apparent. Growth in this pencil economy is thus not a product of some person's choice but rather is a product of the quality of interaction among people, each of whom is seeking to attain more highly desired circumstances. Many different choices must come together in coordinated fashion to achieve growth in the pencil economy. That nexus, moreover, is not something that is constructed by some act of choice, but is also generated through interaction within a nexus of relationships.

For instance, suppose a chemist discovers a compound that reduces the brittleness of the lead without disturbing its writing quality. For this discovery to transmute into growth within the pencil economy, subsequent adjustments will be required throughout the pencil economy. Among other things, there will be a reduced demand for slats from mills. Whether this discovery leads to unemployed resources or reallocations to other activities depends on the properties of the nexus of relationships. The theory of an unhampered market economy describes how readjustments spread throughout the market, and yet the presence of state-based enterprises presents forums that might retard such adjustment. Market economies are both disruptive and progressive, as the desire to secure the value of investments is surely a source of demand for market closures that operate to retard the pace of progress.

In any case, the degree of progress or growth is a property of the nexus of relationships and is not a direct object of choice. The ability of one person's discovery to stimulate increased productivity within the nexus depends on the properties of that nexus and not on the character of that discovery. In a planned economy, a discovery that reduces the brittleness of pencil leads will be contained at that point of discovery. With an unchanged supply of inputs arriving to produce lead, finished pencil lead will now accumulate. Even in a planned economy, such accumulation will eventually lead to efforts at readjustment at other nodes in the nexus. Still, the effect that the invention of the less brittle lead has upon the nexus depends on the relationships among the nodes that comprise the nexus and not just on the node where the invention occurred.

Adam Smith's error regarding progress

In his editorial introduction to Adam Smith's *Wealth of Nations*, Edwin Cannan (Smith 1937: xliii) reports that a contemporary of Smith's, Dugald Stewart, claimed that Smith had an early manuscript where he asserted that:

> Little else is requisite to carry a state to the highest degree of opulence from the lowest barbarism, but peace, easy taxes, and a tolerable administration of justice; all the rest being brought about by the natural course of things.

Smith's three conditions for progress seem simple and straightforward. Opulence is surely universally desired over barbarism. The United States is flooded with immigrants; Haiti and Somalia are not. Not only is opulence universally desired, it is also easy to achieve, according to Smith. All that is required is a modicum of domestic tranquility, relatively low taxation, and an administration of justice that is guided by rules of law and not by arbitrary and capricious edict. We know, of course, that progress has not been easy and general throughout the world. The challenge is to give an economically interesting account of a failure to achieve something that is apparently easy ("natural") and universally desired.

Pondering Adam Smith's error leads one to the nexus of relationships within which people live, for the circumstances that surround one's life are determined largely by the nexus of relationships within which one lives, with valuable treatments of networks and nexuses presented in Buchanan (2002) and Watts (1999). Domestic tranquility, the first of Adam Smith's three easy conditions for facilitating opulence, requires simply that people respect one another's rights of property. This condition seems simple enough, and yet apparently is far from simple to achieve. Simply wishing that people would act to respect one another's property does nothing to bring about this result. But how then might this result be attained? Conflict is inherent in any social setting, so domestic tranquility will require instruments for the resolution of conflict that are not themselves instruments for the incitement of conflict. But what are those instruments? Are they supplied externally, as illustrated by the police? Or are they supplied internally, as qualities residing within the population? And if the latter, how does the requisite mental and moral orientation come about? At a very young age, boys often fight when disputes arise, but leave that behind as they mature. But not always and not everywhere, it also seems.

Low taxes are apparently not so easy to obtain as it might seem at first glance. Some taxation will be required for the administration of justice. But how much will suffice? It seems as though there will never be enough justice in human affairs, and it appears almost self-evident that more justice can be secured if only more taxes are collected. Opulence, moreover, provides targets for those who covet the objects of opulence, and it is easy to translate a desire to secure what has been attained into a need for higher taxation to provide the instruments of security. Moreover, politicians often play upon the lower parts of our nature, which includes a desire to live slothfully upon the efforts of others, and which helps to expand state activity across a wide variety of activities from amusements to zoos, all of which require taxes.

A tolerable administration of justice corresponds to notions of rules of law whereby those who administer justice do so impartially. Yet much legislation is propelled by partiality to support the interests of some people over those of others. A tolerable administration of justice can easily become a casualty of the pursuit of political gain, as can easy taxes and domestic tranquility. It is easy enough for our imaginations to conjure up images of societies wherein energetic and creative people who respect one another's rights of property generate flourishing throughout the societal nexus, with the Venetian Republic for several centuries perhaps being the archetype of such flourishing. But there is no simple recipe for bringing this about, or for maintaining something like that once it has been secured. Indeed, nothing can be secured independently of rightly organized efforts aimed at that end, and even there the gods of unintentional consequences must be kind (Jacobs 2004, Wagner 2006a).

7   From micro to macro through an emergent ecology of enterprises

Macro theory within the neo-Walrasian motif seeks to make the same type of statements that can be made through micro theory, in that one variable is said to act directly on another variable. For instance, changes in the stock of money are said to change an index of prices or changes in government spending are said to change the aggregate volume of employment. Macro theory thus has a choice-theoretic character, as illustrated by efforts to make such statements as "capital spending fell because investors became cautious." A statement that is sensible for an individual is attributed to a society of individuals as well. A society is reduced to an individual by the construction of statistical averages that become the object of theoretical explanation, and with the vehicle of explanation being some model of individual choice.

Within a neo-Mengerian motif, macro theory would address the constitution or generation of economic aggregates. The objects of analysis are still societal aggregates of some sort; however, those aggregates are not treated as bearing some causal relationship to one another. Society is not reduced to an individual through the construction of averages, any more than Colorado is treated as just a higher plateau than Nebraska through averaging elevations across each state. Societies contain structured patterns of relationships which constitute a societal nexus from which various statistical measures can be extracted. As a statistical matter, it is always possible to construct relationships among various variables. Those relationships, however, are empirical and not theoretical or causal. Aggregate variables are the results of structured patterns of interaction and not direct objects of choice, despite the persistence of centralized patterns of thinking that seek to assimilate aggregate patterns to particular acts of choice.

Statements about macro phenomena are not merely scaled-up statements about micro phenomena. The relationship between micro and macro is rather one of simple to complex. Micro phenomena pertain to individual action, the domain of praxeology. Macro phenomena arise out of interaction among individuals, the domain of catallaxy, as recognized in several of the essays collected in Colander (2006). The object of macro-level theorizing thus supervenes on micro-level action but is not reducible to such action. The move from micro to macro is, among other things, a move from relatively simple to more complex phenomena (Hayek 1967).

A macro-economy as an emergent ecology of plans

An emergent approach to macro-level phenomena would seek to connect praxeology to catallaxy. Praxeology is the source of individual plans and actions; catallaxy brings these plans together in the ecology of plans that comprise the catallaxy or society. It is here where the significance of analytical levels comes into play. Macro is not reduced to micro through division. Macro and micro exist on different theoretical levels or planes. The macro level emerges out of interaction among people at the micro level, but the macro-level resultants are phenomena in their own right; those macro phenomena are not independent of the underlying micro phenomena but rather supervene on them.

To make this assertion about levels is not to practice some form of holism. There is no claim here that macro phenomena are uncaused causes of action. Obviously, if everyone but Crusoe were to vanish, society would no longer exist. All kinds of other phenomena would also vanish: there would be no property, no contract, no money, no business firms, no courts, and so on. While those phenomena cannot exist independently of individuals, they are not reducible to individual acts of choice or will. They exist rather at a different level of analysis, just as does the traffic jam examined by Resnick (1994). If people stopped driving there would be no traffic jam. Yet the traffic jam is not just a giant car that is observed to be moving backward while all of the individual cars in the jam are moving forward. The link between micro and macro resides in this relationship between levels, between praxeology and catallaxy.

From this praxeological point of departure, the plan is the prime unit of analysis. All actions that can be placed within a means–ends framework can be construed as plans, but what is of special relevance for macro-level theorizing are the plans of enterprises in the catallaxy. All plans involve intentional action initiated at one moment, but with results that will not be known until some future moment or set of moments. Figure 7.1 presents a general schematic for a stylized enterprise plan, which will operate within the ecology of

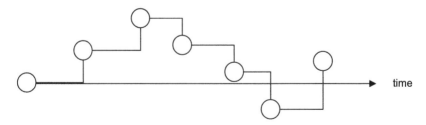

Figure 7.1 A plan as a directed graph.

plans to be considered momentarily. This figure is an amended version of the representation of a plan presented in Figure 4.1. In contrast to Figure 4.1, Figure 7.1 shows subsequent nodes as being displaced from the vision that informed the initial plan. This displacement represents all of the various reasons why a plan might be revised: changing input prices might lead to changes in methods of production or in the characteristics of products produced; beliefs about the desires of consumers might have been revised, inducing in turn changes in the enterprise's plans of operation; the commercial landscape might have changed through the entry of new firms and products, and which required revision in the enterprise's plan. At each node, a firm's plan can be summarized by two projections over some future interval, a projection of revenues and a projection of expenses. These projections in turn reflect myriad considerations relevant to that particular enterprise, and those considerations are not at all captured by or reducible to notions of rational expectations, which is a sensible notion only for a neo-Walrasian program. Not shown in Figure 7.1 is any information about how these plans fit together through entrepreneurial connection. Each plan will make claims on resource inputs that must be obtained through market transactions. Among other things, currently observed conditions in input markets are governed by anticipations and beliefs about the future circumstances at which present action is aimed. In this respect, one source of subsequent plan revision almost surely will be changing input conditions due to changes in plans elsewhere in the ecology of plans.

Figure 7.2 presents a rudimentary sketch of a macro economy conceptualized as an evolving ecology of enterprise plans. Figure 7.2 is constructed by adding three additional plans to the single plan shown in Figure 7.1, and by suppressing the revisions of direction that are shown in Figure 7.1 to avoid the cluttered look that otherwise would result. Figure 7.2 shows four entrepreneurial plans, denoted by A through D, though with the connections among plans suppressed, as are the subsequent revisions to original entrepreneurial plans. Plans A and B are set in motion at the same time, C

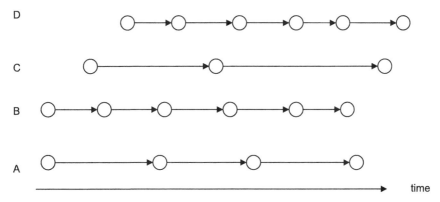

Figure 7.2 A macro ecology of plans.

starts later, and D starts later still. The plans also differ in the frequency with which they are revised, with B and D being revised more frequently than A or C.

There are several notable features of this ecology of plans. One, which is suppressed in Figure 7.2, is that plans form connections with other plans through entrepreneurial action. For any enterprise, some plans connect with other plans to secure inputs while other plans connect with plans that in turn serve as sources of revenue. A further significant feature of the ecology of plans is that the plans evolve in sequential and not in simultaneous fashion. In contrast to the neo-Walrasian formulation, all plans do not start at the same instant, which means in turn that turbulence will be continually injected into the catallaxy as new plans disturb existing plans. The subsequent insertion of a new plan into the ecology will affect the performance of existing plans, which in turn provides one impetus for a subsequent revision of a plan. Changes at one node can influence both positively and negatively the value of other plans in the nexus. Among other things, expansions and contractions at particular nodes can propagate to other locations in the nexus, with the exact pattern of propagation depending on the pattern of connections. This suggests that macro-level variability is a normal feature of an evolving catallaxy; moreover, the amplitude of such variability will depend on both the pattern of connections among enterprises and on the sizes of enterprises that are revising plans, for it is plan revision (and also creation and extinction) rather than execution that is the source of turbulence.

Yet another feature of the ecology of plans is that the customary distinction between short run and long run vanishes at the societal level though not at the enterprise level. It vanishes at the societal level because entrepreneurial action does not start in unison, nor do all entrepreneurs act upon the same planning horizon. As an epistemological matter, it is quite likely that the neo-Walrasian program would pass conventional empirical muster even though this program analogizes societies to parades. Within a full ecology of plans, which Figure 7.2 sketches in starkly adumbrated fashion, consider any vertical slice of time through that ecology. That slice will catch most enterprises in their operating phases. Only a relatively small number will be creating new plans, shifting to revised plans, or abandoning plans. With the execution phase analogous to flying a plane on automatic pilot, firms in the execution phase would appear to be in a condition of stasis. If we suppose that at any point of observation 95 percent of such plans are in their execution stages, by customary significance tests we could not reject the hypothesis that our observations reflected a steady state or stasis, even though the systemic observations are constructed upon a presumption of ongoing evolutionary change. It is the five percent of enterprises that at any moment are not in stasis that are inducing movement in the remainder of the catallaxy; the neo-Walrasian reduction to averages and representative agents nullifies the injection and propagation of novelty that provides the dynamic motion through time.

The centralized mindset

There is all the difference in the world between a scientific enterprise aimed at the study of relationships among economic aggregates and one aimed at the constitution or generation of those aggregates, for in the latter case macro variables do not act directly upon one another. Mitchel Resnick (1994) claims that all too often we fall into a centralized mindset that leads us to characterize and explain aggregate phenomena as if they reflected conscious decisions to act in unison when they did not. Where Resnick used computational modeling to convey his theme, Thomas Schelling (1978) explored the same theme in a more prosaic manner. In both cases, aggregate patterns were identified that were not products of some collective intention but were simply unintentional by-products of interactions among individual intentions. The range of phenomena examined in this manner included such things as seating patterns in auditoriums when seats are not assigned in advance, patterns of segregation in residential housing, the flight patterns of flocks of geese, the spatial properties of epidemics, and the backward movement of traffic jams even though all cars are moving forward.

Standard macro theory operates with this same centralized mindset, even if this is not always readily apparent. Representative agent models in macro are no different than treating a beehive as a gigantic bee or a traffic jam as a gigantic car moving in reverse. More generally, macro theorizing is filled with formulations where one macro variable acts directly upon another macro variable. For instance, an increase in the supply of money increases the price level. Alternatively, an increase in the marginal rate of tax lowers aggregate output. In both of these cases and many others, one macro variable is treated as acting directly on another macro variable, without undergoing any intermediation through interaction among the people who constitute that macro economy. In such formulations as these, macro theory conforms to Resnick's description of the centralized mindset. This, moreover, should probably not be too surprising, as macro theory, along with the concomitant construction of national income accounting, was rooted in the belief in the efficacy of national economic planning that seized the western world starting early in the twentieth century. While that belief is deeply ensconced in institutionalized practice, emergent-style theorizing uncovers some of the problematic features of this centralized mindset.

With respect to macro-level theory, I shall first give an abstract rendition of what I have in mind, and will then advance a substantive illustration of that point. Figure 7.3 presents an abstract illustration of the distinction between centralized and emergent approaches to macro phenomena. In the standard macro formulations, one macro variable acts directly on another macro variable. Figure 7.3 can be used to illustrate either one of two possible forms of relationship. One concerns a relationship between the stock of money and the level of prices, as illustrated by the claim that an increase in the stock of money increases the level of prices. The other concerns a relationship

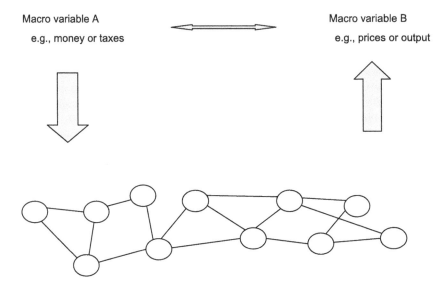

Figure 7.3 Abstract representation of centralized vs. emergent macro.

between tax rates and output, as illustrated by the claim that an increase in the marginal tax rate reduces aggregate output. Both of these relationships have, of course, received extensive treatment in various bodies of literature, and from the orientation of a centralized mindset where one aggregate variable acts directly upon another aggregate variable. The standard macro statements are about averages, as if everyone is locked together and acting in unison: the many cars that comprise a traffic jam are locked together and are moving backward; the geese are wired together and fly as a single unit. This common presumption is illustrated by the double-ended arrow between the two sets of variables: money acts on prices and taxes act on output; moreover, these variables have no relevant structural properties because all individual units are wired together, similar to presumptions about the geese in a flock. In this set up it is only natural to regress one variable on another, and to interpret the results as indicating the direction and strength of the relationship.

The alternative, emergent approach asserts that aggregates do not act directly upon each other, but rather are intermediated through interactions among people within the relevant society. This type of relationship is indicated by the two broad arrows in Figure 7.3, one pointing down and the other pointing up. If money is increased, that increase initially accrues to some particular people and not others. If taxes are increased, they are increased for some people and not for others. In consequence of these changes in money or taxes, particular people alter their economic conduct in numerous ways, which in turn *generates* the aggregative consequences depicted by the upward arrow. The same amount of monetary injection could thus have different patterns of consequence, depending on patterns of injection and subsequent interaction.

It is the same for tax increases. With respect to tax increases, however, it should be noted that it is methodologically impossible to posit an aggregate tax increase without some offsetting change of equivalent aggregate magnitude. One such possible change would be an increase in state expenditures. Another possible change would be a reduction in government's holding of debt, which in turn could lead to a contraction in the money supply. For my purposes of illustrating the centralized mindset, these complicating considerations can be ignored even though they would have to be incorporated to secure analytical consistency and completeness.

Suppose $100 billion of increased taxation is imposed on the economy. There are an indefinitely large number of ways this could be done. For instance, personal exemptions could be reduced. The estate tax could be increased. The personal income tax could be increased at the upper end of the income scale. Alternatively, it could be increased at the lower end of the income scale. As can be easily imagined, there are numerous particular ways that taxes can be increased. However a tax is increased (or money injected, for that matter), numerous kinds of economic readjustments will occur, and out of this will emerge some volume of tax collection along with some measure of aggregate output. Suppose there were 20 different patterns of tax increase of the same aggregate magnitude, and with 20 different measures of the impact on aggregate output resulting. The centralized macro mindset would characterize this by the functional relationship $O = f(T)$, with $f' < 0$. The estimated relationship would entail both an average impact and a variance, and with the variance described simply as an error term. Within an emergent formulation, this is not truly an error term but is an illustration of the misspecified character of the model. What has really happened is that different tax measures of the same aggregate volume had different outcomes in the aggregate, depending on the patterns of interaction and adjustment that were set in motion within the underlying micro structure.

The discussion to this point has treated the money expansion or the tax increase as exogenous shocks to illustrate the point that aggregate variables do not act directly on one another because the aggregate impact of any policy injection depends on both on where it enters the catallaxy and on the structure of catallactical relationships. Such aggregate variables, however, are themselves products of internal emergence and not acts of outside intervention. Parliamentary assemblies and central banks operate within a nexus of catallactical relationships, wherein so-called policy measures are products of interaction among interested participants, and with those participants typically having differing interests and desires and most certainly not being wired together to act as a single unit.

An emergent approach to macro theory would represent a radically micro-centric approach to macro. It would involve micro-foundations for macro, only those micro-foundations would be emergent-theoretic and not choice-theoretic. The result would be more of a unification of economic theory, whereby the micro–macro distinction would vanish in some respects and would strengthen in other respects. It would vanish in that all economic phenomena are treated as emerging out of individual action to replace less desired with more desired circumstances; all societal phenomena would reflect the common principle of economizing action. That distinction between micro and macro would also intensify in that theorizing would now operate on distinct analytical levels, as illustrated, for instance, by Jason Potts (2001) and also Potts and Morrison's (2007) distinction among micro, meso, and macro levels of analysis. Among other things, it would be necessary to consider macro foundations for micro theory as well as micro foundations for macro theory.

Micro-foundations for macro; macro-foundations for micro

The interest in micro-foundations for macro theorizing arose out of a growing disenchantment with the so-called neoclassical synthesis. According to that synthesis, there was no connection between micro theory and macro theory. Standard micro theory was fine so long as the aggregate economy was at full employment. This latter condition, however, was not a central tendency of a market economy but could only be secured by government action to secure and maintain full employment through its use of policy instruments. Macro theory sought to illuminate just what a government should do to maintain full employment, with such things as antitrust policy presumably working at the micro level to keep markets competitive according to some textbook vision of perfect competition.

The interest in micro-foundations grew in response to several criticisms of various prescriptions about macro policy. For instance, the fiscal policy analysis of tax cuts was conveyed by notions of Keynesian multipliers that made no micro sense once it was realized, following Friedman (1957), that temporary changes in disposable income would be mostly saved, so would generate little to no multiplier. It was the same with a fiscal policy that increased expenditure. The Keynesian multiplier was buried beneath the Ricardian equivalence of debt and taxes (Barro 1974), leaving only second-order effects attributable to such things as debt illusion and incomplete bequest motives. More generally, Robert Lucas (1976) explained that it was necessary to take into account how policy measures might change the values of parameters that had been estimated under a previous policy regime before gauging the probable impact of some proposed policy measure.

Real business cycle theorists have been in the forefront of the search for micro foundations, and have done so by reducing an aggregate economy to a representative individual who responds to various exogenous shocks. By doing this, the appearance of a theoretical relationship between macro variables is established even though there is no genuine basis for such a relationship.

There can be statistical regularities among macro variables, at least until parameters no longer work and new ones must be estimated. To establish statistical regularity is not to establish a theoretical micro-foundation. A problem with a purely statistical regularity, of course, is that it can change. Indeed, the central claim of the Lucas Critique is that policy measures should be expected to change parameters. Hence, policy can rely on old parameters only so long as it isn't changed. The real business cycle theorists accepted the Lucas Critique and sought to provide choice-theoretic foundations for macro by transforming all aggregate variables into miniature, person-sized representations. The only difference between Crusoe and society is a simple matter of scalar multiplication.

An emergent approach to micro-foundations for macro analysis would seek to connect praxeology to catallaxy, and would start by recognizing that there are no choice-theoretic foundations for macro theory, at least so long as macro theory is conceptualized as dealing theoretically with relationships among aggregate variables. Praxeology is the source of individual plans and actions; catallaxy brings these plans together in the ecology of plans that comprise the catallaxy or society. It is here where the significance of analytical levels comes into play. Macro is not reduced to micro through division. Macro and micro exist on different theoretical levels or planes, and the macro is not reducible to the micro. The macro level emerges out of interaction among people at the micro level, but the macro-level resultants are phenomena in their own right; those macro phenomena are not independent of the underlying micro phenomena but rather supervene on them. To make this assertion about levels is not to practice some form of holism. There is no claim here that macro phenomena are uncaused causes of action. Obviously, if everyone but Crusoe were to vanish, society would no longer exist. All kinds of other phenomena would also vanish: there would be no property, no contract, no money, no business firms, no courts, and so on. While those phenomena cannot exist independently of individuals, they are not reducible to individual acts of choice or will. They exist rather at a different level of analysis, just as does the traffic jam examined by Resnick (1994). The link between micro and macro resides in this relationship between levels, between praxeology and catallaxy.

Price rigidity plays a big role in orthodox macro theory. This is a topic that is warped both by equilibrium theorizing and by a misguided sense of what sensible micro-foundations entail. Suppose there is postulated a general increase in the demand for money. If all prices are fully flexible, prices will fall sufficiently to leave aggregate output unchanged. This result is compelled by the hard core of the problem statement of the neo-Walrasian program. In the absence of full flexibility, aggregate output will fall as inputs become unemployed due to inflexible prices. Hence, markets are prone to failure; moreover aggregate demand management that inflates the stock of money is thought to be superior in light of downward rigidity of prices.

One troubling feature of this formulation is the presumption that full price flexibility is desirable or even possible, and with price inflexibility being a source of imperfection. This seems to be one more example where equilibrium, pre-coordinated thinking goes astray. All firms are treated as acting as a single unit in setting prices: the course of economic activity can be explained by considering a representative firm. A different insight about pricing and inflexibility arises once we realize that an economy is constituted as a population of semi-independently acting units that cannot meaningfully be reduced to some representative or average unit.[1]

At the level of praxeology, plans require some degree of inflexibility in pricing, as well as in other attributes of a plan. Information must be accumulated and processed before it can be acted upon. Accumulation and processing are activities that require the passing of time. During any such time interval, prices will be inflexible for that entity. This does not mean that prices are inflexible for all firms within the catallaxy, for some firms will be in a better position to change prices than other firms. Plans are often revised, and only a fool would stick with some original plan totally impervious to any kind of evidence that might suggest the merits of some revision or perhaps even abandonment. Still, the very idea of plans and an ecology of plans means that some degree of inflexibility is part of a well-working catallaxy. To be sure, in a population there will always be units that are revising or reformulating plans, and which will provide a leading source of flexibility.

Symmetry requires at least some recognition that the macro foundations for micro theory are also a sensible concern. Micro foundations for macro are concerned with how to build up from individual action to aggregate configurations. For the emergent or interactive orientation pursued here in place of the orthodox, choice-theoretic orientation, the relationship of macro to micro is one of supervention and not reduction. On the one hand, micro-level interaction generates macro-level configurations; on the other hand, macro-level configurations shape and influence micro-level actions and interactions.

Neutral money

Richard Cantillon was roughly one generation ahead of David Hume, both in birth and in death. Each advanced formulations about the effect of money on economic activity. Both asserted that the injection of money exerted economic consequences, but there the similarity between the two ended. Figure 7.4 is a simple graphical representation of the differences between the two. In both panels, the nodes represent enterprises and the box with an M inside it represents a monetary authority or a point of monetary injection. The Hume model is a densely connected graph. In that figure, there is also a reference to viscosity being low. What this means is that even though money may enter at one particular point, its low viscosity means it is diffused quickly throughout the catallaxy. This gives the simple quantity theory result that money works simply as a scalar upon prices, leaving real economic relationships and patterns unaffected.

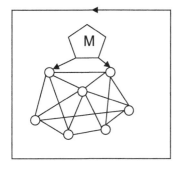
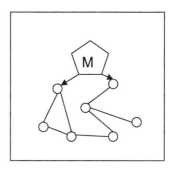

Panel A	Panel B
Hume model	Cantillon model
Connections = dense	Connections = sparse
Viscosity = low	Viscosity = high

Figure 7.4 Two models of monetary expansion.

The Humean formulation dominates economic theory today, though it has been amended a bit in light of modern sensibilities about economic modeling. That amendment concerns expectations and monetary surprises. It is now acknowledged that within the Humean framework a monetary change can exert aggregate impacts only so long as that change surprises people. This gives the result represented by the Lucas supply function, where actual aggregate output equals natural aggregate output, plus or minus some disturbance to represent unanticipated monetary change.

In the Humean formulation it makes no difference which path the monetary injection follows. With dense connections and low viscosity, monetary injection can disturb equilibrium relationships only through surprise. Otherwise, monetary injection operates indiscriminately upon the overall nexus, as if that nexus were a balloon whose air pressure can be increased or decreased. What we have is a stark illustration of how an analytical model can serve to focus attention in a way that denies the very possibility of examining many alternative lines of explanation. If observations are presumptively observations of equilibriums, a field theory model with low viscosity forces the Humean formulation, updated in light of modern formulations of rationality of expectation, as the only analytical possibility.

In the Cantillon formulation, money (and also credit) enters at particular points in the network of transactions that comprise the catallaxy, as explored in Horwitz (2000). Two possible points of entry are sketched in Panel B. For the locus of monetary or credit injection to matter, it is necessary to work with an analytical schema that allows the dimensions of such mattering to reveal themselves. This is impossible with the hedonic erasure of all structure that equilibrium modeling imposes. For structure to matter, equilibrium cannot be presumed, for in the absence of equilibrium the possibility is kept open that changes in the course of money and credit can influence the structure of economic activity. What we have here is another illustration of the non-additive architectonics of theoretical frameworks, which means that they cannot be pulled apart. If you work with equilibrium, you cannot allow structure to be anything other than a sideshow. If you want structure to matter, you cannot work with equilibrium. Conventional Austrian macro formulations are thus off-base in seeking to make structure important while working with notions of equilibrium that neuters structure. To render structure economically significant, equilibrium theorizing must be replaced with emergent-style theorizing.

Consider one illustration of how this line of thought might be pursued. The illustration I give is stylized to make the point, and other such illustrations could also be developed. Suppose that increased credit enters at one point in Panel B. We can assume that other people in the nexus would like to gain some access to that credit, but how do they do so? One possibility is that those who are generally closest to the point of injection will be more successful in gaining access. To be sure, this distance allusion can take several substantive forms. One is pure geographical distance. Another might be some notion of social distance. Yet a third could be some notion of commercial distance. The central point, however it might be illustrated substantively, is that propinquity matters.

Let's stick with geography for now, because the illustration can be sketched more quickly than could other possible illustrations. In this case, people who are located relatively close to the point of injection will be more successful in competing for credit than those located farther away. The point of injection creates a kind of commercial amenity, after a fashion. Within this kind of framework, it would be plausible to expect to see alternative patterns of commercial location, depending on the point of credit injection. Land close to the point of injection will become more valuable and population densities will rise, as compared with places far from the point of injection.

One intriguing feature of this formulation is that the effects of monetary arrangements do not show up in any kind of aggregate magnitude, but rather show up through changes in the structural pattern of economic activity, and particularly through changes in the prices of land. Such a model, moreover, could easily be constructed so as to keep aggregate land rents unchanged, so that nothing appeared to happen at the aggregate level. Other concepts of propinquity could easily be pursued. Within the universe of new commercial ideas, only some will receive support and only some of those will subsequently prove viable. It is surely plausible to think that at the structural level different patterns of credit injection can thereby influence the pattern of commercial activity through time, even though standard aggregate measures might appear to show that nothing has happened. This result, however, would not testify to the strength of standard macro modeling but to its limits.

This remark about structure leads to an inquiry into what central banking is really about. It cannot really be about administering wise monetary policy because even hyper-active monetary policy wouldn't require many people to conduct it. Central bank employment of professional people is surely orders of magnitude higher than what would be required for a hyper-active monetary regime. A modest sampling of Congressional hearings on monetary matters, moreover, gives a strong impression that what is of foremost interest is who can get credit on what terms, and similar types of questions. This recognition fits better with the Cantillon framework than with the Humean framework, for it suggests that central banking operates to the advantage of some clienteles within society and at the expense of others, as against operating to provide some general benefit to all.

Monetary policy is, of course, a curious concept. Money is a form of property; it is an asset that can easily be exchanged for other assets. Monetary policy might thus seem to be concerned with securing those assets against predation. Yet what is denoted as monetary policy seems clearly to be mostly organized predation that takes the form of diluting the real value of existing monetary claims on assets by issuing additional claims without creating new assets to offset those claims. To be sure, much of the literature on monetary policy supports but modest predation as illustrated by modest rates of increase in the issuing of such claims. Still, monetary policy is a curious concept as it involves a claim that collectively sponsored counterfeiting can be a good thing, as explored and explained in such places as Siegel (1984), Selgin (1996), Yeager (1997b), and White (1999).

Austrian-style cycle theory

Standard Austrian cycle theory (ACT) adopts a neo-Walrasian point of departure, and then engages in a two-stage form of comparative statics in place of the typical one-stage analysis, as explained by Roger Garrison (2001). Hence you get a monetary expansion that initially leads to an expansion in the capital goods industries. This happens because the fall in the market rate of interest below the natural rate increases particularly strongly the apparent profitability of long-term capital projects, setting in motion an expansion in relatively capital intensive projects. This expansion phase is identical to what would have happened had people generally decided to save more, as illustrated by a general decrease in time preference. The problem with the credit expansion that is not the result of a fall in time preference is that the lengthening of the structure of production cannot be sustained. The structure of production initially shifts in a capital-intensive direction, but consumers have not reduced their desire to buy consumer goods. A conflict is set in motion that can be eased only by a subsequent contraction, wherein the initial boom in the capital goods industries is replaced by a subsequent bust. Thus you get a kind of concertina-like effect: an initial expansion followed by a contraction, with both set in motion by the initial credit expansion and with both the expansion and the contraction reflecting economic mis-coordination (O'Driscoll 1977).

Most macro theorists do not even know about ACT. Of those that do, nearly all dismiss it on expectational grounds. Robert Lucas's (1975) model of the islands was actually a variation of ACT, and Lucas abandoned his support for this construction as soon as he realized the problem that anticipation created.[2] But how, exactly, does anticipation create a problem, and for whom? In a world where loans are mostly for commercial purposes, credit expansion promotes new production plans of a higher-order character, according to standard ACT. The critics claim that this can work only for monetary surprises. Within the neo-Walrasian world within which ACT is typically framed, the critics are right.

The neo-Walrasian framework is the same as the Humean set-up described in Figure 7.4. If you take away the surprise nothing can happen of real significance. It is the same when ACT is played on the neo-Walrasian field, for Cantillon-like considerations are neutered on that field. The problem with ACT is not that it is wrongheaded but that it has been conveyed with intellectual vehicles that are not suited to the task (Witt 1997). You cannot start with a presumption of pre-coordinated equilibrium and then inject credit expansion, because you will fall on your own expectational sword. Credit expansion in this case operates as a simple scalar imposed uniformly on the economic nexus, and any changes that result necessarily are purely nominal (Horwitz 2000).

ACT can be rendered sensible only by working with non-equilibrium models, as illustrated by an ecology of continually changing plans and as explored in Wagner (1999b) and Oprea and Wagner (2003). Such an alternative conceptual framework casts different illumination on credit expansion. In the usual equilibrium story there are no latent enterprises that are superior to those enterprises that are already being supported. In consequence, the resulting comparative static exercise will show no real change but only a nominal, scalar impact on prices. Figure 7.5 illustrates this point. Suppose current time preferences support the interest rate r_1 which in turn supports the capital structure denoted by c_1. The standard Austrian formulation distinguishes between two sources of a fall in the rate of interest to r_2: a fall in time preference and an increase in bank credit without the increase in saving that accompanies the fall in time preference. The fall in time preference simply leads to a lengthening of the structure of production. The credit expansion starts the same way but then reverses direction.

When this Austrianesque analysis is conveyed within an equilibrium framework, it verges on incoherence. Suppose the capital-axis in Figure 7.5 maps into the number of enterprises. The increase in bank credit then is claimed to lead entrepreneurs denoted by $c_2 - c_1$ to create new enterprises. Yet the given conditions for equilibrium support only c_1 enterprises. Thus those new enterprises are destined to fail because their value added is not worthwhile in light of prevailing time preferences. Since there are no monetary surprises and since there is no reason to postulate some alternative

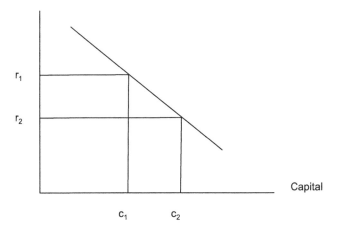

Figure 7.5 Credit expansion and structure of production.

equilibrium configuration, the same $c_2 - c_1$ firms that are born will be the ones that will die, and the owners and investors will know this. Being rational, they will forsake such illusory and losing investments for such things as investments in government bonds, and the expansion will never happen in the first place. The expansion doesn't happen because it violates the initial equilibrium conditions in conjunction with the presumption of full knowledge of those conditions and of the credit injection.

It is different in a non-equilibrium framework. At any instant within the ecology of enterprises there are some firms that are on their deathbeds while there are other firms that are in the throes of birth. Credit injection, moreover, does not operate as some uniformly-spread liquid, but comes in lumps to particular enterprises. Within this alternative frame of reference, a credit expansion may well facilitate some firms that prove to be successful, as well as exerting subsequent negative consequences. The overall impact, thus, cannot be captured only by some time series of aggregate measures, for those aggregates are composed of structural elements whose components are subject to variation.

The truly central feature of ACT is cousin to claims about the impossibility of collective planning (Hayek 1935, Boettke 1998). Idealize for a moment a catallaxy that is fully privately ordered. In standard equilibrium thinking, any aggregate measure of activity would show a flat line to indicate the steady state quality of the model. Catallaxy modeled in non-equilibrium fashion would not give any flat-line portrayal in the aggregate. Enterprises do not die instantly, to be replaced by new ones, again instantly. Not all plans mesh fully. Sometimes they collide, with debris scattered about. We speak of a construction industry, but a chunk of that activity is devoted to remodeling and renovation. Think about remodeling and renovation for a moment. They make sense only in the presence of failed plans that require reformation and revision. Some degree of variability is surely to be expected as a normal feature of a well-ordered catallaxy, although it is not at all clear what kind of aggregate indicator could be used to express this idea, since the customary aggregates are sensible only in light of a presumption of equilibrium.

Now introduce a government that seeks to manipulate economic outcomes. There may well be zones where it can achieve some desired objective, though this will entail unsettling relationships elsewhere in the catallaxy. A government might subsidize particular lines of long-term investment, but this doesn't mean that those enterprises will find commercial success. ACT is fundamentally a story about how the operation of market *processes* is distorted through policy-induced changes in the availability of credit. The word *processes* is pivotal in the preceding sentence. A neo-Walrasian equilibrium is not a process, it is the end of a process and stands outside any notion of process. A process, at least when meant within a catallactical frame of reference, is not an equilibrium and requires instead some non-equilibrium approach to modeling.

In equilibrium theorizing, much is made about the presumption that the mean forecast error is zero. This means that people are not systematically wrong, so that the claim of equilibrium appears to be sensible. Such an argument would be used to claim that it doesn't matter if particular entrepreneurs judge wrongly so long as the mean error is zero. This widespread claim is one more illustration of how a presumption of equilibrium neuters structure. You can assimilate this statement to forecasting the air pressure in a balloon. Perhaps the mean forecasted pressure is equal to the actual pressure at 28 pounds per square inch, with a variance of 2 p.s.i. This corresponds to rational expectations in New Classical macro models.

The situation looks different within a non-equilibrium framework where structure matters and does important work (or at least reflects important work). Most significantly, it means that a mean forecast error of zero means nothing. If there is any work to be done by such a statistic, it is to be done by the variance and not the mean, and it does so because the variance points to structure, which is not at all captured by allusions to air pressure. An increase in error means an increased volume of particular lines of subsequently ill-fated commercial activity. These failed lines of activity have particular shape: people acquire special skills, tools and equipment are fabricated, and so on. While these resources can always be redeployed, often this can be done only at some loss as compared with what would have been the case had the original plans worked out successfully.

Fiscal stimulus within the macro ecology of plans

How might a large increase in government spending be analyzed in terms of the macro ecology of plans? This question points in two directions moving away from the stimulus program. One direction would seek to explain how such a program emerges out of a catallaxy. This topic will be explored in the next chapter, where policy is treated as an emergent feature of a network of catallactical relationships and not as the action of some planning agent who imposes a policy blanket on society. The other direction, the one explored here, explores the consequences of such a measure when inserted into a network of catallactical relationships.

One thing that should be said immediately about such measures is that there is no such thing as a genuine stimulus. After all, a stimulus refers to some insertion into a system from someplace outside that system. What is called fiscal stimulus is not some insertion into the market economy from outside of it. Rather, it is a rearrangement or redistribution within the market. The consequences of that rearrangement are something to be explored, but that exploration cannot proceed under the presumption that there has been a net addition to aggregate spending because the added government spending is made possible by restrictions on the ability of people to spend in their private capacities.

There are different ways of accomplishing this restriction of private spending. The most direct way is through an increase in taxation. Government borrowing is an alternative way, but this is just a substitution of future for present taxation, and with the present value of those future taxes being equivalent to the borrowing under principles of double-entry accounting. Yet a third way is inflationary finance through money creation, which is just a form of taxation imposed on the money balances that people hold.

Any such program is really a change in the distribution of property rights within a society, with initial recipients of the added spending receiving title to resources that were transferred away from other people. It is sometimes claimed that this transfer comes from idle money balances. This is a misnomer because the appellation idle implies that there is no point to the idleness. To claim this is to take an instantaneous view of economic activity. Once it is recognized that activity proceeds through plans, it is also necessary to recognize that plans entail the passing of time. What are idle balances when interpreted in terms of a presumption that economic activity is instantaneous become components of plans once the temporal character of economic activity is recognized. Therefore, a stimulus program will promote some nodes within the ecology of enterprises while suppressing other nodes. The aggregate impact will depend on how the entire operation works out, and is a complex matter that has not been truly explored, though the problems it presents bear a family resemblance to Austrian cycle theory once that theory is separated from the neo-Walrasian veneer that accompanied its initial formulation.

Game theoretic formulations of macro-level coordination failure

While macro theorizing is dominated by presumptions of coordinated general equilibrium, there have been some efforts to treat the degree of coordination as a variable to be explained, usually in game theoretic terms. I shall consider briefly two such formulations of macro-level mis-coordination: the currency game and the stag hunt game.

The currency game is presented in Table 7.1 and is discussed in Young (1998) among other places. The central assumption is that people can bring one of two types of currency to market, but not a mixture of both. The payoffs, moreover, accrue only if both participants bring the same currency. Those payoffs reveal that neither party cares which currency is used, for all that matters is that each carry the same currency. The game theoretic analytics proceeds in several directions. The proportions of people who carry each currency can be varied. People can be modeled as Bayesians who update their expectations based on what they discover during their preceding visit to the market. Some random element can be introduced, perhaps to represent experimentation where some people simply decide to switch currencies regardless of their prior experience. The general features of simulations of this game show both a strong tendency for one currency to dominate and occasional shifts to the other currency within a relatively short number of rounds of play.

Before commenting on this approach to macro-level coordination, it will be useful to describe the stag hunt game, as presented in Bryant (1994) among other places, because both of these games seek to make the same point on the one hand and raise the same type of analytical problem on the other hand. Table 7.2 characterizes a stag hunt game. In this game, people can choose how much effort to supply to some common endeavor, and where individual consumption depends on the outcome of that common endeavor. This situation fits the name of the game, as a stag hunt conveys an image of people

Table 7.1 Currency game

	Gold	Silver
Gold	3,3	0,0
Silver	0,0	3,3

Table 7.2 Stag hunt game

	$E = 1$	$E = 2$
$E = 1$	1, 1	1, 0
$E = 2$	0, 1	2, 2

looking for game and with all hunters sharing equally in the catch. As shown in the payoff table, each hunter's consumption is determined by the minimum effort supplied by one of the hunters. While maximum consumption results when each supplies two units of effort, individual rationality can easily lead to the supply of one unit of effort.

I have no desire to comment directly upon these games, and wish to comment instead on their ability to render intelligible the phenomena under examination, namely macro-level coordination and failures of such coordination. To do this, it is necessary to recur to the earlier distinction (Chapter 1) between outside-in and inside-out approaches to modeling. Standard game theory starts from the outside and moves in. By this I mean that the actions and strategies are posited in advance of play, and the properties of rational play are subsequently deduced. The structure of the game is in place first, with the players subsequently playing the game: the analytical order flows from the outside shell to the inside where the players reside. By inside-out I mean the reverse order: you start with players who in turn generate their strategies and actions. One of the things this means is that the situation represented by the game will evolve in complexity as the players interact. That growing complexity, moreover, will transform the character of the social setting in the direction of increased coordination.

With respect to the currency game it can be wondered why players can take only one form of currency with them. But suppose this is so. The payoff pattern shows that trades can be made only if both parties carry the same currency. We may agree that the lack of a common currency prevents trade by throwing the participants back to a barter setting. But surely it is not reasonable to think that the societal patterns represented by this game matrix will remain unchanged. Among other things, we would surely expect middlemen to emerge who would carry both currencies and serve as money changers. The absence of money changers within the setting described by the currency game does generate failures of people to conclude mutually profitable trades, but at the same time it presents profit opportunities for someone who can devise ways of facilitating those trades. Peter Howitt and Robert Clower (2000) developed a computational model of the emergence of money, wherein the societal architecture transformed through profit seeking from barter to a money economy. Something similar would surely lead to transformation within the currency game.

The stag hunt game likewise describes a particular societal architecture wherein consumption is in common regardless of individual contributions toward production. It is easy enough to recognize the tendencies for shirking that would exist in such an environment, but it is difficult to imagine how such an environment would persist. To be sure, cooperative forms of organization exist even in modern societies, but even these are not organized along the lines of a stag hunt. The stag hunt game describes a purely communal society. Actual cooperatives include such practices as monitoring and the assessment of merit that, while perhaps falling short of thoroughgoing residual claimacy nonetheless are far removed from stag hunt communism. An inside-out approach to modeling might start with the stag hunt scenario as representative of life at an early stage of civilization. But that approach would also recognize that individual efforts to remove uneasiness, perhaps as stimulated by seeing some lazy bum who nonetheless feasts at the table, will transform the initial setting in the direction of a growing complexity that likewise generates mutual gains.

This distinction between inside-out and outside-in modeling is related to the distinction between private ordering and public ordering. With private ordering, individual participants can generate whatever contractual practices and organizational frameworks they choose, as all such outcomes are manifestations of people's use of their rights of property. The game matrix is generated by the participants and is not specified in advance. The situation is different with public ordering. There, a game matrix is specified in advance, or at least some elements are specified and others are prohibited.

Growth theory, aggregate and otherwise

Contemporary theorizing about growth has been approached primarily at the macro level through the construction of models that articulate direct relationships among aggregate variables. For the most part, those efforts at articulation have been developed by performing exercises on aggregate production functions, and with this approach to articulation being inspired by Robert Solow (1956). Within these formulations, aggregate output is explained as a function of the supply of inputs, and qualitative features concerning those inputs and their combination in production. This framework can be illustrated by the Cobb-Douglas representation of aggregate production denoted by $Y = AK_a(hL)^{1-\alpha}$, where Y denotes output, K and L denote capital and labor respectively, where h denotes some hedonic index of human capital that is erected upon a base of common labor, and where A denotes some type of efficiency parameter, which as a residual is meant to include whatever of relevance is excluded from the quantitative measures of K and hL.

Growth refers to the rate of change in output over some interval, and is typically expressed in per capita terms by dividing the production function by L and expressing the production function as a rate of change. The rate of change in per capita output thus depends on changes in A, h, and K/L. Moreover, changes in h and K/L can affect steady state levels of output but can exert only transitory effects on rates of growth. Permanent effects on rates of growth must enter through A in these formulations. A, it should be noted, is a portmanteau variable that represents a compound of conceptually distinct elements. One element refers to advances in knowledge and technology that shifts production functions (Mokyr 1990, Romer 1990). Another element refers to the level of technical efficiency in the combination of inputs, what Leibenstein (1966, 1979) characterizes as X-efficiency. In this vein,

Parente and Prescott (2000) note that output per worker in coal mining declined by about 50 percent in the United States between 1969 and 1978. This decline was attributed to union work rules that created technically inefficient input combinations. After 1978, this decline was reversed in response to increased competition from two sources: (1) western coal which was produced without unionized labor and (2) oil, for which the price underwent a significant decline.

These macro-level formulations also seek to explore the possible effects on growth of other macro-level variables, and these efforts represent yet further efforts to decompose that portmanteau variable A. For instance, one line of inquiry seeks to relate growth to inequality in the distribution of income (Barro 2000). Another line of inquiry seeks to relate growth to forms of government (Barro 1997, Acemoglu, Johnson, and Robinson 2001). Throughout this macro-grounded literature, a notion of an aggregate production function is used as a vehicle for organizing thought about growth, both over time and among societies at some particular time. Differences in per capita output are thus attributed to differences in systemic efficiency denoted by A, differences in capital per worker denoted by K/L, or differences in human capabilities denoted by h.

The aggregate production function has the appearance of a recipe for organizing thought, but any effort to put that recipe into some kind of use would quickly induce a movement to a lower analytical level, wherein growth is treated as an emergent feature of a nexus of relationships. How, for instance, might h be increased? Typically, h is measured by some aggregate quantity of schooling, which gives the impression that all schooling is identical in its aggregate impact. If it is thought that the subjects people study are significant or if it is thought that schools can differ in their quality of instruction, the explanation of growth is moved from the macro to the micro level.

In this respect, the presence of the efficiency parameter A is puzzling and further illustrates the disjunction between macro and micro thinking (Stigler 1976). Micro theory is based upon the presumption that inputs are combined with technical efficiency. A cost function is defined as a boundary that separates possibility from impossibility. It is possible to produce some particular output at higher cost but never at lower cost. Average cost is simply the locus of points where inputs are combined optimally to produce that output. As for why economists would think that inputs would always be combined in their least cost fashion, the answer surely lies in the universal recognition that people seek to be effective rather than ineffective in whatever they attempt. When people are residual claimants to the difference between revenues and outlays, people have strong incentive to combine inputs in least cost fashion. The theory of a market economy is thus based on the presumption that efficiency prevails, so that the efficiency parameter A has no work to do because it is a constant. Alternatively, to allow A to vary is to undermine one of the conceptual pillars of orthodox equilibrium analysis.

Aggregate statistics in the conduct of human affairs

The neo-Walrasian orientation toward macro-level theory reflects a form of marriage between aggregate accounting and low-level collective planning. I refer to low-level planning to denote something that is not generally thought of as planning. These days, no one advocates the thoroughgoing planning that derives from Marxist desires to abolish commodity production by eliminating the alienability of property. Neither does anyone advocate pseudo-market planning of the Lange-Lerner sort, wherein consumer goods would be organized through market transactions while production was organized through planning without markets.[3] Market-based relationships are robust even if their particular forms are subject to great variability across time and place. Yet planning in the sense of some collective articulation of objectives, along with the subsequent development of state policy aimed at achieving those objectives, is widespread and growing. Anything for which a statistic can be collected can be transformed into an object of planning and collective action.

It is common to use various aggregate measures as indicators of some kind of performance of some facet of society. Aggregate statistics present objects at which policy-induced effort can be directed. This is the attention-arresting power of numbers: they can create policy targets regardless of the value of the target or the accuracy of the aim. This use of aggregate statistics invites the notion of social engineering and is also an understandable feature of human nature. How much do governments invest in collecting statistics? Who are the clients for those statistics? Statistical agencies have limited budgets and must compete with other agencies for appropriations. The statistics they collect must be valued more highly by some set of people who matter than other statistics that might have been or could have been collected. Several different types of motivation are likely to be in play. For instance, some population statistics must be collected in the US to satisfy a constitutional requirement to reapportion Congressional representatives among the states. The preponderance of statistics, however, has nothing to do with constitutional requirements and everything to do with legislation, in at least two respects. In one respect, legislation creates a demand for statistics; in the other respect, the existence of statistics can also serve as a focal point for the creation of a legislative program.

If statistics show that reading scores have gone down, these can operate to create a point of orientation for groups of interested parties to seek to secure higher budgets through pursuing policies to raise those scores. If statistics show that some measure of occupational health is lower in some parts of the country than elsewhere, this can serve as an instrument for advocating a new program or shifting emphasis within some existing program. For instance, people are now using statistical relationships between cholesterol levels and heart disease to pursue policies that regulate the foods restaurants can serve, and which if successful may some day lead to regulations regarding what foods can be produced in the first place. Behind all such sets of proposals are various statistics that have been collected by government agencies. So people pay taxes for governments to collect statistics, and those statistics are then used as instruments to help drive taxes higher still. This is perhaps what we should expect to get from the marriage of national income accounting and aggregate theorizing within the neo-Walrasian motif.

Within the neo-Walrasian analytical motif, macro-level phenomena are equally simple as micro-level phenomena. Macro theory has the same analytical structure as micro theory, only the magnitudes of the variables are larger because individual choices are added together to yield the aggregate macro outcome. It is as if a model of an individual driving down a road was multiplied by the number of drivers to generate a macro-level model. Once it is recognized that a traffic jam is a distinct object from the individual cars through which the jam is constituted, an alternative, interactive approach to macro-level theorizing comes into the analytical foreground.

When aggregate variables are recognized to be products of often complex interaction and not as simple and direct objects of choice, a change in orientation also arises with respect to the treatment of what is called macro-level policy. It is no longer reasonable to treat policy measures as acting on society as a single, equilibrated unit: they are not like a blanket that falls uniformly across society. Rather, policy measures are injected at particular nodes within a societal nexus, and with that nexus being a network of relationships and not a field. How far those measures spread and how fast depend on their acceptability to other nodes, which in turn depends on how they support or contradict the plans that are in motion at those nodes. It also depends on the forms and amounts of force that are brought to bear on those other nodes in the absence of voluntary compliance from those nodes. It is easy for policy measures to yield results that are quite at variance with some set of articulated intentions, once society is recognized to be an order of minds with each mind possessing its own objectives and not an organization with objectives embraced by all participants. The problem of policy with respect to a moving crowd of pedestrians is categorically different from the problem of policy that is faced by a parade marshal.

8 Politics, markets, and political economy

Entangled, not separated

For the most part, economists have embraced a conceptual antinomy in their treatments of markets and states. Markets are treated as polycentric networks of human relationships, and with prices being essential for securing coordinated activity within that network. While there is disagreement among economists over just how well or smoothly that coordination takes place, nearly all economists deny the possibility of economy-wide planning without prices, as illustrated even by James Yunker's (2001) treatment of what he calls pragmatic socialism. The situation is different when it comes to states and politics. States are treated as organizations that exist apart from those market relationships, and with states using planning to intervene into an economy. This conceptual antinomy is widely held despite widely divergent appraisals of the impact of such state intervention: where some think the state mostly corrects market failures, others think it mostly or even wholly creates market impediments. In either case, however, there is nearly universal agreement that state is to be treated as a unitary agent of intervention into an economy.

The contrasting alternative sketched here is one in which state too is conceptualized as an order in which numerous organizations participate, as was sketched during the examination of property rights in Chapter 2. State, like market, describes a process of interaction among participants and not some coherent set of optimizing choices. Organizations can be characterized by such choice-theoretic coherence but orders cannot. Where state and market are typically treated as separable spheres of existence and action, they are treated here as non-separable components of activities that emerge within the same sphere of existence, as set forth in Wagner (2007). Hence, political economy does not denote the union of separate spheres of polity and economy. Rather, it denotes an entangled network of enterprises that are constituted under different institutional arrangements that generate a continually evolving admixture of cooperation and conflict.

Organization-theoretic Political Economy

It was 1896 when Knut Wicksell lamented that the theory of public finance was still based on a presumption of political absolutism even though absolutist regimes had long given way to various forms of representative government (Wicksell 1958: 82). Things haven't changed a lot since Wicksell voiced his lamentation, as it is still common to refer to the state as some acting and choosing entity. The neo-Walrasian program leads inescapably to an organization-based or choice-theoretic political economy. Within the framework of this program, there is plenty of scope for different theories about the relations and interactions between those two distinct entities, polity and economy. Whatever the particular theoretical framework, agents will optimize with relevant knowledge and outcomes will be equilibrium states.

Prior to the emergence of public choice, polity was construed as acting autonomously into an economy in some presumptively benevolent fashion, as conveyed nicely by Tinbergen's (1952) treatment of policy in terms of achieving a matching of goals and instruments. Public choice challenged this treatment of political action, mostly by postulating something other than benevolence, and dropping in the process the presumption that polity operated independently of economy. In an interesting turn of events, the pre-public choice orientation has been resuscitated in the name of a newer version of political economy, as exemplified by Persson and Tabellini (2000) and Besley (2006). According to these models, candidates compete to secure support from the median voter. The median voter selects the candidate who injects polity into economy, in contrast to the earlier view where policy presumably conformed to some textbook standard of good governance. In both cases, however, the conceptualization of political economy is the same: one point-mass entity acts upon another, as illustrated by one billiard ball striking another.

It seems easy enough to understand the popularity of the orthodox, organization-based approach to political economy: it is both easy to work with and presents a prominent role for the economist as policy advisor. It construes the policy-maker as a mechanic who works on a sputtering engine. To be sure, some engines are quite complex and diagnosis is sometimes difficult. Still, the conceptual framework is simple and elegant, with the mechanic state tuning the engine economy, and with the orthodox political economist advising the policy mechanic. Organization-theoretic political economy treats the state as a person or enterprise. While there have been extensive debates over how competent the mechanic state might actually be, those debates occur within a presumed disjunction between polity and economy.

Figure 8.1 depicts graphically the social relationships that would correspond to the antinomy conveyed by this hierarchical conceptualization of political economy. This graph portrays the architectural pattern of social relationships that are implicit in conventional political economy, wherein the state is treated as intervening into a market economy. The circles in the bottom part of Figure 8.1 denote the individual enterprises that operate within the market economy. The edges of the graph denote the various commercial

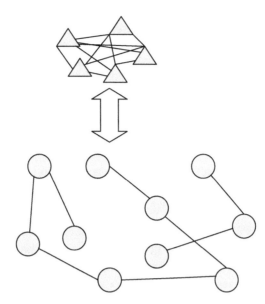

Figure 8.1 Hierarchical political economy.

relationships among those enterprises, while the nodes represent the location of those enterprises in some abstract commodity space. This graph is only partially connected, which indicates that those enterprises comprise a poly-centric order. Those enterprises constitute a network and not a field, which means that the order contained within the entire system is not duplicated within any particular node: the system of nodes cannot be reduced to some representative node. No particular node possesses the ability to make a pencil, and yet the system is capable of producing pencils.

The triangles at the top of Figure 8.1 denote the individual agencies that comprise the state. These agencies are represented as a fully connected graph to indicate that they act as a single entity when intervening into the market economy. That intervention is denoted by the arrow that lies between state and market. The state acts as a coherent entity to intervene into the market economy, changing the market-generated configuration of relationships in the process. In this graph-theoretic representation, state policy would be denoted by a shift in the pattern of relationships, just as would chiropractic adjustment. While no node or enterprise or person in the market economy can truly duplicate all of the detailed actions required to make a pencil, the state has the ability to improve the making of pencils by using policy to re-configure the nexus of market-generated relationships. This, anyway, is the primal presumption of organization-theoretic political economy. The state is treated as an organization that stands outside the market economy and inter-venes into it according to a logic that is orthogonal to that which propels market participants.

Order-theoretic political economy

The alternative conceptual framework that is congruent with the neo-Mengerian research program entails interdependence and entanglement among political and economic entities. Polity contains many organizations and is not itself an organization. Political entities are presumed to act on the same basis of distributed knowledge as economic entities. Moreover, political entities no more act in unison than do commercial entities. Both cooperation and conflict occur among political entities just as they do among economic entities. Moreover, political and economic entities coexist on the same plane of densely intertwined relationships, and not on the distinct planes that separate the mechanic from the engine, as Wagner (2007) elaborates. Polity, just like economy, denotes multiple participants who differ both in what they know and in what they desire. Hence, policy emerges out of interaction among interested participants. It is just as metaphorical to assert that the state does something as it is to assert that the market does something. What we denote as state activity, just as market activity, emerges out of complex patterns of interaction.

The order-theoretic or neo-Mengerian orientation toward political economy asserts that there is no such locus of action that stands outside of and above the ordinary people and their interactions that constitute civil society. Acts of government arise on the same plane of societal activity as the acts of all other entities within society. "State" does not denote a unitary, goal-directed firm; rather, it is a portmanteau concept that denotes a large number of distinct enterprises that often are antagonistic to one another. Furthermore, state enterprises do not act independently of market and civil society but rather interact with enterprises established within the market and civil society. Society cannot be captured by simple addition across independent entities denoted by state, market, and civil society, for the resulting patterns of social activity depend significantly both on interactions among its various participants and on the institutional framework that governs those interactions. The relation between polity and economy is not separable and additive but rather is entangled. State agencies and offices act within society as part of the self-organizing motion of society, and do not stand outside of society and act on it.

Figure 8.2 illustrates what I mean by order-theoretic political economy. It describes an alternative, polycentric model of political economy; this alternative has been a central thrust of Vincent Ostrom's scholarly oeuvre, illustrated by such works as Ostrom (1962), (1973), (1987), and (1997), which in turn are surveyed in Wagner (2005). Figure 8.2 is a transformation in two respects of the organization-theoretic sketch. First, the political agencies no longer comprise a fully connected graph. They do not speak with one, coherent voice, but rather comprise a competitive ensemble, sometimes harmonizing with other political agencies and sometimes clashing. Second, political agencies no longer stand outside and above the market economy, but

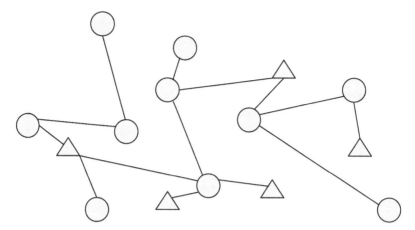

Figure 8.2 Polycentric political economy.

rather operate on the same plane of action as all other enterprises in society. We can reasonably expect coherence from a consumer's choices, as well as from a firm's or from an individual state office. We should, however, expect no more coherence from the aggregate constellation of state enterprises than we would expect from the entire constellation of market enterprises. States and markets are both orders and not organizations. This distinction matters greatly for understanding and explaining state activity.

States as polycentric networks of ordered relationships

When state is recognized to be an order and not an organization, we enter a situation where there is not one locus of sovereignty where action in the name of state can be either initiated or withheld. What we have is what in a different context Gordon Tullock (1965), in amplifying and extending Ludwig von Mises (1944), described as bureaucratic free enterprise. If state denotes an arena and not a firm, it is an arena that contains many distinct firms, as Figure 8.2 illustrates. We should no more expect coherence among the activities undertaken within the state than we find among activities undertaken within the market. Markets generate some products to encourage people to smoke cigarettes and drink alcoholic beverages; they also generate products to dissuade people from smoking or drinking, including nicotine patches and pills to make alcohol taste revolting. Similarly, states generate police-like products to enhance personal security while at the same time degrading security by opposing the incorporation of martial arts and marksmanship into school curricula. Alternatively, there are programs created to subsidize the acquisition of skills while at the same time other programs are created to subsidize unemployment. The Tullock-Mises notion of bureaucratic free enterprise was articulated in the context of the state as a firm, only one that had grown so large that it became uncontrollable. Hence, individual units within the state apparatus practiced a form of free enterprise. Once the state is recognized to be an order and not an organization, a form of free enterprise becomes recognized as the state's ordinary mode of operation and not some aberration.

Plans are action directed at future objectives. Entrepreneurial plans provide the propulsive energy through which societies generate their own transformation. It is straightforward to characterize entrepreneurship within the market, for it is induced by beliefs about profits that can be captured by seizing tomorrow by initiating a plan today. Entrepreneurship within the state arena has the same formal character, for the effort to replace less desired states with more desired states is a universal quality of human action; indeed, we couldn't even recognize ourselves if it weren't true.

The substance of state-based entrepreneurship must take shape differently from that taken by market-based entrepreneurship, due to differences in the forms of property and property-based relationships in the two settings. Profit simply signifies that gains from trade have been captured. Within the market, much of that capture takes the form of capital appreciation. Within the state arena, however, there can be no direct capital appreciation. The absence of capital appreciation is a historical feature that accompanies the absence of transferable ownership within the state arena. The search for gain, however, is a universal feature of humanity. Within the state arena, profit must be captured in other forms than capital appreciation.

Refer again to the enterprise map represented by Figure 8.2. That map depicts ten market-based enterprises and five state-based enterprises, to reflect some rough correspondence with various aggregate measures of market and state activity. The pattern of connections shown in Figure 8.2 has a story to tell that reflects a presumption about the capture of profit from state-based enterprises. Market-based enterprise establish connections with other market-based enterprises, often many of them. This is sensible, as all such enterprises exist within a chain of transactions, providing output to some enterprises and receiving input from other enterprises.

The pattern of connections is different with state-based enterprises. As shown in Figure 8.2, state-based enterprises establish connections with market-based enterprises but not with other state-based enterprises. This is not to suggest that connections among state-based enterprises are never created, but is only to note that they are not as dense as are connections among market-based enterprises. Connections between state-based and market-based enterprises can be important conduits by which profit is extracted from state-based enterprises. A state-based enterprise that had no connections with market-based enterprises would be unable to appropriate profit from its activities. The nonprofit status of state-based enterprises does not eliminate profit but only changes the concrete forms it takes. Those forms, moreover, are surely myriad. As an abstract matter, profits can be transferred through market-based enterprises either by increasing the prices paid for inputs or reducing the prices charged for outputs. Which form this transfer of profits takes, moreover, will depend on the identity and position of the genuine owners and sponsors of any particular state-based enterprise.

Economists are, of course, accustomed to thinking of profit in monetary form. This is the normal form within market-based arrangements, due to the alienability of property. We should remember, however, that profit simply denotes successful action, and the range of potentially successful action is wider than the range of action that can be monetized. Nonprofit forms of enterprise surely offer greater scope for non-monetary forms of profit extraction, in addition to indirect extraction through market-based enterprises (Auteri and Wagner 2007). One seemingly growing form of such extraction could perhaps be described as a form of sport whose popularity has grown with increasing wealth. Some people spend more time in athletic forms of sporting activity, as reflected in the growing membership of and participation in gymnasiums and health clubs throughout the land. Other people spend more of that released time in non-athletic forms of sporting activity, as reflected in the growth in an enormous array of interest group activities. While a significant portion of interest group activity surely represents investment in the search for profit, it is also surely the case that a significant portion represents a desire to participate in sporting activities in a collective setting of some sort. Indeed, it is probably the union of both that gives them political salience, as a form of Baptist-and-bootlegger as set forth by Bruce Yandle (1983, 1999).

Elections, political competition, and rationality

Following Anthony Downs' (1957) adumbration of Harold Hotelling's (1929) analysis of spatial competition, public choice theorists have treated voters as having preferences over policies, and politicians as competing to satisfy those voter preferences. Electoral competition is the arena where policy is chosen. There is an analogy in form between the ballot box and the supermarket: consumers secure their groceries through competition among supermarkets while voters secure policies through competition among candidates. To be sure, political competition faces voters with bundles of items through a form of full-line forcing that contrasts with the ability of consumers to choose among individual items from supermarkets. In both cases, however, what is regarded as central is the competitive effort of vendors to secure support, with only the circumstances by which success is judged varying between the two settings.

It is easy enough to treat voting from a purely formal orientation as a matter of comparing gain and cost: according to the standard rational-choice calculus, if the value they place upon voting exceeds the cost (i.e. the value they place on the alternative to voting), people will vote. Judged by participation rates in democratic elections, a significant number of people appear to regard the gain from voting as worth the cost. Yet this outcome is problematic if voting is construed as the instrument of policy choice because the value of voting is approximately zero in any moderate-sized electorate. The cost of voting is generally not high in modern democracies. It might involve an hour or two of time, but not much else. There are no poll taxes, though in some jurisdictions being registered to vote can make one eligible for jury duty.

While the cost of voting seems generally low, so too does any reasonable sense of instrumental return to voting. Within the ordinary calculus of voting, $V = U(P_1 - P_2)^\lambda - C$, where C denotes the cost of voting and the preceding term denotes the value of voting. This value term has two elements. One is the difference in the evaluation of the anticipated policies to be enacted by the alternative candidates, $P_1 - P_2$. The other, denoted by λ, describes the likelihood that the voter's vote will be decisive for the outcome. With $\lambda \approx 0$, the value of voting is nearly zero, and by any reasonable standard surely in excess of cost.

And yet people vote, which calls for further effort to explain voting. Within the framework of rational choice, two types of amendments have been advanced to the previous expression, which produces $V = U(P_1 - P_2)^\lambda - C + D + E$. In this expression, D and E describe two alternative amendments that have been added to maintain the form of rational voting while evading the substantive possibility that voting is not properly analogized to consumer choice among policies, even if it does represent choice among candidates. D, illustrated by Riker and Ordeshook (1968), incorporates a return from performing a civic duty into the return from voting. E, illustrated by Brennan and Lomasky (1993) and Brennan and Hamlin (1998), incorporates a form of entertainment value, much as the spectators to an athletic event are entertained. These formulations seek to maintain the formal framework of a rational voting calculus by invoking considerations that have nothing to do substantively with rational deliberation or calculation. As an instrument of policy choice based on deliberation among policy options, voting cannot be explained. Yet voting must be explained if policy is to be explained, because the models locate voting as the arena where policy is selected. Hence, non-rational additions are made to the returns from voting; however, those amendments do nothing to boost the deliberative input into electoral choice: we are left with a situation where politicians articulate programs but voters have no reason to pay attention, which should mean in turn that the rational content, substantively speaking, of elections should dwindle toward zero, making it difficult to analogize ballot boxes to supermarkets.[1]

Some significant difficulties arise in trying to treat voting as the instrument by which a set of policies is selected from among the options proffered by competing politicians. For one thing, the information that is conveyed during a political campaign concerns but a tiny portion of the policy activities of governments. Moreover, those issues are addressed in a casual and cursory manner; campaigns do not even remotely resemble a parade of academic seminars. As a formal matter one could claim that voters use the proffered sample of policy positions to estimate the full panoply of policy positions.

Doing this would be to cover a lack of substance by an emphatic embrace of form; the talent required to conduct such estimation is in rare supply within electorates. Furthermore, democratic polities are polycentric and not hierarchical (Ostrom 1997). There is no elected office that selects an office of "policy-maker." What we characterize as policy emerges through interaction among interested parties; even though those participants may differ in the influence they exert over that interactive process, there is no position where it can be truthfully said that policy is imposed by an act of will that exists apart from the process through which it is identified. Policies emerge out of interaction among a set of interested participants, and do not genuinely represent a choice by one of those participants.

The paradox of voting is doubly paradoxical. As commonly formulated, it is strenuous electoral competition that keeps policy in line with voter desires. At the same time, however, voters have no basis either for listening to this political conversation or for voting. It's hard to go from civic duty or entertainment to the gathering of information prior to making significant choices. And political choices are significant. For most people housing is their largest item of personal expenditure. In most democracies taxes are on the order of twice what people spend on housing. With this simple comparison, it might be thought that people would dig more deeply into political options than housing options, let alone options for other items of private expenditure. This is most clearly not the case. If voters are consumers, the extent of knowledge that is in play in electoral processes pales in comparison to that which operates within market processes. To be sure, the situation is no different with most advertising, for advertising does little to nothing to provide experiential information about product characteristics. But one doesn't look to advertising as the locus of knowledge that circulates within market processes. By the same token, one shouldn't look to elections as providing the locus of knowledge that flows within political processes.

The orthodox model presents elections as moments where some preceding equilibrium is punctuated by the insertion of new policies in consequence of the election. The alternative model I have in mind would treat elections as but ephemeral events within an ongoing process of continual political competition. The articulation of policies and the selection of policies is not the province of elections but is a feature of a competitive process that never ceases. My thesis, which I will now proceed to sketch, can be stated thusly: as a first-order matter, the substantive content of democratic politics is independent of elections. What matters is the casting of votes per se; how they are cast is irrelevant. In one regime people could listen to speeches and read newspapers prior to voting. In the other regime people could do none of that and simply flip a coin before deciding which lever to pull. My thesis is that as a first-order matter the two regimes would be indistinguishable. There may be second-order differences, and these can be significant, but they do not operate directly within the arena of policy choice. The locus of democratic competition is not an election but rather takes place within the political process, which is intensely competitive, always.

It shouldn't be necessary to ask "why" voters vote. We observe that many of them do, and from this observation we must conclude that they prefer to devote that time to voting than to whatever else they might have done with their time. As for the sources of value or the character of the alternative uses of time, they surely differ among people and there is no need to be concerned with such matters because voting is not the instrument of policy choice. People follow athletic teams without thinking that they are choosing winners of contests. We neither inquire into the choice to follow a team nor seek to connect those choices with the results of athletic contests. The same situation pertains to politics and political competition.

If voting is not an instrument for the selection of policy, what might it accomplish that would not, perhaps, be accomplished through random selection among candidates? Suppose, as illustrated by Wagner (2007), human nature entails desires for both autonomy and solidarity, though with the substantive content of those desires differing among people. Within this framework, let autonomy map into market action while solidarity maps into non-market action which I associate with civic association as well as government.

Think back on Shakespeare's character Jaques in *As You Like It*: "All the world's a stage, and all the men and women merely players." Suppose we adopt this Shakespearean orientation of all being performers in a drama (or perhaps a comedy, divine or otherwise) in which we write our own parts, though in doing so seek to make connections with other parts and participants. Where on this cosmic stage is a person's action located? Partly this is a matter of preference and choice, though it is also influenced by choices that other people make, much as a person's motion in a crowd of pedestrians is influenced by other pedestrians.

Joseph Schumpeter (1934) noted that in a capitalist society leadership to seize the future is provided largely by entrepreneurs. This claim seems reasonably descriptive of nineteenth-century industrial capitalism. The center of the stage of social life was occupied by entrepreneurs. To follow Shakespeare's analogy, political figures operated largely in the background, serving as stagehands and in similar capacities. All such capacities are necessary for the cosmic drama to proceed, but the differences in roles are noticeable all the same. Schumpeter's time is long behind us, and we have evolved into a different societal arrangement than what Schumpeter designated as capitalist. While societal evolution has proceeded, the same ceaseless contest for space and location on stage continues without end, only with some of the stagehands moving into more central locations, sometimes displacing entrepreneurs while at other times being invited by them (perhaps to keep other entrepreneurs in the background).

Within this framework, might not voting, in contrast to selection by lot, be something that helps politicians to move more to the center of the stage?

With selection by lot, politics as an activity would be less prominent. Term limits, moreover, might operate with somewhat similar effect by reducing brand-name recognition. Hence, voting can exert significant effects on society even if it is not an instrument for selecting policies. In this alternative formulation, voting would do its work by altering the prominence of certain positions in the societal drama, and not by selecting substantively among policy options that emerge within that nexus. Within the context articulated by Norbert Elias (1982), voting might serve as one type of civilizing process within society even if it is not an instrument for selecting among policy options.

In raising this prospect, I would note that to speak of a civilizing process is not to offer some kind of welfare judgment. Tocqueville in *Democracy in America*, in his chapter on democratic despotism (Tocqueville 1966: vol. 2, 335–41), described a civilizing process by which people became placid sheep to be herded and guarded. Perhaps such placidity has positive survival value in an increasingly densely populated planet, in which case it might be judged historically to have been beneficial. But whatever that historical judgment, it seems likely that election campaigns, especially in conjunction with modern electronic technology, work to strengthen the political articulation of much of the uneasiness that propels human action and which at an earlier time was perhaps more the province of entrepreneurial articulation. For instance, political competition has surely created a greater awareness that our activities can influence our global environment even if the outcomes that emerge from that process might be inferior to other outcomes that can be imagined.

Stated differently, elections would seem to be part of a continuing process within which policy options are articulated, contested, adopted, revised, and rejected. Those activities can also take place without elections, so the contribution of elections would not seem so much to be policy selection as an element of a particular constitutional framework within which policies emerge through rule-governed interaction among interested participants.

Democratic legislatures as peculiar investment banks

Within the architecture of a democratically organized polity, a parliamentary assembly is a peculiar form of investment bank. Like an ordinary investment bank, a parliamentary assembly intermediates between people who have enterprises for which they are seeking support and people who have the means to support enterprises. With an ordinary investment bank, both sides of the transaction arise contractually through agreement among the participants. With the peculiar investment bank denoted by a parliamentary assembly, investors are forced and not contractual investors, or at least a good number of investors are forced investors. Not all investors can be forced investors, for then the enterprise would have no advocates. Nonetheless, taxation creates scope for the creation of forced investors.

Whether investment is voluntary or forced, the parliamentary assembly is an arena for the supply of intermediary services. However people acquire membership in a parliamentary assembly, the assembly operates as a form of intermediary organization within the polity, and does not itself encapsulate the polity. People acquire membership in the parliamentary assembly through some form of electoral process, and the assembly operates according to some managerial framework that governs relations among the members of the assembly, as explained in McCormick and Tollison (1981). A parliamentary assembly provides intermediary services much as do banks. It is reasonable to think that the members of a parliamentary assembly will be united in preferring a robust parliament to an anemic one. The individual members of a parliament will typically differ in their preferred patterns of investment, while agreeing that a robust parliament is better than an anemic one. Hence, parliamentary organization will, among other things, match members to activities in a manner that promotes parliamentary robustness through an internal division of labor.

It should be noted, moreover, that to treat a parliamentary assembly as a peculiar investment bank is to locate political processes and outcomes within the penumbra of market processes and not in some location outside it. While a parliament is a peculiar investment bank, its members still must engage in economic calculation. Decisions must be made about which enterprises to support and to what extent. Economic calculation is necessary for a parliamentary assembly to operate. In undertaking such calculation outside of direct market organization, political enterprises act parasitically upon the market economy and create a form of societal tectonics in the process, as will be explored shortly.

Collective bodies cannot choose or otherwise act in any direct fashion, but can only do so through some constitutive framework of parliamentary procedure. Parliamentary outcomes are products of interaction among members within some framework of procedural rules, and are not products directly of choice. Among other things, the members of parliament will typically differ among themselves in how much support they would prefer to give to the different enterprises. The competing political enterprises, moreover, can engage in many types of action to strengthen their competitive position. Only some of those activities will take place within the confines of parliament, perhaps as illustrated best by lobbying. Many activities will occur at other precincts within the polity and will be aimed at influencing what is often described as the climate of opinion. For instance, political enterprises can advertise and in numerous particular ways. One enterprise might work with the producers of a popular television program. Another enterprise might offer materials for use in schools, and perhaps even have people available to make supporting presentations. In these ways, public enterprises use public relations to gain competitive advantage just as do private enterprises.

The institutional framework for political calculation

Politics is an activity that attracts a significant volume of people and capital. Political activity is a subset of the activities that comprise the division of labor within a society. There is good reason to think that people will pursue their comparative advantages in deploying talent and capital across all activities in society. There is also good reason to think that among any cohort of people, those who are most talented and energetic will rise the highest in their chosen fields of activity. It is pointless to dispute that elections attract and select people who are relatively good at running for office: people who are better at politics will tend to have greater electoral success. Whether this also selects for some disinterested quality of public-spiritedness is a different matter. It's quite possible for electoral selection to generate a political class populated with significant numbers of knaves and charlatans even though still populated by people who are particularly good at what they do.

The theory of agency provides a useful framework for exploring democratically organized polities.[2] Political practice, like medical practice, academic practice, or any other form of practice, tends to select among entrants according to how well they practice their craft. Successful democratic politicians tend to be good at doing things that return support when elections are at hand. Takeovers are rare in the corporate world, and it's surely plausible to claim that this rarity attests to the generally high quality of corporate management. While democratic polities provide regular opportunities for the submission of takeover bids, the success rate of challengers is quite low. Successful politicians, like successful corporate managers, are good at what they do. But form does not determine substance. After all, all athletic competitions have the same form, and yet their substantive characteristics differ hugely from one another. In like manner, successful embezzlers and thieves are likewise good at what they do, as their competence has been demonstrated through competitive selection.

The formal theory of agency posits a common interest among citizens that politicians receive zero rents for their work. Political campaigns, following Persson and Tabellini (2000), can be summarized by the government's budget constraint supported by each candidate: $B \equiv tY = g^* + r$, where t is a flat-rate tax applied to a comprehensive income base Y, and with g^* denoting the budget that corresponds to some presumed efficiency standard and r denoting the rents that politicians capture. When confined by this formalization, an increase in rents will require some combination of higher taxes and less provision of valued public goods. Political competition will tend to drive rents toward zero; moreover, politicians who support rents in the post-election period will be more susceptible to subsequent electoral defeat than politicians who do not.

Within this formal framework, political outcomes are assimilated to standard concepts of economic efficiency, at least as a first-order matter. To be sure, the formal literature also gives scope for second-order inefficiency and positive political rents, mostly by introducing presumptions that campaign statements do not translate perfectly into political outcomes. My interest here, however, lies not in different formalizations but in bridging the gulf between form and substance. And a wide gulf it is, and it remains to be seen whether it can be bridged.

The absence of a market for ownership shares in political corporations means that competing claims about managerial competence cannot be reduced to a common dimension through monetary calculation. Where corporate campaigns are centered on projections of corporate value, political campaigns are spread across the various attributes of policy that would have fed into corporate value in the presence of transferable ownership. Vectors of programmatic characteristics will not be reducible to a scalar measure of value. Political campaigns reside in the cheap talk world, as no equivalent to a tender offer is advanced. Tender offers would seem to have rectitude on their side, due to the residual claimant position of those who proffer such offers. With political forms of takeover bid being limited to cheap talk, we should surely expect some movement away from rectitude toward verisimilitude or even mendacity to result because those who advance claims are never placed in the position of betting on those claims.

The very notion of a principal carries an ambiguity in politics that it does not have in commerce. Transferable ownership creates unanimity among shareholders regarding actions that influence corporate value (De Angelo 1981, Makowski 1983). This feature does not operate so strongly in politics because there can be divisions among principals that are represented by wealth transfers among principals. These possibilities are obscured by the representative agent formulation described above, by the government's budget constraint, as well as by models of probabilistic voting which accomplishes the same thing. All such formulations neuter structure through their initial set-up. An agent might be judged positively by some principals and negatively by others, and for reasons that have nothing to do with some aggregate or general value and everything to do with being in the winning or losing end of redistributions of value. Principals need no longer speak with the same voice because they no longer share in the value consequences of corporate choices according to their shareholdings.[3] To put the point differently, what is called "vision" becomes more significant for nonprofit enterprises of all forms because vision is a vector of characteristics that is not reduced to a scalar through transferable ownership, as Auteri and Wagner (2007) explain.

Suppose hotel management is deliberating whether to eliminate some rooms to provide daycare facilities for employees and guests (this illustration is based on Wagner 2007: 108–10). Both managers and shareholders may well hold different appraisals of the commercial consequence of this decision; nonetheless, they will share in the commercial result of that decision and have good reason to be soberly realistic in their judgments and appraisals. The situation changes when the setting is shifted to a political body. There will never be any firm value against which competing claims could be potentially tested, so people can appraise the choice based on their conjectures about the consequences to them.

This replacement of substantive with formal agency seems likely to produce some diminution of rectitude in personal and public expression (Kuran 1995). With substantive agency, people may honestly and openly hold different conjectures about the future value consequences of present actions. In this setting, people can engage in an open process of conjecture and refutation (Popper 1962) as best they can, realizing always the inescapable difficulty involved in seeking to compare some past experience with some future that is created as an act of imagination. Where some might think the conversion of some rooms to a daycare facility might increase the value of the enterprise, others can honestly hold the opposite conjecture. Regardless of the particular conjecture held, the value of the enterprise provides a focal point around which the discussion can be organized, as well as providing some subsequent test of past conjectures.

When substantive agency is replaced by purely formal agency, the scope for honest and truthful deliberation would seem to narrow. No one will advocate support for converting rooms to daycare because they will secure personal gain that exceeds their share of the fall in the aggregate value of the enterprise. To be sure, there is no aggregate value of the enterprise because there is no transferable ownership. That aside, the speaker would doubtless seek to camouflage such recognition by speaking in terms of some generalized or aggregate interest that cannot be put to any test, other than an acceptance or rejection of the proposal, which is not the same thing.

In the absence of substantive agency, participants become involved in discourse that easily can become dishonest, or at least self-deceptive (Cowen 2005). With respect to Pareto's (1935) formulation, the gap between derivations (the public rationalizations people advanced to explain their actions) and residues (the foundational sentiments that informed action) would surely widen. Despite these possibilities, elections will still tend to select for people who are good at winning elections just as commerce selects for people who are good at creating profitable enterprises. To postulate a close similarity if not identity between the two forms of competition is on the one hand a necessary conclusion of a sufficiently abstract formalization, while on the other hand it cannot bridge the chasm that separates form from substance. There is no sense in arguing with the claim that strong competitors tend to win over weak competitors. This gives no reason to think that basketball selects the same athletic qualities as billiards.

Parasitical political pricing and tectonic societal landscapes

The enterprise map presented in Figure 8.2 appears still because its medium of presentation leaves no alternative. If the enterprise sea charted by Figure 8.2 were to be animated, it would not be still: it would contain relatively placid regions along with tectonic zones of turbulence of variable intensity. Ordinary contract among holders of private property is generally placid as both parties gain through trade, though private law also reveals that market-based relationships are also accompanied by turbulence, as illustrated by bankruptcy and by the birth and death of enterprises. Another source of turbulence arises when relationships cross various boundaries between political- and market-based enterprises. Relationships between market-based enterprises and state-based enterprises will typically generate turbulence beyond that which arises among market-based enterprises. The landscape on which market-based enterprises interact can be reasonably approximated by a surface that is continuous and twice differentiable, but that landscape develops tectonic regions when state-based enterprises are incorporated into the catallaxy. In a similar vein, Jason Potts (2000) distinguishes between integral and non-integral geometries, only he refers to market relationships generally. I do not dispute Potts' formulation in this respect, but I want to place the focus on the different forms of relationship among alternative forms of enterprise.[4]

Tectonic relationships can take any of several forms. One form arises when some combination of state enterprises and market enterprises restricts the competitive efforts of other market-based enterprises. A good deal of regulatory activity takes the form of imposing particularly high costs on incipient competitors, thereby conferring advantages on established competitors. This process involves a tectonic clash among enterprises, but this clash does not typically array along a private–public dichotomy; rather it involves some alliance among public and private enterprises to the detriment of other private enterprises. This reference to tectonics brings to mind Maffeo Pantaleoni's (1911) treatment of parasitical political pricing, which is discussed in Wagner (1997). Pantaleoni developed his model with reference to two bazaars. One bazaar denoted the ordinary market arrangement. The other bazaar denoted a politically organized bazaar where prices were political in nature. For instance, a tax that is in proportion to income creates a system of political pricing where prices rise in proportion to income. People with lower incomes will pay lower prices in the political bazaar, while people with higher incomes will pay lower prices in the market bazaar. The movement of customers would set in motion various changes in the bazaars, because the loss of buyers who were charged higher prices by the political bazaar would erode the ability of the political bazaar to offer lower prices to other buyers.

At this stage, the analysis can proceed in any of several directions. The creation of the political bazaar does not change the universal applicability of economic law, but it does change the particular way that such law plays out in a society. What happens subsequently is a course of development that can be rendered intelligible as a playing out of the societal tectonics that is set in motion by the injection of political pricing into a society.[5] The low prices that enterprises inside the political bazaar offer to some buyers are made possible by the high prices those enterprises charge to other buyers. If people who are charged high prices take their business to enterprises located in the market bazaar, the viability of enterprises located within the political bazaar will be threatened. This possibility sets in motion clashes of interest within the society, and those clashes can play out in any number of ways. However they might play out, they are intelligible features of the non-optional character of economic law.

It is surely noteworthy that in their treatise on *Crime and Human Nature*, James Wilson and Richard Herrnstein (1985) limited the crimes they treated to what they called "natural crimes." These were things like murder, robbery, theft, rape, and incest. The crimes they didn't treat could reasonably be called "political crimes" to denote that they represented efforts within a political regime to suppress forms of activity that supporters of that regime want to suppress. Legislation, however, cannot repeal natural law any more than a surfer on a board can repeal physics. Natural crimes have no defenders, and even guilty parties know they are wrong and try to avoid detection.

The situation is very different with politically-defined crimes. For instance, such a straightforward activity as buying and selling stock is criminal under a wide variety of circumstances even though many and perhaps most people see nothing wrong in doing so without filing notice or asking permission from the Securities and Exchange Commission. Just because the Congress and the SEC say such trades shouldn't be made doesn't make them wrongful to most people. It means instead that people should be cautious, and in many cases will be inventive in developing new forms of contract and enterprises that will allow otherwise proscribed transactions to go forward. This situation will induce governing officials to spy on ordinary citizens. This in turn, would seem to transform a "we" into an "us and them." By this, public officials morph from being people who help to facilitate commerce into being people who lord it over society, thereby transforming I–Thou into I–It relationships (Buber 1958) by replacing contract-based relationships with status-based relationships.

I–Thou relationships are between equals, and with both parties acting within a framework of mutuality and respect. I–It relationships arise when one person regards the other not also as a subject but as an object to be acted upon and manipulated. Market-based relationships seem typically to be of I–Thou form, where the focus of the conversation between the parties is on whether they can arrange something that will be for their mutual benefit. In contrast, political relationships would seem to involve significant elements of I–It relationships. Compare visiting a grocery store with visiting a motor vehicle department. Not every visit to a grocery store goes smoothly, but they mostly proceed in a friendly and engaged manner. For a motor vehicle department, a visit would not be described as friendly and engaging. Alternatively, compare two distinct approaches to personal identification and security. Federal legislation has now made it illegal to renew driver's licenses online, and apparently will often even require multiple visits in person to do so. This is detachment-squared or even cubed, as the people who will have to run this gauntlet are objects to be moved about according to various rules that constitute administrative procedure. Yet banks and other financial institutions deal with the same concerns and situations, and handle them in generally friendly and engaging ways with their customers, doubtlessly because they have to attract patronage as against compelling it.

Economists have often claimed that state-based enterprises are more costly producers than market-based enterprises, though the empirical claims in this regard have a good deal of ambiguity. However strong those empirical claims might be, they have analytical cogency on their side. That cogency speaks to technical efficiency in combining inputs. Buber (1958) calls our attention to a different quality of human existence, where we can ask whether the organizational arrangements we generate can influence the ways in which people relate to one another. The use of people as objects and not as subjects is surely a cardinal operating principle of state-based enterprises, as Jacobs (1992) recognizes, and thus presents another reason for constricting the sphere of state even though that sphere will not and, indeed, cannot dissolve.

It is perhaps particularly ironic to consider the state of Paretian welfare economics in light of these considerations. A utility-possibility frontier is derived by maximizing one person's utility while setting other utility levels at various arbitrary levels. One interpretation of welfare economics is that it seeks to present an economically coherent and organized treatment of ethics. Yet its central framework for doing so construes the central relationship as one of I–It form: there is an I whose utility is being maximized and there is a remnant brigade of Its who are treated as objects in that maximization.

Parasitical calculation and public square catallaxy

Orthodox political economy pursues a sequential mode of analysis where people write the first draft of the manuscript of social life, as it were, through their efforts in the precincts of market and civil society, and with the state subsequently revising and polishing the manuscript. The alternative, polycentric orientation pursued here leads to a coeval or simultaneous mode of analysis, in which the manuscript of social life is generated through continual interaction among participants within the precincts of market, state, and civil society. What is of particular significance is that the value of political activity can be calculated only in light of how that activity is refracted through market activity. Economic calculation requires prices as tools of calculation. But prices emerge only in the presence of alienable property. Collective property is inalienable. The internal economy of the state cannot generate prices. Prices can arise only within that part of society where property is alienable, and which is denoted as the market. Thus in a technical sense the state must act parasitically upon the market economy, as recognized both by Maffeo Pantaleoni (1911) and Joseph Schumpeter (1918), and elaborated in Wagner (1997). Political entities must use market prices as calculational aids even if they make incomplete use by staying within the state as against joining the market.

How much support will a highway department or a dredging department acquire from parliament? How will these enterprises choose their patterns of activity? How can such activities as these be given a catallactical explanation without falling into the snare of treating them as if they were ordinary market outcomes? The fundamental catallactical relationship is an exchange of support for payment. We can explain the size of marinas, hotels, restaurants, and such things in this manner. But what about road maintenance, beach replenishment, and harbor dredging? There are public enterprises organized on the public square that provide such services. What might a theory of emergent political economy look like? It would have to disavow both the planning that emanates from the treatment of polity as an organization and the reduction of polity to just another market participant. Polity is different from economy, and yet the resulting political economy must be emergent and transactional to match the nature of the object under examination.

To start on such an endeavor, I would call upon two analytical tools. One is Maffeo Pantaleoni's (1911) formulation of parasitical political pricing; the other is the theory of tie-in sales. Each of these conceptual formulations offers insight that seems potentially useful for approaching a catallactically-centered theory of political economy, recognizing that I do not limit catallaxy to voluntary transactions but extend it to duress, as illustrated by the aphorism "going along to get along."

Political agencies that maintain highways and dredge harbors do not sell their services directly, so there is no way of generating independent estimates of the value of services or of the value of the enterprises. There are many possible places where silt could be dredged and beaches replenished. Scarcity is present here as it is everywhere else. Such issues as how many operations the agency can staff, where they operate, and to what extent are not answered in the same manner they would be if they were organized truly through market transactions. For Pantaleoni, a system of political prices was treated as existing parasitically upon the system of market prices. Pantaleoni's prime interest resided in interaction between the two price systems. Mine is somewhat different, though related, and likewise involves parasitical relationships: while enterprises within the polity cannot calculate directly through market prices, they nonetheless must use prices to achieve calculational guidance, though they do so in peculiar and indirect ways as befits their position as *peculiar* investment banks.

It is here where the theory of tie-in sales enters. One use of tied sales is to avoid price controls. The classic illustration is a rent-controlled apartment that can be leased only by also buying furniture at a price that exceeds the market price. The rent control creates a situation were there is a shortage at the controlled price. Thus demanders seek to gain a competitive advantage, which they can do by paying more in secondary market transactions. In some cases ordinances can seek to prevent such tie-ins, which in turn would set in motion a further search for ways of competing for apartments when competition through price is not allowed. Regardless of the particular form that such tied sales might take, the underlying principle in operation is that a restriction on alienability for one service will tend to induce a bundling of services to secure economic calculation in the absence of alienability for the controlled service.

Getting a road repaired or a harbor dredged is particularly valuable to enterprises whose operations depend on those facilities. We may think of the demand for marina services as a variable that depends on the quality of beach and harbor maintenance. In an open market, a marina owner would purchase the amount of such service that obtains the maximum value for the marina. But these services are not directly priced. Public-private interaction must still be catallactical, only this must be indirect and involve secondary markets, as with tie-in sales. Indeed, we can think of road and harbor maintenance as available at zero price, which is below the market clearing price.

What we should thus expect to find are other types of transaction that operate equivalently to the sale of furniture in cases of rent control. As a conceptual matter, we can say that such channels must exist for harbors to get dredged and in orderly fashion, with some people getting dredging done more quickly than others. What cannot be determined is the particular channel that might be used. Indeed, there could be and probably are multiple channels in use. Some channels could be quite venal, as in bribery. Other channels would be less so, as illustrated by contributions to political campaigns. Invitations to speak before civic clubs and even charitable contributions that support activities valued highly by relevant politicians are other possible channels that are farther removed from the exchange of service directly for money, and which work to secure standing all the same.

It is easy to imagine yet other channels that are less direct still, and yet which can be intelligible features of efforts to gain competitive advantage. The marina might take out a full-page advertisement for a high school dramatic production where the relevant bureau chief has children attending school there and with those children possibly even having roles in the production. We are dealing with an open range of possibilities here, all of which are intelligible as efforts to gain competitive advantage. There is a deep entanglement achieved between polity and economy in this formulation. Figure 8.3 sketches what I have in mind. Panel A describes an ordinary market relationship between two enterprises denoted by the large circles. The mutual profitability of that relationship is denoted by the removal of profits denoted by the appended small circles.

Panel B sketches what I have in mind by a parasitical relationship between polity-based and market-based enterprise, with the polity-based enterprise denoted by the square. As with Panel A, the relationship is catallactical, and is presumed to be profitable to supporters of both enterprises. Yet the collective enterprise is nominally non-profit. This does not mean it doesn't return profits, for the expectation of profit is the raison d'être for its support. The

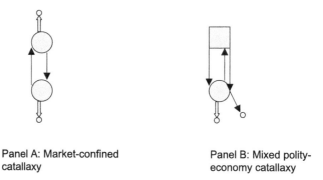

Panel A: Market-confined   Panel B: Mixed polity-
catallaxy   economy catallaxy

Figure 8.3 Catallactical relationships in political economy.

second small circle on the lower right side of the market-based enterprise, in conjunction with the third arrow connecting the two enterprises, indicates that there is some path by which profit is returned to supporters of the collective enterprise.

These matters are necessarily more complex than they are for relationships between market-based enterprises. Yet any effort to explain the operation of public-private interaction in polycentric fashion with widely dispersed and distributed knowledge must start from the presumption that collective enterprises have sponsors who receive gains in excess of what they could expect to receive through market employments of their capital. To be sure, political enterprises bring along forced investors as well, but my interest here resides only with those who support the enterprise and who are its effective owners. Publicly sponsored firms compete both with one another and with market-based firms, while at the same time fabricating networks of cooperative and mutually supportive relationships. Budgeting isn't a top-down, hierarchical process; it is an interactive, polycentric process. For instance, publicly sponsored firms advertise as methods of garnering support. Not only might a marina owner contribute to political campaigns, but he might also belong to civic clubs that invites speakers from particular public agencies, while also contributing selectively to charities that in turn have connections that impact positively both the marina and the relevant public enterprises. This scene and countless more like them illustrate entangled political economy in action.

A constitutional peroration

The formulation presented here treats polities as orders and not as organizations (Hayek 1973, Ikeda 2003). Thinking about orders and their reform is different from thinking about organizations and their reform because there is no singular source of reforming activity within an order. There are many sources of reforming effort, with various relations of complementarity and antagonism among those efforts. Outcomes are emergent and not chosen. A conductor can change the direction of the band's movement in an instant. Changing the movement of a crowd of pedestrians is a different matter; for instance, some people will climb over barricades rather than take the longer and slower path around the barricade. For emergent phenomena, the constitutional rules of the game, and the order of actions that emerge out of those rules, replace the position of the ruler-as-conductor as the focal point for addressing issues arising out of recognition that an emergent order might have generated undesirable features.

In the opening paragraph of *Federalist* No. 1, Alexander Hamilton asked "whether societies of men are really capable or not of establishing good government from reflection and choice, or whether they are forever destined to depend for their political constitutions on accident and force." Hamilton's formulation framed the task of securing good government as a form of societal agriculture, as Vincent Ostrom (1987) explains in his examination of the political-economic theory behind the *Federalist*. Both normative and positive elements are involved, and they must work to congruent effect. On the one hand reside questions of what is valued and what is not; on the other hand reside questions of the ability of alternative institutional frameworks to support or impair those values.

It might be thought normatively that social relationships should be grounded on principles of equality, mutuality, and reciprocity, and not on feudal-like principles involving status relationships of superior and subordinate. While no such principles can be reasonably treated as absolute conditions, it is nonetheless possible to recognize how varying degrees of institutional congruity or incongruity can arise. For instance, market-based relationships are both based on and promote relationships based on equality and mutuality, as conveyed by the idea of gains from trade. The degree to which polity-based relationships are congruent with equality and mutuality depend on the constitutive framework within which political processes operate. Political relationships are never as openly competitive as market relationships, but under some settings they come close, in which case the ability to use power and domination to extract rents is comparatively weak.

The relation between polity and economy was central to the development of *Ordnungstheorie*, literally translated as "order theory," which was articulated seminally by Walter Eucken (1952) and elaborated in Kaspar and Streit (1998). This theory recognized something like a polycentric arrangement of political economy, and sought to specify principles or rules for the conduct of state enterprises that would allow them to support rather than undermine the market economy. Ordnungstheorie was a forerunner to what has since become known as constitutional political economy. The key feature of this theory is its bi-level analytical framework: the constitutional level concerns the establishment and maintenance of rules of just conduct; the operational level concerns the patterns of human activity and organization that people generate through interaction within that framework of constitutive rules.

One of the significant features of this analytical framework is expressed by the principle of market conformability. This principle would not prevent state action, but would only hold that state action should be consistent with the constitutive principles of a market economy: property, contract, and liability. With respect to the activities of the welfare state, for instance, it would be market conformable to require people to participate in programs where they contributed to accounts to support their retirement and medical care. To be sure, no constitutional rule is free from contention and controversy. The Fifth Amendment to the American Constitution is a good illustration of this. It states a simple principle clearly when it declares that private property cannot be taken by a government unless that government pays just compensation and has a genuine public use for that property. The huge volume of litigation and the intensity of the continuing controversy over takings of private property (Epstein 1985) show that mere parchment is never sufficient to maintain a constitutional framework against erosion. Yet once it is recognized that the polity also constitutes a spontaneously generated order, the constitutional framework of rules that order the actions of participants within the political economy becomes the proper arena for addressing issues that arise from what might appear to be undesirable though emergent features of that order.

There seem to be two reasons why people study economics: (1) to understand how society works and (2) to improve society (and with resisting deterioration also denoting improvement). With respect to the dichotomy between engineering and science, reason #2 recalls engineering while reason #1 recalls science. Engineering accomplishments are, of course, made possible by scientific understanding. A question that is sometimes raised with respect to this neo-Mengerian research program concerns the place of the economist and economic knowledge in securing social betterment. The neo-Walrasian framework provides what appears to be a vantage point for pronouncing on matters of betterment, while the neo-Mengerian framework does not. While this difference seems to be a commonly held perception, what is perceived is nonetheless an illusion promoted by the neo-Walrasian framework.

The neo-Walrasian program does allow room for assertions to be made about market failure, and with the judge of any such claim being the median voter who chooses among competing candidates. This program places the economist in the position of seeking to instruct the median voter, and with it being the median voter who makes policy choices, as exemplified by Persson and Tabellini (2000). This framework offers a vision of an economist sitting at the right hand of an official called "Policy Maker" who controls levers that can shift society to some new equilibrium. The presence of Policy Maker is an illusion created by the research program, as conveyed by the comparison between Figures 8.1 and 8.2.

The neo-Walrasian program generates a program of political economy that almost invariably must support whatever political activity is in place. After all, observations are of equilibria among optimizing agents. There can be room for second-order differences of the sort that might speak to minor departures from Pareto efficiency, due possibly to certain categories of imperfection in processes of political competition. The neo-Walrasian program also allows room for exogenous shocks to disrupt existing relationships, causing consequent capital losses. What is central to this program, however, is the impossibility of giving an account of the systemic generation of what would be widely perceived as losses, for this possibility is excluded from the realm of possibility by the hard core of the research program.

In contrast, the neo-Mengerian program allows scope for systemic sources of losses even though it provides no space for Pareto efficiency. Political economy within the neo-Mengerian program would be one of emergent entanglement, in contrast to the neo-Walrasian program of equilibrated additivity. In medicine, there are maladies that arise as exogenous shocks: broken arms and legs are examples. In many cases, however, as illustrated by cancers, those maladies are generated within the body. The challenging opportunity facing a neo-Mengerian orientation toward political economy is one of explaining the internal generation of societal cancers. Adolf Hitler, after all, came to power through a democratic process; Japan was a democracy in the 1930s.

As for what would be recognized to be the equivalent of societal cancers, some of the central claims of the natural law tradition provide a good point of departure. There is, of course, considerable variation among those claims, and they come in both theological and secular varieties, as illustrated by such works as Budziszewski (2003), Miller (1995), Pinker (1997), and Tooby and Cosmides (1990). Such an effort would represent, perhaps, an inversion of Thomas Schelling's (1978) treatment of *Micromotives and Macrobehavior*. Where Schelling sketched instances where individual actions generated social outcomes that most of the participants would have regarded as undesirable, the alternative line of analysis would explore how what are unavoidably parasitical relationships among carriers of the commercial and guardian moral syndromes can escape relatively benign limits as growing entanglement between the different types of carriers generates monstrous moral hybrids (Jacobs 1992). Such emergent phenomena can be rendered intelligible within a neo-Mengerian political economy as the dark side of parasitism, as illustrated by Mitchell and Simmons (1994), whereas it can be nothing but an external shock within a framework of neo-Walrasian political economy, is illustrated by Wittman (1995).

Notes

1 Social economy: some preliminaries on scope and method

1 Three treatments of economic methodology that I have found helpful are Blaug (1992), Caldwell (1982), and Pheby (1988). On economics as social theory, see Lawson (1997, 2003) and the essays collected in Lewis (2004).
2 Expositions of emergence are presented in Holland (1998), Johnson (2001), Strogatz (2003), and Miller and Page (2007).
3 For thoughtfully absorbing biographical treatments of Hayek, see Caldwell (2004) and Ebenstein (2001). Also perceptive on Hayek is the laudatory treatment by Steele (1993) and the critical treatment by Kley (1994).
4 Anthropology and geography are also social sciences, but their domains exist inside those of the core social sciences. Hence anthropology deals with all social sciences in the context of non-literate societies while geography deals with the impact of location on patterns of human activity. Psychology, moreover, is often listed as a social science; however, its object of inquiry is the individual and not society, save for social psychology.
5 In terms of Carrol Quigley's (1961: 49–62) formulation, the cell phone arose as an instrument and transmuted into an institution. In related fashion, Makowksy and Wagner (2009) explore the metamorphosis of cost-benefit analysis from an instrument into an institution.
6 For a lucid statement of the principle that models in the social sciences should aim to generate their relationships and not just postulate them, see the essays in Epstein, ed. (2006). Moreover, the distinction between neo-Walrasian and neo-Mengerian is similar to the distinction Meir Kohn (2004) makes between what he calls the value paradigm and the exchange paradigm. For a symposium on Kohn's treatment, see the *Review of Austrian Economics* 20 (2007).
7 Boehm (1992) describes the short-term flourishing of this research program during the inter-war period. Backhaus and Wagner (2005a, 2005b) explore the dissipation of that program through genocide and the geographic dispersion of remnants. Vaughn (1990) traces the various strands at work in the revival of interest in Austrian economics over the past generation to Carl Menger.
8 See, for instance, Alexander Rosenberg (1992), who argues that the very concern with intentional action makes prediction incoherent because it becomes impossible to distinguish crisply between desires and beliefs.

2 Society, property, and human action

1 To say this does not imply that patterns of property rights are wholly conventional and capable of acquiring any imaginable configuration. Human nature surely places bounds on those patterns, as explained to some extent by Pinker (2002).

2 This treatment of conflict as central to social organization falls within the conflict tradition of sociological theory (Collins 1994), and which Collins contrasts with what he describes as the utilitarian tradition. To be sure, Collins seems to treat these as separable and additive, where I don't, as I explain below. On the related sociological theory of Max Weber, see Collins (1986) and Wallace (1994).
3 For a related examination of how commercial relationships are governed only modestly by the formal articulations of courts and legislatures, see Stewart Maccaulay (1963).
4 Becker and Mulligan (1997) treat time preference within a household management model of the formation of patience that reinforces itself through its positive effect on wealth.
5 159 F.2d 169 (2d Cir. 1947).
6 115 Ill. App. 2d 35, 253 N.E.2d 56 (1969).
7 227 N.Y 208, 125 N.E. 93 (1919).

3 Economizing, calculation, and purposive action

1 By this I mean that it is possible to predict the general features of emergent patterns without being able to predict the precise details that constitute those patterns. One can establish that an increased price will reduce the aggregate amount people buy without establishing how that reduction is apportioned among the set of buyers. See, for instance, Hayek (1967) on pattern prediction.
2 Within a closed equilibrium model, one could, of course, model time spent in conversation by using the same formal framework as employed in search theorizing. Any set of observations can in principle be organized by a closed model. What is at issue isn't the ability to organize such observations, however, but is the ability to render intelligible the underlying societal configurations and processes through which this happens. My own earlier effort to deal with some of these issues, only without so clear a recognition of the open–closed dichotomy, is Wagner (1994).
3 Charles Hampden-Turner (1981) provides a catalog of maps of the mind that scholars have constructed; Barbara Montero and Mark White (2007) provide a collection of essays that examine facets of the relationship between mind and economics.

5 Markets and prices as emergent patterns of human interaction

1 Barabási (2002) provides a useful framework for exploring linkages and their generation.
2 For an alternative treatment of these issues see Esteban Thomsen (1992).
3 For a discussion of degeneracy in biological systems see Tononi, Sporns, and Edelman (1999).

6 Competition and its social organization

1 It would, of course, also be possible for a manufacturer to create minimum prices as a feature of contracts with retailers. This possibility brings the same setting of potential contestation into play because retailers who think they are disadvantaged by such a requirement can always file suit or seek legislative remedy.
2 384 U.S. 270 (1966).
3 To be sure, the owner of the store might contribute to the election campaign of the uncle of the chairman of the county zoning board that has to approve an expansion in the size of the grocery store.

7 From micro to macro through an emergent ecology of enterprises

1 A set of people, each of whom constructs a survey to gather information to use in revising an enterprise plan, is characterized by independent action. Should those people instead use information from the same public source, their actions would be only semi-independent.

2 For a comparison of Austrian and New Classical styles of macro-level theorizing, see Van Zijp (1993).

3 James Yunker (2001) argues in support of what he calls pragmatic socialism, where capital income would be pooled and distributed as dividends in proportion to wage income.

8 Politics, markets, and political economy: entangled, not separated

1 In this respect, Caplan (2007) pushes a claim for irrationality over the standard claim of rational ignorance. I don't see any need to select between rational ignorance and rational irrationality because, as I explain below, I dispute the presumption that elections are arenas within which policies are selected. I might also note that I don't believe that irrational is a useful concept. In this regard I follow Max Weber (1964) and Vilfredo Pareto (1935) in distinguishing between logical (deliberative) and non-logical action. This doesn't mean that the two types of action are disconnected or even antagonistic, for this would be to commit Descartes' Error (Damasio 1994) and would fail to acknowledge the intelligence of emotions (Nussbaum 2001).

2 For a symposium on agency and politics, centered on Besley (2006), see the *Review of Austrian Economics* 22 (no. 2, 2009).

3 Common or plural agency is also relevant here, as illustrated by Bernheim and Whinston (1986), and Dixit, Grossman, and Helpman (1997).

4 I take the tectonic character of state-market interaction from Robert Young (1991), although he takes tectonic in a different direction than I take it here.

5 It is also a course of development that was illustrated nicely by the American experience with Prohibition, and is also well illustrated by contemporary experiences of a similar sort.

Bibliography

Acemoglu, D., Johnson, S., and Robinson, J. A. (2001) "The Colonial Origins of Comparative Development: An Empirical Investigation," *American Economic Review* 91: 1369–1401.

Aghion, P. and Howitt, P. (1992) "A Model of Growth through Creative Destruction," *Econometrica* 60: 323–51.

Akerlof, G. (1970) "The Market for 'Lemons': Quality, Uncertainty, and the Market Mechanism," *Quarterly Journal of Economics* 84: 488–500.

Alchian, A. A. (1950) "Uncertainty, Evolution, and Economic Theory," *Journal of Political Economy* 58: 211–21.

—— (1965) "Some Economics of Property Rights," *Il Politico* 30: 816–29.

—— (2006) *The Collected Works of Armen A. Alchian*, Vol, II, Indianapolis, IN: Liberty Fund.

Alchian, A. A. and H. Demsetz. (1972) "Production, Information Costs, and Economic Organization," *American Economic Review* 62: 777–95.

Allen, J. F. *et al.* (1991) *Reasoning about Plans*, San Mateo, CA: Morgan Kaufmann Publishers.

Alston, L. J., Eggertsson, T., and North, D. C. (eds) (1996) *Empirical Studies in Institutional Change*, Cambridge: Cambridge University Press.

Anderson, G. M., Shughart, W. F., and Tollison, R. D. (1988) "A Public Choice Theory of the Great Contraction," *Public Choice* 59: 3–23.

Angello, R. J. and Donnelley, L. P. (1975) "Property Rights and Efficiency in the Oyster Industry," *Journal of Law and Economics* 18: 521–33.

Auteri, M. and Wagner, R. E. (2007) "The Organizational Architecture of Nonprofit Governance: Economic Calculation within an Ecology of Enterprises," *Public Organization Review* 7 (2007): 57–68.

Backhaus. J. (ed.) (2003) *Evolutionary Economic Thought*, Cheltenham, UK: Edward Elgar.

Backhaus, J. G. and Wagner, R. E. (2005a) "From Continental Public Finance to Public Choice: Mapping Continuity," *History of Political Economy*, Annual Supplement 37: 314–32.

—— (2005b) "Continental Public Finance: Mapping and Recovering a Tradition," *Journal of Public Finance and Public Choice* 23: 43–67.

Baier, A. (1997) *The Commons of the Mind*, Chicago: Open Court.

Banfield, E. C. (1958) *The Moral Basis of a Backward Society*, Glencoe, IL: Free Press.

—— (1970) *The Unheavenly City: The Nature and Future of Our Urban Crisis*, Boston: Little, Brown.

Barabási, A-L. (2002) *Linked: The New Science of Networks*, Cambridge, MA: Perseus.

Barro, R. J. (1974) "Are Government Bonds Net Wealth?" *Journal of Political Economy* 82: 1095–1117.

—— (1997) *Determinants of Economic Growth: A Cross-Country Empirical Study*, Cambridge, MA: MIT Press.

—— (2000) "Inequality and Growth in a Panel of Countries," *Journal of Economic Growth* 5: 5–32.

Barzel, Y. (1989) *Economic Analysis of Property Rights*, Cambridge: Cambridge University Press.

Becker, G. S. (1976) *The Economic Approach to Human Behavior*, Chicago: University of Chicago Press.

Becker, G. S. and Mulligan, C. B. (1997) "The Endogenous Determination of Time Preferences," *Quarterly Journal of Economics* 112: 729–58.

Benson, B. L. (1990) *The Enterprise of Law*, San Francisco: Pacific Research Institute.

Bergh, A. and Höijer, R. (2008) *Institutional Competition*, Cheltenham, UK: Edward Elgar.

Berman, H. (1983) *Law and Revolution: The Formation of the Western Legal Tradition*, Cambridge, MA: Harvard University Press.

Bernheim, B. D. and Whinston, M. D. (1986) "Common Agency," *Econometrica* 54: 923–42.

Besley, T. (2006) *Principled Agents? The Political Economy of Good Government*, Oxford: Oxford University Press.

Bikhchandaini, S., Hirshleifer, D. and Welch, I. (1992) "A Theory of Fads, Fashion, Custom, and Cultural Change as Information Cascades," *Journal of Political Economy* 100: 992–1026.

Blaug, M. (1992) *The Methodology of Economics*, 2nd ed., Cambridge: Cambridge University Press.

Blumenfeld, S. L. (ed.) (1974) *Property in a Humane Economy*, LaSalle, IL: Open Court.

Boehm, S. (1992) "Austrian Economics between the Wars: Some Historiographical Problems," in B. J. Caldwell and S. Boehm (eds) *Austrian Economics: Tensions and New Directions*, Boston: Kluwer, pp. 1–30.

Boettke, P. J. (1993) *Why Perestroika Failed*, London: Routledge.

—— (1997) "Where Did Economics Go Wrong? Modern Economics as a Flight from Reality," *Critical Review* 11: 11–64.

—— (1998) "Economic Calculation: The Austrian Contribution to Political Economy," *Advances in Austrian Economics* 5: 131–58.

—— (2001) *Calculation and Coordination*, London: Routledge.

—— (2002) "Information and Knowledge: Austrian Economics in Search of its Uniqueness," *Review of Austrian Economics* 15: 263–74.

Böhm–Bawerk, E. (1899 [1959]) *Positive Theory of Capital*, South Holland, IL: Libertarian Press.

Boulding, K. E. (1978) *Ecodynamics: A New Theory of Societal Evolution*, Beverly Hills, CA: Sage.

Bowden, R. C. (1989) *Statistical Games and Human Affairs: The View from Within*, Cambridge: Cambridge University Press.

Bowles, S. and Gintis, H. (1993) "The Revenge of Homo Economicus: Contested Exchange and the Revival of Political Economy," *Journal of Economic Perspectives* 7: 83–102.

Brancato, K. and Wagner, R. E. (2004) "Inefficient Market Pricing: An Illusory Economic Box," *Journal of Public Finance and Public Choice* 22: 3–13.

Brennan, G. and Lomasky, L. (1993) *Democracy and Decision: The Pure Theory of Electoral Preference*, Cambridge: Cambridge University Press.

Brennan, H. G. and Hamlin, A. P. (1998) "Expressive Voting and Electoral Equilibrium," *Public Choice* 95: 149–75.

—— (2000) *Democratic Devices and Desires*, Cambridge, Cambridge University Press.

Bryant, J. (1994) "Coordination Theory, the Stag Hunt, and Macroeconomics," in J. W. Friedman (ed.) *Problems of Coordination in Economic Theory*, Boston: Kluwer Academic Publishers, pp. 207–25.

Buber, M. (1958) *I and Thou*, New York: Scribner's.

Buchan, J. (2004) *Crowded with Genius: the Scottish Enlightenment*, New York: Perennial.

Buchanan, J. M. (1964) "What Should Economists Do?" *Southern Economic Journal* 30: 213–22.

—— (1969) *Cost and Choice*, Chicago: Markham.

Buchanan, J. M. and Thirlby, G. F. (eds) (1973) *L.S.E. Essays on Cost*, London: Weidenfeld and Nicolson.

Buchanan, J. M. and Yoon, Y. J. (eds) (1994) *The Return to Increasing Returns*, Ann Arbor: University of Michigan Press.

Buchanan, M. (2002) *Nexus: Small Worlds and the Groundbreaking Science of Networks*, New York: Norton.

Buckle, S. (1991) *Natural Law and the Theory of Property: Grotius to Hume*, Oxford: Oxford University Press.

Budziszewski, J. (2003) *What We Can't Not Know*, Dallas: Spence.

Butos, W. N. and Koppl, R. G. (1993) "Hayekian Expectations: Theory and Empirical Applications," *Constitutional Political Economy* 4: 303–29.

Caldwell, B. (1982) *Beyond Positivism: Economic Methodology in the Twentieth Century*, London: George Allen and Unwin.

—— (2004) *Hayek's Challenge: An Intellectual Biography of F. A. Hayek*. Chicago: University of Chicago Press.

Camerer, C. F. and Thaler, R. (1995) "Anomalies: Dictators, Ultimatums, and Manners," *Journal of Economic Perspectives* 9: 209–19.

Cantillon, R. (1931 [1755]) *An Essay on the Nature of Commerce in General*, London: Macmillan.

Caplan, B. (2007) *The Myth of the Rational Voter*, Princeton: Princeton University Press.

Casson, M. (1982) *The Entrepreneur: An Economic Theory*, Totowa, NJ: Barnes and Noble.

Cheung, S. N. S. (1975) "Roofs or Stars: The Stated Intents and Actual Effects of a Rents Ordinance," *Economic Inquiry* 13: 1–21.

Clower, R. W. (1995) "Axiomatics in Economics," *Southern Economic Journal* 62: 307–19.

Coase, R. H. (1937) "The Nature of the Firm," *Economica* 4: 386–405.

—— (1960) "The Problem of Social Cost," *Journal of Law and Economics* 3: 1–44.

Colander, D. (ed.) (2006) *Post Walrasian Macroeconomics*, Cambridge: Cambridge University Press.

Colander, D., Holt, R. P. F., and Rosser, J. B. Jr. (2004) "The Changing Face of Mainstream Economics," *Review of Political Economy* 16: 485–99.

Coleman, J. S. (1990) *Foundations of Social Theory*, Cambridge, MA: Harvard University Press.

Collins, R. (1986) *Weberian Sociological Theory*, Cambridge: Cambridge University Press.

—— (1988) *Theoretical Sociology*, San Diego, CA: Harcourt Brace Jovanovich.

—— (1994) *Four Sociological Traditions*, New York: Oxford University Press.

—— (1998) *The Sociology of Philosophies: A Global Theory of Intellectual Change*, Cambridge, MA: Harvard University Press.

Coser, L. A. (1964) *The Functions of Social Conflict*, New York: Free Press.

Cournot, A. A. (1838 [1927]) *Researches into the Mathematical Principles of the Theory of Wealth*, New York: Macmillan.

Cowen, T. (2005) "Self-Deception as the Root of Political Failure," *Public Choice* 124: 437–51.

Currie, M. and Steedman, I. (1990) *Wrestling with Time*, Ann Arbor: University of Michigan Press.

Daiches, D, Jones, P., and Jones, J. (1986) *A Hotbed of Genius: The Scottish Enlightenment, 1730–1790*, Edinburgh: Edinburgh University Press.

Damasio, A. R. (1994) *Descartes' Error: Emotion, Reason, and the Human Brain*, New York: Putnam.

De Angelo, H. (1981) "Competition and Unanimity," *American Economic Review* 71: 18–27.

Demmert, H. and Klein, D. B. (2003) "Experiment on Entrepreneurial Discovery: An Attempt to Demonstrate the Conjecture of Hayek and Kirzner," *Journal of Economic Behavior and Organization* 50: 295–310.

Demsetz, H. (1967) "Toward a Theory of Property Rights," *American Economic Review*, Proceedings 57: 347–59.

Dietze, G. (1963) *In Defense of Property*, Chicago: Regnery.

Dixit, A., Grossman, G. M., and Helpman, E. (1997) "Common Agency and Coordination: General Theory and Application to Government Policy Making," *Journal of Political Economy* 105: 752–69.

Dixit, A. K. (2004) *Lawlessness and Economics*, Princeton: Princeton University Press.

Douglas, M. (1979) *The World of Goods*, New York: Basic Books.

Downs, A. (1957) *An Economic Theory of Democracy*, New York: Harper & Row.

Durkheim, E. (1933 [1893]) *The Division of Labor in Society*, New York: Macmillan.

Easterlin, R. A. (2000) "The Worldwide Standard of Living since 1800," *Journal of Economic Perspectives* 14: 7–26.

Ebenstein, A. (2001) *Friedrich Hayek*, Chicago: University of Chicago Press.

Elias, N. (1982) *The Civilizing Process*, New York: Pantheon Books.

—— (1991) *The Society of Individuals*, Oxford: Basil Blackwell.

Elster, J. (1989) *The Cement of Society*, New York: Cambridge University Press.

Epstein, J. M. (ed.) (2006) *Generative Social Science: Studies in Agent-Based Computational Modeling*, Princeton: Princeton University Press.

Epstein, R. A. (1980) "The Static Conception of the Common Law," *Journal of Legal Studies* 9: 253–75.

—— (1993) *Bargaining with the State*, Princeton: Princeton University Press.

—— (1995) *Simple Rules for a Complex World*, Cambridge, MA: Harvard University Press.

Eucken, W. (1952 [1990]) *Grundsätze der Wirtschaftpolitik*, 6th edn, Tübingen: J. C. B. Mohr.

Fama, E. F. (1980) "Agency Problems and the Theory of the Firm," *Journal of Political Economy* 88: 288–307.

Fama, E. F. and Jensen, M. C. (1983) "Agency Problems and Residual Claims," *Journal of Law and Economics* 26: 327–49.

Fellner, W. J. (1965) *Probability and Profit: A Study of Economic Behavior along Bayesian Lines*, Homewood, IL: Richard D. Irwin.

Foldvary, F. (1994) *Public Goods and Private Communities*, Cheltenham, UK: Edward Elgar.

Foss, N. (1993) "Theories of the Firm: Contractual and Competence Perspectives," *Journal of Evolutionary Economics* 3: 127–44.

Frank, R. F. (1987) "If Homo Economicus Could Choose His Own Utility Function, Would He Want One with a Conscience?" *American Economic Review* 77: 593–604.

Frey, B. S. and Stutzer, A. (eds) (2007) *Economics and Psychology: A Promising New Cross-Disciplinary Field*, Cambridge, MA: MIT Press.

Friedman, D. D. (2000) *Law's Order*, Princeton: Princeton University Press.

Friedman, M. (1953) "The Methodology of Positive Economics," in idem, *Essays in Positive Economics*, Chicago: University of Chicago Press, pp. 3–46.

—— (1957) *A Theory of the Consumption Function*, Princeton: Princeton University Press.

Friedman, M. and Savage, L. J. (1948) "The Utility Analysis of Choices Involving Risk," *Journal of Political Economy* 56: 270–304.

—— (1952) "The Expected-Utility Hypothesis and the Measurability of Utility," *Journal of Political Economy* 60: 463–74.

Galbraith, J. K. (1990) *A Tenured Professor*, New York: Houghton Mifflin.

Garrison, R. W. (2001) *Time and Money: The Macroeconomics of Capital Structure*, London: Routledge.

Gladwell, M. (2008) *Outliers: The Story of Success*, New York: Little, Brown.

Gloria-Palermo, S. (1999) *The Evolution of Austrian Economics: From Menger to Lachmann*, London: Routledge.

Gordon, S. (1954) "The Economic Theory of a Common Property Resource: The Fishery," *Journal of Political Economy* 62: 124–42.

Groenewegen, P. D. (2007) *Alfred Marshall*, Basingstoke: Palgrave Macmillan.

Grossman, S. J. and Stiglitz, J. E. (1976) "Information and Competitive Price Systems," *American Economic Review* 66: 246–53.

—— (1980) "On the Impossibility of Informationally Efficient Markets," *American Economic Review* 70: 393–408.

Hamilton, A. Madison, J., and Jay, J. (n.d. [1961]) *Federalist*, New York: New American Library.

Hampden-Turner, C. (1981) *Maps of the Mind*, London: Mitchell Beazley.

Hardin, G. (1968) "The Tragedy of the Commons," *Science* 162: 1243–48.

Harper, D. A. (1996) *Entrepreneurship and the Market Process: An Inquiry into the Growth of Knowledge*, London: Routledge.

Hayek, F. A. (1932) *Monetary Theory and the Trade Cycle*, New York: Harcourt Brace.

—— (ed.) (1935) *Collectivist Economic Planning*, London: Routledge and Kegan Paul.

—— (1935) *Prices and Production* 2nd edn, London: Routledge and Kegan Paul.

—— (1945) "The Use of Knowledge in Society," *American Economic Review* 35: 519–30.

—— (1952) *The Sensory Order*, London: Routledge and Kegan Paul.
—— (1955) *The Counter-Revolution of Science: Studies on the Abuse of Reason*, Glencoe, IL: The Free Press.
—— (1967) "The Theory of Complex Phenomena," in idem, *Studies in Philosophy, Politics, and Economics*, Chicago: University of Chicago Press, pp. 22–42.
—— (1973) *Rules and Order*, Chicago: University of Chicago Press.
Heffernan, G. M. (2003) "Path Dependence, Behavioral Rules, and the Role of Entrepreneurship in Economic Change: The Case of the Automobile Industry," *Review of Austrian Economics* 16: 45–62.
High, J. (1990) *Maximizing, Action, and Market Adjustment*, Munich: Philosophia.
Himmelfarb, G. (1992) *Poverty and Compassion: The Moral Imagination of the Late Victorians*, New York: Vintage.
Hirshleifer, J. (2001) *The Dark Side of the Force: Economic Foundations of Conflict Theory*, Cambridge: Cambridge University Press.
Hirschman, A. O. (1977) *The Passions and the Interests: Political Arguments for Capitalism before Its Triumph*, Princeton: Princeton University Press.
—— (1982) *Shifting Involvements: Private Interest and Public Action*, Princeton: Princeton University Press.
—— (1992) *Rival Views of Market Society*, Cambridge, MA: Harvard University Press.
Hogue, A. R. (1966) *Origins of the Common Law*, Bloomington, IN: Indiana University Press.
Holland, J. M. (1998) *Emergence: From Chaos to Order*, Reading, MA: Addison-Wesley.
Homans, G. C. (1958) "Social Behavior as Exchange," *American Sociological Review* 29: 597–606.
—— (1974) *Social Behavior: Its Elementary Forms*, New York: Harcourt Brace.
Horwitz, S. (2000) *Microfoundations and Macroeconomics: An Austrian Perspective*, London: Routledge.
Hotellling, H. (1929) "Stability in Competition," *Economic Journal* 39: 41–57.
Howitt, P. and Clower, R. (2000) "The Emergence of Economic Organization," *Journal of Economic Behavior and Organization* 41: 55–84.
Huber, P. (1988) *Liability: The Legal Revolution and Its Consequences*, New York: Basic Books.
Ikeda, S. (1997) *Dynamics of the Mixed Economy*, London: Routledge.
—— (2003) "How Compatible are Public Choice and Austrian Political Economy," *Review of Austrian Economics* 16: 63–75.
Irving, W. (1819) *The Sketch Book of Geoffrey Crayon*, New York: C. S. Van Winkle.
Jacobs, J. (1992) *Systems of Survival*, New York: Random House.
—— (2004) *Dark Age Ahead*, New York: Random House.
Jaffé, W. (1965) *Correspondence of Léon Walras and Related Papers*, Amsterdam: North-Holland.
—— (1976) "Menger, Jevons, and Walras De-Homogenized," *Economic Inquiry* 14: 511–24.
Jevons, W. S. (1871 [1965]) *The Theory of Political Economy*, New York: Augustus M. Kelley.
Johnson, S. (2001) *Emergence: The Connected Lives of Ants, Brains, Cities, and Software*, New York: Scribner.
Kahneman, D., Knetsch, J., and Thaler R. (1990) "Experimental Test of the Endowment Effect and the Coase Theorem," *Journal of Political Economy* 98: 1325–1348.

Kaspar, W. and M. E. Streit. (1998) *Institutional Economics: Social Order and Public Policy*, Cheltenham, UK: Edward Elgar.

Kass, L. R. (1993) "Introduction: The Problem of Technology," in A. M. Meltzer, J. Weinberger, and M. Zinman (eds) *Technology in the Western Political Tradition*, Ithaca, NY: Cornell University Press, pp. 1–24.

Katzner, D. (1998) *Time, Ignorance, and Uncertainty in Economic Models*, Ann Arbor: University of Michigan Press.

Kenny, C. (1999) "Does Growth Cause Happiness, or Does Happiness Cause Growth?" *Kyklos* 52: 3–26.

Keynes, J. M. (1936) *The General Theory of Employment, Interest, and Money*, New York: Harcourt, Brace.

—— (1951) *Essays in Biography*, New York: Norton.

Kirman, A. P. (1992) "Whom or What Does the Representative Individual Represent?" *Journal of Economic Perspectives* 6: 117–36.

Kirzner, I. M. (1960) *The Economic Point of View*, Kansas City: Sheed and Ward.

—— (1973) *Competition and Entrepreneurship*, Chicago: University of Chicago Press.

—— (1979) *Perception, Opportunity, and Profit*, Chicago: University of Chicago Press.

—— (1985) *Discovery and the Capitalist Process*, Chicago: University of Chicago Press.

Klein, D. B. (ed.) (1997) *Reputation: Studies in the Voluntary Elicitation of Good Conduct*, Ann Arbor: University of Michigan Press.

—— (1999) "Discovery and the Deepself," *Review of Austrian Economics* 11: 47–76.

—— (2000) *Assurance and Trust in a Great Society*, Irvington, NY: Foundation for Economic Education.

Kley, R. (1994) *Hayek's Social and Political Thought*, Oxford: Oxford University Press.

Knight, F. H. (1921) *Risk, Uncertainty, and Profit*, Boston: Houghton-Mifflin.

—— (1924) "Some Fallacies in the Interpretation of Social Cost," *Quarterly Journal of Economics* 38: 582–606.

Koestler, A. (1964) *The Act of Creation*, New York: Macmillan.

—— (1978) *Janus*, London: Hutchinson.

Kohn, M. (2004) "Value and Exchange," *Cato Journal* 24: 303–39.

Koppl, R. (2002) *Big Players and the Economic Theory of Expectations*, New York: Palgrave Macmillan.

—— (2006) "Austrian Economics at the Cutting Edge," *Review of Austrian Economics* 19: 231–41.

Kruger, A. O. (1974) "The Political Economy of the Rent-Seeking Society," *American Economic Review* 64: 51–70.

Kuran, T. (1995) *Private Truths, Public Lies: The Social Consequences of Preference Falsification*, Cambridge, MA: Harvard University Press.

Lachmann, L. (1956) *Capital and Its Structure*, London: Bell and Sons.

—— (1971) *The Legacy of Max Weber*, Berkeley, CA: Glendessary Press.

—— (1977) *Capital, Expectations, and the Market Process*, Kansas City: Sheed Andrews and McMeel.

Laibson, D. (1997) "Golden Eggs and Hyperbolic Discounting," *Quarterly Journal of Economics* 112: 443–77.

Lakatos, I. (1970) "Falsification and the Methodology of Scientific Research Programs," in I. Lakatos and A. Musgrave (eds) *Criticism and the Growth of Knowledge*, New York: Cambridge University Press, pp. 91–196.

—— (1976) *Proofs and Refutations*, Cambridge: Cambridge University Press.

—— (1978) *The Methodology of Scientific Research Programs*, Cambridge: Cambridge University Press.

Landes, W. M. and Posner, R. A. (1987) *The Economic Structure of Tort Law*, Cambridge, MA: Harvard University Press.

Lasswell, H. D. (1935) *Politics: Who Gets What, When, How?* New York: Meridian.

Latour, B. (2005) *Reassembling the Social: An Introduction to Actor-Network Theory*, Oxford: Oxford University Press.

Latsis, S. (ed.) (1976) *Method and Appraisal in Economics*, Cambridge: Cambridge University Press.

Lawson, T. (1997) *Economics and Reality*, London: Routledge.

—— (2003) *Reorienting Economics*, London: Routledge.

Leeson, P. T. (2006) "Cooperation and Conflict: Evidence on Self—Enforcing Arrangements and Heterogeneous Groups," *American Journal of Economics and Sociology* 65: 891–907.

—— (2007) "An-arrgh-chy: The Law and Economics of Pirate Organization," *Journal of Political Economy* 115: 1049–94.

Leibenstein, H. (1966) "Allocative Efficiency vs. X-Efficiency," *American Economic Review* 56: 392–415.

—— (1979) "The General X-Efficiency Paradigm and the Role of the Entrepreneur," in M. J. Rizzo (ed.) *Time, Uncertainty, and Disequilibrium*, Lexington, MA: D. C. Heath, pp. 127–39.

Leipold, H. and Pies, I. (eds) (2000) *Ordnungstheorie und Ordnungspolitik: Konzeptionen und Entwicklungsperspektiven*, Stuttgart: Lucius & Lucius.

Lewin, P. (1999) *Capital in Disequilibrium*, London: Routledge.

Lewis, P. (ed.) (2004) *Transforming Economics*, London: Routledge.

Lijenberg, A. (2004) "The Infusion of Relational Market Obligations into the Austrian Agenda: Some Lessons Learned from Economic Sociology," *Review of Austrian Economics* 17: 115–33.

Lindahl, E. (1939) *Studies in the Theory of Money and Credit*, London: Allen & Unwin.

Loasby, B. (1982) "The Entrepreneur in Economic Theory," *Scottish Journal of Political Economy* 29: 235–45.

—— (1991) *Equilibrium and Evolution*, Manchester: Manchester University Press.

—— (1998) "The Organization of Capabilities," *Journal of Economic Behavior and Organization* 35: 139–60.

Loewenstein, G. (1999) "Because It Is There: The Challenge of Mountaineering . . . for Utility Theory," *Kyklos* 52: 315–43.

Lovejoy, A. O. (1961) *Reflections on Human Nature*, Baltimore: Johns Hopkins University Press.

Lucas, R. E., Jr. (1975) "An Equilibrium Model of Business Cycles," *Journal of Political Economy* 83: 1113–44.

—— (1976) "Econometric Policy Evaluation: A Critique," in K. Brunner and A. Metzer (eds) *The Phillips Curve and Labor Markets*, Amsterdam: North Holland, pp. 19–46.

MacCallum, S. (1970) *The Art of Community*, Menlo Park, CA: Institute for Humane Studies.

McCann, C. R. (1994) *Probability Foundations of Economic Theory*, London: Routledge.

Maccaulay, S. (1963) "Non-Contractual Relations in Business: A Preliminary Study," *American Sociological Review* 28: 55–67.

McChesney, F. (1997) *Money for Nothing: Politicians, Rent Extraction, and Political Extortion*, Cambridge, MA: Harvard University Press.

Machovec, F. (1995) *Perfect Competition and the Transformation of Economics*, London: Routledge.

McCloskey, D. N. (2006) *The Bourgeois Virtues: Ethics for an Age of Commerce*, Chicago: University of Chicago Press.

McCormick, R. E. and Tollison, R. D. (1981) *Politicians, Legislation, and the Economy*, Boston: Kluwer Academic Publishers.

McKean, R. and. Minasian, J. R. (1966) "On Achieving Pareto Optimality—Regardless of Cost," *Economic Inquiry* 4: 14–23.

McNulty, P. (1968) "Economic Theory and the Meaning of Competition," *Quarterly Journal of Economics* 82: 639–56.

Makowski, L. (1983) "Competition and Unanimity Revisited," *American Economic Review* 73: 329–39.

Makowsky, M. and Wagner, R. E. (2009) "From Scholarly Idea to Budgetary Institution: The Emergence of Cost-Benefit Analysis," *Constitutional Political Economy* 20: 57–70.

Marchionatti, R. (1999) "On Keynes' Animal Spirits," *Kyklos* 52: 415–39.

Marshall, A. (1890) *Principles of Economics*, London: Macmillan.

Meckling, W. H. and Jensen, M. C. (1976) "Theory of the Firm: Managerial Behavior, Agency Costs, and Ownership Structure," *Journal of Financial Economics* 3: 305–60.

Menger, C. (1871 [1981]) *Principles of Economics*, New York: New York University Press.

—— (1883 [1985]) *Investigations into the Method of the Social Sciences*, New York: New York University Press.

—— (1892) "On the Origin of Money," *Economic Journal* 2: 238–55.

Merton, R. K. (1936) "The Unanticipated Consequences of Purposive Social Action," *American Sociological Review* 1: 894–904.

Miller, F. D., Jr. (1995) *Nature, Justice, and Rights in Aristotle's Politics*, Oxford: Oxford University Press.

Miller, G. A. (1956) "The Magical Number Seven, Plus or Minus Two," *Psychological Review* 63: 81–97.

Miller, J. H. and Page, S. E. (2007) *Complex Adaptive Systems*, Princeton: Princeton University Press.

Minsky, M. (1986) *The Society of Mind*, New York: Simon and Schuster.

Miron, J. A. and Zwiebel, J. (1991) "Alcohol Consumption during Prohibition," *American Economic Review*, Proceedings 81: 242–47.

Mirowski, P. (1989) *More Heat than Light: Economics as Social Physics*, Cambridge: Cambridge University Press.

—— (2002) *Machine Dreams*, Cambridge: Cambridge University Press.

Mises, L. (1912 [1936]) *The Theory of Money and Credit*, London: Jonathan Cape.

—— (1933) *Epistemological Problems of Economics*, New York: New York University Press.

—— (1944) *Bureaucracy*, New Haven, CT: Yale University Press.

—— (1957) *Theory and History*, New Haven, CT: Yale University Press.

—— (1966) *Human Action*, Chicago: Henry Regnery.

Mitchell, W. C. and Simmons, R. T. (1994) *Beyond Politics: Markets, Welfare, and the Failure of Bureaucracy*, Boulder, CO: Westview Press.

Mokyr, J. (1990) *The Lever of Riches: Technological Creativity and Economic Progress*, New York: Oxford University Press.

Montero, B. and White, M. D. (eds) (2007) *Economics and the Mind*, London: Routledge.

Morgenstern, O. (1972) "Thirteen Critical Points in Contemporary Economic Theory," *Journal of Economic Literature* 10: 1163–89.

Mueller, D. C. (1987) "Voting Paradox," in C. K. Rowley (ed.) *Democracy and Public Choice*, Oxford: Basil Blackwell, pp. 77–99.

Murphy, L. and Nagel, T. (2002) *The Myth of Ownership*, Oxford: Oxford University Press.

Murray, C. (1984) *Losing Ground*, New York: Basic Books.

—— (1988) *In Pursuit of Happiness and Good Government*, New York: Simon and Schuster.

Nelson, R. R. and Winter, S. G. (1982) *An Evolutionary Theory of Economic Change*, Cambridge, MA: Harvard University Press.

Neyman, J. (1950) *First Course in Probability and Statistics*, New York: Henry Holt.

North, D. C., Wallis, J. J., and Weingast, B. R. (2009) *Violence and Social Orders*, Cambridge: Cambridge University Press.

Noteboom, B. (2007) "Methodological Interactionism: Theory and Application to the Firm and to the Building of Trust," *Review of Austrian Economics* 20: 137–53.

Noyes, C. R. (1936) *The Institution of Property*, New York: Longmans, Green.

Nussbaum, M. C. (2001) *Upheavals of Thought: The Intelligence of Emotions*, Cambridge: Cambridge University Press.

O'Driscoll, G. P. (1977) *Economics as a Coordination Problem*, Kansas City: Sheed Andrews and McMeel.

O'Driscoll, G. P. and Rizzo, M. J. (1985) *The Economics of Time and Ignorance*, Oxford: Basil Blackwell.

Olson, M. (1996) "Big Bills Left on the Sidewalk," *Journal of Economic Perspectives* 10: 3–24.

Oprea, R. D. and Wagner, R. E. (2003) "Institutions, Emergence, and Macro Theorizing: A Review Essay on Roger Garrison's Time and Money," *Review of Austrian Economics* 16: 97–109.

Ostrom, E. (1990) *Governing the Commons*, Cambridge: Cambridge University Press.

—— (2005) *Understanding Institutional Diversity*, Princeton: Princeton University Press.

Ostrom, V. (1962) "The Water Economy and Its Organization," *Natural Resources Journal* 2: 55–73.

—— (1973) *The Intellectual Crisis in American Public Administration*, University, AL: University of Alabama Press.

—— (1987) *The Political Theory of a Compound Republic* 2nd edn, Lincoln: University of Nebraska Press.

—— (1997) *The Meaning of Democracy and the Vulnerability of Societies: A Response to Tocqueville's Challenge*, Ann Arbor: University of Michigan Press.

Pantaleoni, M. (1911) "Considerazioni sulle proprieta di un sistema di prezzi politici," *Giornale degli Economisti* 42: 9–29, 114–33.

Parente, S. and Prescott, E. (2000) *Barriers to Riches*, Cambridge, MA: MIT Press.

Pareto, V. (1935) *The Mind and Society: A Treatise on General Sociology*, New York: Harcourt Brace.

Parsons, T. (1931) "Wants and Activities in Marshall," *Quarterly Journal of Economics* 45: 101–40.

—— (1949) *The Structure of Social Action*, Glencoe, IL: The Free Press.

—— (1951) *The Social System*, Glencoe, IL: The Free Press.

—— (1967) *Sociological Theory and Modern Society*, New York: The Free Press.

Penrose, E. T. (1959) *The Theory of the Growth of the Firm*, Oxford: Oxford University Press.

Persson, T. and Tabellini, G. (2000) *Political Economics: Explaining Economic Policy*, Cambridge, MA: MIT Press.

Pheby, J. (1988) *Methodology and Economics*, Armonk, NY: M. E. Sharpe.

Phlips, L. (1988) *The Economics of Imperfect Information*, Cambridge: Cambridge University Press.

Pinker, S. (1997) *How the Mind Works*, New York: W. W. Norton.

—— (2002) *The Blank Slate: The Modern Denial of Human Nature*, New York: Viking.

Polanyi, M. (1958) *Personal Knowledge*, Chicago: University of Chicago Press.

Popper, K. (1959) *The Logic of Scientific Discovery*, New York: Basic Books.

—— (1962) *Conjectures and Refutations*, London: Routledge and Kegan Paul.

Potts, J. (2000) *The New Evolutionary Microeconomics: Complexity, Competence, and Adaptive Behaviour*, Cheltenham, UK: Edward Elgar.

—— (2001) "Knowledge and Markets," *Journal of Evolutionary Economics* 11: 413–31.

Potts, J. and K. Morrison. (2007) "Meso Comes to Markets," *Journal of Economic Behavior and Organization* 63: 307–12.

Pribram, K. H. (1971) *Languages of the Brain*, Englewood Cliffs, NJ: Prentice Hall.

Quigley, C. (1961) *The Evolution of Civilizations: An Introduction to Historical Analysis*, New York: Macmillan.

Quine, W. V. O. (1951) "Two Dogmas of Empiricism," *The Philosophical Review* 60: 20–43.

Radomysler, A. (1946) "Welfare Economics and Public Policy," *Economica* 13: 190–204.

Read, L. (1958) *I, Pencil*, Irvington, NY: Foundation for Economic Education.

Reder, M. W. (1982) "Chicago Economics: Permanence and Change," *Journal of Economic Literature* 20: 1–38.

Reinert, E. S. (2003) "Austrian Economics and 'the Other Canon': the Austrians between the Activistic-Idealistic and the Passivistic-Materialist Traditions of Economics," in J. G. Backhaus (ed.) *Evolutionary Economic Thought*, Cheltenham, UK: Edward Elgar, pp. 160–207.

—— (2007) "Towards an Austro-German Theory of Uneven Economic Development: A Plea for Theorizing by Inclusion," *Review of Austrian Economics* 20: 155–70.

Rescher, N. (2000) *Process Philosophy*, Pittsburgh: University of Pittsburgh Press.

Resnick, M. (1994) *Turtles, Termites, and Traffic Jams: Explorations in Massively Parallel Microworlds*, Cambridge,MA: MIT Press.

Richardson, G. B. (1960) *Information and Investment*, Oxford: Oxford University Press.

Riker, W. H. and Ordeshook, P. C. (1968) "A Theory of the Calculus of Voting," *American Political Science Review* 62: 25–42.

Rizzo, M. J. (1980) "Law Amid Flux: The Economics of Negligence and Strict Liability," *Journal of Legal Studies* 9: 291–318.

Rizzo, M. J. and Whitman, D. G. (2003) "The Camel's Nose Is in the Tent: Rules, Theories, and Slippery Slopes," *UCLA Law Review* 51: 539–92.

Robbins, L. (1932) *An Essay on the Nature and Significance of Economic Science*, London: Macmillan.

Roberts, P. C. (1971) *Alienation and the Soviet Economy*, Albuquerque: University of New Mexico Press.

Romer, P. M. (1990) "Endogenous Technological Change," *Journal of Political Economy* 98: S71–S102.

Röpke, W. (1958) *Jenseits von Angebot und Nachfrage*, Zürich: Eugen Rentsch.

Rosen, S. (1997) "Austrian and Neoclassical Economics: Any Gains from Trade?" *Journal of Economic Perspectives* 11: 139–52.

Rosenberg, A. (1992) *Economics: Mathematical Politics or Science of Diminishing Returns?* Chicago: University of Chicago Press.

Rosenberg, N. (1960) "Some Institutional Aspects of the *Wealth of Nations*," *Journal of Political Economy* 68: 557–70.

Rothbard, M. N. (1962) *Man, Economy, and State*, Los Angeles: Nash.

Rowley, C. K., Tollison, R. D., and Tullock, G. (eds) (1988) *The Political Economy of Rent Seeking*, Boston: Kluwer Academic Publishers.

Runde, J. (1996) "On Popper, Probabilities, and Propensities," *Review of Social Economy* 54: 465–85.

Samuelson, P. A. (1947) *Foundations of Economic Analysis*, Cambridge, MA: Harvard University Press.

Sautet, F. (2000) *An Entrepreneurial Theory of the Firm*, London: Routledge.

Schelling, T. C. (1978) *Micromotives and Macrobehavior*, New York: Norton.

—— (1984) *Choice and Consequence*, Cambridge, MA: Harvard University Press.

Schlicht, E. (1998) *On Custom and the Economy*, Oxford: Clarendon Press.

Schmitz, S. W. (2004) "Uncertainty in the Austrian Theory of Capital," *Review of Austrian Economics* 17: 67–85.

Schoeck, H. (1969) *Envy: A Theory of Social Behavior*, New York: Harcourt Brace.

Schumpeter, J. A. (1934) *Theory of Economic Development*, 2nd edn, New York: Oxford University Press.

—— (1954) *A History of Economic Analysis*, New York: Oxford University Press.

—— (1954 [1918]) "The Crisis of the Tax State," *International Economic Papers* 4: 5–38.

Seager, H. R. (1893) "Economics at Berlin and Vienna," *Journal of Political Economy* 1: 236–62.

Selgin, G. (1996) *Bank Deregulation and Monetary Order*, London: Routledge.

Shackle, G. L. S. (1961) *Decision, Order, and Time in Human Affairs*, Cambridge: Cambridge University Press.

—— (1968) *Uncertainty in Economics and Other Reflections*, Cambridge: Cambridge University Press.

—— (1972) *Epistemics and Economics*, Cambridge: Cambridge University Press.

Shavell, S. (1987) *Economic Analysis of Accident Law*, Cambridge, MA: Harvard University Press.

Shionoya, Y. (2005) *The Soul of the German Historical School*, Dordrecht: Springer.

Shoven, J. B. and Whalley, J. (1992) *Applying General Equilibrium*, Cambridge: Cambridge University Press.

Siegel, B. N. (ed.) (1984) *Money in Crisis*, Cambridge, MA: Ballinger.

Simmel, G. (1900 [1978]) *The Philosophy of Money*, London: Routledge.

Simon, H. (1959) "Theories of Decision-Making in Economics and Behavioral Science," *American Economic Review* 49: 253–83.

—— (1978) "Rationality as Process and as Product of Thought," *American Economic Review*, Proceedings 68: 1–16.

Smith, A. (1759 [1976]) *The Theory of Moral Sentiments*, Indianapolis, IN: Liberty Fund.

—— (1776 [1937]) *An Inquiry into the Nature and Causes of the Wealth of Nations*, New York: Modern Library.

Smith, V. L. (2008) *Rationality in Economics*, Cambridge: Cambridge University Press.

Snowdon, B., Vane, H., and Wynarczyk P. (1994) *A Modern Guide to Macroeconomics: An Introduction to Competing Schools of Thought*, Cheltenham, UK: Edward Elgar.

Solow, R. (1956) "A Contribution to the Theory of Economic Growth," *Quarterly Journal of Economics* 70: 65–94.

Sparks, N. (2007) *The Choice*, New York: Grand Central Publishing.

Spencer, H. (1884) *Principles of Sociology*, New York: D. Appleton.

Spengler, J. J. (1954) "Richard Cantillon: First of the Moderns," *Journal of Political Economy* 62: 281–95, 406–24.

Starr, R. M. (1997) *General Equilibrium Theory*, Cambridge: Cambridge University Press.

Steele, G. R. (1993) *The Economics of Friedrich Hayek*, London: Macmillan.

Stigler, G. J. (1957) "Perfect Competition, Historically Contemplated," *Journal of Political Economy* 65: 1–17.

—— (1961) "The Economics of Information," *Journal of Political Economy* 69: 213–25.

—— (1975) *The Citizen and the State*, Chicago: University of Chicago Press.

—— (1976) "The Xistence of X-Efficiency," *American Economic Review* 66: 213–16.

Stigler, G. J. and Becker, G. S. (1977) "De gustibus non est disputandum," *American Economic Review* 67: 76–90.

Storr, V. (2008) "The Market as a Social Space," *Review of Austrian Economics* 21: 135–50.

Strogatz, S. (2003) *Sync: The Emerging Science of Spontaneous Order*, New York: Theia Books.

Sutton, J. (2000) *Marshall's Tendencies: What Can Economists Know?* Cambridge, MA: MIT Press.

Swedberg, R. (1994) "Markets as Social Structures," in N. J. Smelser and R. Swedberg (eds) *The Handbook of Economic Sociology*, Princeton: Princeton University Press, pp. 255–82.

Szasz, T. (1961) *The Myth of Mental Illness: Foundations of a Theory of Personal Conduct*, New York: Harper & Row.

Thébaud, O. and Locatelli, B. (2001) "Modelling the Emergence of Resource-Sharing Conventions: An Agent-based Approach," *Journal of Artificial Societies and Social Simulation* 4: no. 2, article 3.

Thompson, E. A. (1974) "Taxation and National Defense," *Journal of Political Economy* 82: 755–82.

Thomsen, E. (1992) *Prices and Knowledge*, London: Routledge.

Thornton, M. (1991) *The Economics of Prohibition*, Salt Lake City: University of Utah Press.

Tinbergen, J. (1952) *On the Theory of Economic Policy*, Amsterdam: North-Holland.

Tocqueville, A. (1835–40 [1966]) *Democracy in America*, 2 vols, New Rochelle, NY: Arlington House.

Tollison, R. D. (1982) "Rent Seeking: A Survey," *Kyklos* 35: 575–602.

Tononi, G., Sporns, O., and Edelman, G. M. (1999) "Measures of Degeneracy and Redundancy in Biological Networks," *Proceedings of the National Academy of Sciences* 96: 3257–52.

Tooby, J. and Cosmides, L. (1990) "On the Universality of Human Nature and the Uniqueness of the Individual," *Journal of Personality* 58: 17–67.

Tullock, G. (1965) *The Politics of Bureaucracy*, Washington: Public Affairs Press.

—— (1967) "The Welfare Costs of Tariffs, Monopolies, and Theft," *Economic Inquiry* 5: 224–32.

—— (1994) *The Economics of Non—Human Societies*, Tucson, AZ: Pallas Press.

Tversky, A. and Kahneman, D. (1991) "Loss Aversion in Riskless Choice," *Quarterly Journal of Economics* 106: 1039–61.

Vanberg, V. J. (1988) "Ordnungstheorie as Constitutional Economics: The German Conception of a 'Social Market Economy'," *ORDO* 39: 17–31.

—— (1992) "Organizations as Constitutional Systems," *Constitutional Political Economy* 3: 223–53.

—— (1994) *Rules and Choice in Economics*, London: Routledge.

Van Zijp, R. (1993) *Austrian and New Classical Business Cycle Theories*, Cheltenham, UK: Edward Elgar.

Vaughn, K. I. (1990) "The Mengerian Roots of the Austrian Revival." *History of Political Economy*, Annual Supplement 22: 379–407.

—— (1994) *Austrian Economics in America*, Cambridge: Cambridge University Press.

Vickers, D. (1994) *Economics and the Antagonism of Time*, Ann Arbor: University of Michigan Press.

Viner, J. (1972) *The Role of Providence in the Social Order*, Princeton: Princeton University Press.

Volokoh, E. (2003) "The Mechanisms of the Slippery Slope," *Harvard Law Review* 116: 1026–1138.

Vriend, N. J. (2002) "Was Hayek an Ace?" *Southern Economic Journal* 68: 811–840.

Wagner, R. E. (1992) "Crafting Social Rules: Common Law vs. Statute Law, Once Again," *Constitutional Political Economy* 3: 381–97.

—— (1994) "Economic Efficiency, Rent Seeking, and Democracy: Zenoistic Variations on Coasian Themes", *Advances in Austrian Economics* 1: 129–44.

—— (1997) "Parasitical Political Pricing, Economic Calculation, and the Size of Government: Variations on a Theme by Maffeo Pantaleoni," *Journal of Public Finance and Public Choice* 15: 135–46.

—— (1999a) "Understanding the Tobacco Settlement: The State as a Partisan Plaintiff." *Regulation* 22, no. 4: 38–41.

—— (1999b) "Austrian Cycle Theory: Saving the Wheat while Discarding the Chaff," *Review of Austrian Economics* 12: 65–80.

—— (2005) "Self—Governance, Polycentrism, and Federalism: Recurring Themes in Vincent Ostrom's Scholarly Oeuvre," *Journal of Economic Behavior and Organization* 57: 173–88.

—— (2006a) "Retrogressive Regime Drift within a Theory of Emergent Order," *Review of Austrian Economics* 19: 113–23.

—— (2006b) "States and the Crafting of Souls: Mind, Society, and Fiscal Sociology," *Journal of Economic Behavior and Organization* 59: 516–24.

—— (2007) *Fiscal Sociology and the Theory of Public Finance*, Cheltenham, UK: Edward Elgar.

—— (forthcoming) "Change within Permanence: Time and the Bivalent Logic of Economic Analysis," *Advances in Austrian Economics*.

Wallace, W. L. (1994) *A Weberian Theory of Human Society*, New Brunswick, NJ: Rutgers University Press.

Walras, L. (1874 [1954]) *Elements of Pure Economics*, Homewood, IL: Richard D. Irwin.

Watts, D. J. (1999) *Small Worlds: The Dynamics of Networks between Order and Randomness*, Princeton: Princeton University Press.

Watts, R. and Zimmerman, J. (1983) "Agency Problems, Auditing, and the Theory of the Firm," *Journal of Law and Economics* 26: 613–33.

Weber, M. (1964) *The Theory of Social and Economic Organization*, Glencoe, IL: The Free Press.

Weintraub, E. R. (1993) *General Equilibrium Analysis: Studies in Appraisal*, Ann Arbor: University of Michigan Press.

White, L. H. (1999) *The Theory of Monetary Institutions*, Oxford: Blackwell.

Wicksell, K. (1958 [1896]) "A New Principle of Just Taxation," in R. A. Musgrave and A. T. Peacock (eds) *Classics in the Theory of Public Finance*, London: Macmillan, pp. 72–118.

Wicksteed, P. H. (1910) *The Common Sense of Political Economy*, London: Macmillan.

—— (1914) "The Scope and Method of Political Economy," *Economic Journal* 24: 1–23.

Williamson, O. E. (1996) *The Mechanisms of Governance*, New York: Oxford University Press.

Wilson, E. O. (1971) *The Insect Societies*, Cambridge, MA: Harvard University Press.

—— (1975) *Sociobiology: The New Synthesis*, Cambridge, MA: Harvard University Press.

Wilson, J. Q. and Herrnstein, R. J. (1985) *Crime and Human Nature*, New York: Simon and Schuster.

Wiseman, J. (1989) *Cost, Choice, and Political Economy*, Aldershot, UK: Edward Elgar.

Witt, U. (ed.) (1992a) *Explaining Process and Change*, Ann Arbor: University of Michigan Press.

—— (1992b) "Turning Austrian Economics into an Evolutionary Theory," in B. Caldwell and S. Boehm (eds) *Austrian Economics: Tensions and New Directions*, Boston: Kluwer, pp. 215–36.

—— (1997) "The Hayekian Puzzle: Spontaneous Order and the Business Cycle," *Scottish Journal of Political Economy* 44: 44–58.

Wittman, D. (1995) *The Myth of Democratic Failure*, Chicago: University of Chicago Press.

Yandle, B. (1983) "Bootleggers and Baptists," *Regulation* 7: 12–16.

—— (1999) "Bootleggers and Baptists in Retrospect," *Regulation* 22: 5–7.

Yeager, L. B. (1997a) "Austrian Economics, Neoclassicism, and the Market Test," *Journal of Economic Perspectives* 11: 153–65.

—— (1997b) *The Fluttering Veil: Essays on Monetary Disequilibrium*, Indianapolis, IN: Liberty Fund.

Young, H. P. (1998) *Individual Strategy and Social Order: An Evolutionary Theory of Institutions*, Princeton: Princeton University Press.

Young, R. A. (1991) "Tectonic Policies and Political Competition," in A. Breton *et al.* (eds) *The Competitive State*, Dordrecht: Kluwer Academic Publishers, pp. 129–45.

Yunker, J. A. (2001) *On the Political Economy of Market Socialism*, Aldershot, UK: Ashgate.

Zanotti, G. J. (2007) "Intersubjectivity, Subjectivism, Social Sciences, and the Austrian School of Economics," *Journal of Markets and Morality* 10: 115–41.

Index

In this index tables and figures are indicated in bold. Notes are indicated by n.

T - #0083 - 230425 - C0 - 234/156/12 - PB - 9780415750011 - Gloss Lamination